I0120923

FACING ASIA

A History of the Colombo Plan

FACING ASIA

A History of the Colombo Plan

Daniel Oakman

THE AUSTRALIAN NATIONAL UNIVERSITY

E PRESS

ANU

E PRESS

Published by ANU E Press
The Australian National University
Canberra ACT 0200, Australia
Email: anuepress@anu.edu.au

This title is also available online at: http://epress.anu.edu.au/facing_asia _citation.html

National Library of Australia Cataloguing-in-Publication Entry
  Author: Oakman, Daniel.
  Title: Facing Asia : a history of the Colombo Plan / Daniel Oakman.
  ISBN: 9781921666926 (pbk.) 9781921666933 (eBook)
  Notes: Includes bibliographical references.
  Subjects: Economic assistance--Southeast Asia--History.
      Economic assistance--Political aspects--Southeast Asia.
      Economic assistance--Social aspects--Southeast Asia.
  Dewey Number: 338.910959

All rights reserved. No part of this publication may be reproduced, stored in a retrieval system or transmitted in any form or by any means, electronic, mechanical, photocopying or otherwise, without the prior permission of the publisher.

Cover design by Emily Brissenden

Cover: Lionel Lindsay (1874–1961) was commissioned to produce this bookplate for pasting in the front of books donated under the Colombo Plan.
Sir Lionel Lindsay, Bookplate from the Australian people under the Colombo Plan, nla.pic-an11035313, National Library of Australia

Printed by Griffin Press

This edition © 2010 ANU E Press
First edition © 2004 Pandanus Books

For Robyn and Colin

Acknowledgements

Thank you: family, friends and colleagues.

I undertook much of the work towards this book as a Visiting Fellow with the Division of Pacific and Asian History in the Research School of Pacific and Asian Studies, The Australian National University. There I benefited from the support of the Division and, in particular, Hank Nelson and Donald Denoon. I am especially grateful to those who made constructive and reassuring comments about drafts of this book: Colin Jones, Warwick Gullett, Michael Pretes, Robert Nichols and Jodi Oakman.

For permission to reproduce images, I thank the Department of Foreign Affairs and Trade, the National Library of Australia and the Herald and Weekly Times Photographic Collection. I also thank Sally White for permission to quote from the published papers of her father, Osmar White; Peter Edwards for use of the Tange interview held at the National Library of Australia; the State Library of South Australia for permission to quote from the diaries of Sir Walter Crocker, and Jane MacGowan for permission to quote from the papers of Lord Casey held at the National Library of Australia.

Finally, and most importantly, I thank Robyn and Colin Jones, without whose unswerving faith and support this book would not have been written.

Daniel Oakman

CONTENTS

1. INTRODUCTION

For most of their history, Australians have seen themselves as a beleaguered white outpost of the British Empire, perched precariously between the hordes of Asia and the edge of the world. They looked north with a mixture of ignorance, wonder and fear, and always through the prism of imperial design and racism. But by the middle of the 20th century the turmoil of the Second World War, communism and decolonisation had ended any possibility that the region could be ignored. 'No nation can escape its geography', warned Percy Spender, Australia's Minister for External Affairs, in 1950, 'that is an axiom which should be written deep in the mind of every Australian'.[1] Threats that seemed to emanate from Asia compelled Australia to take action and reassess its place in the region: Britain's 'Far East' became Australia's 'Near North'. And so, in the early 1950s, Australia embarked on its most ambitious attempt — outside of war — to engage with Asia: the Colombo Plan.

Once a conspicuous symbol of Australia's engagement with the region, the Colombo Plan has since faded from popular memory. But many Australians remember the Asian students who came — first in their hundreds, then in their thousands — to study at Australian tertiary institutions. Those students, along with privately-funded Asian scholars, were among the first people from South and South–East Asia whom Australians encountered. For those who taught, befriended, or provided board and lodgings for these students, the impact on their lives was personal, immediate, and enduring. But few Australians are aware that the Colombo Plan extended far beyond the giving of scholarships. They do not know how and why the Colombo Plan was created, nor how it served as an instrument of Australian foreign policy in the fight against communism, or what the political and racial anxieties were upon which the scheme was built.

Historians of post-war Australia, too, have overlooked the Colombo Plan. They have considered it, and all forms of foreign aid, as tangential to the history of Australia's foreign policy and relations with Asia. Instead, attention has been devoted to relations with the Western world, particularly the desire to cement a military alliance with the United States, at the expense of Australian efforts to engage with the region. Another reason for the Colombo Plan's minor place in post-war historiography is that it was an international creation, established by Commonwealth, and not exclusively Australian, policy-makers. Australia certainly played a prominent role in the creation of the Colombo Plan, but it was not 'our' aid program. Later historians have interpreted the seemingly inconsequential volume of funds spent by Australia as an indicator of political and cultural insignificance. This book seeks to address these oversights and explain how giving financial and technical assistance to Asia — a region hitherto ignored or reviled — became an indispensable plank of the Menzies Government's policy towards Asia.

For Percy Spender, the man who pushed the idea of an aid program for the region through to reality, the Colombo Plan became a feather in his cap. It was, he wrote proudly in his memoirs, 'a dramatic example of how a small nation ... may influence history'.[2] Setting aside the egotistical fervour, his assertion captures the degree of hope and confidence invested in the plan. Part of the Colombo Plan's success came from its longevity (still operating today, it is the world's longest-running bilateral aid program), but also because it crossed deep divides in Australian politics. Although grounded in Cold War politics, the Colombo Plan was one of the few post-war creations that achieved consistent, bipartisan support and allowed the humanitarian internationalist and the Australian nationalist, fearful of the outside world, to come together.

The Colombo Plan reached into almost every aspect of Australian foreign policy, from strategic planning and diplomatic initiatives, to economic and cultural engagement. More generally, it encouraged officials and politicians to define an Australian approach to the Cold War and the challenges of decolonisation. This book explores the public and private agenda behind Australia's foreign aid diplomacy and reveals the strategic, political and cultural objectives that drove the Colombo Plan. It examines the legacy of the Second World War, how foreign aid was seen as crucial to the achievement of regional security, and the debates which led to the establishment of the Colombo Plan in the early 1950s. The book gives particular attention to Spender's successor as foreign minister, Richard Casey, and his role as chief defender and promoter of an Australian aid program. Other themes touched on include the way the Colombo Plan was sold to Australian and Asian audiences, the type of assistance offered under the program, the limitations and effectiveness of Australian aid projects, and the changing nature of Australia's attitude towards its connections with the Empire, the British Commonwealth and the United States. Also considered are questions about sponsored Asian students: who they were, what they studied, what community support they received, and what impact they had on Australia's reputation as a racist and anti-Asian country. Encompassing all these issues is the question of how Australia sought to assert a stronger international presence and project itself into the region; in effect, how Asia was introduced into Australian consciousness.

The Colombo Plan was a cultural creation as much as a political and strategic one. As such, it offers an important way to investigate Australian hopes and assumptions about their future next to Asia. Indeed, this book tries to capture the wide-ranging impact of Australian assistance to Asia and locate the Colombo Plan not only in national history but in the lives of those who helped create it. It aims to deepen our understanding of the relationship between aid and foreign policy and to illuminate the complex mix of self-interest, condescension and humanitarianism that characterised Australia's early ventures into Asia. Most of all, this book tells the story of how an insular society, deeply scarred by the turbulence of war, chose to face its regional future.

Footnotes

[1] *Commonwealth parliamentary debates: House of Representatives*, vol. 6, 9 March 1950, p. 628

[2] P. Spender, *Exercises in diplomacy: ANZUS and the Colombo Plan*, Sydney, Sydney University Press, 1969, p. 200

2. THE ROAD TO COLOMBO

The decaying gun emplacements dotted around Australia's coast stand as an epitaph to an idea once central to Australian civilisation: that freedom and security were best preserved by building physical barriers and deterrents against a hostile world. 'We live in an unstable era', warned founding father and future Prime Minister Alfred Deakin in 1888, 'from the far east and the far west alike we behold menaces and contagion'.[1] Safe behind their defences, Australians populated and cultivated their continent largely unfettered by outsiders who, many believed, looked rapaciously at an empty, undeveloped country. Indeed, hard work and the fruitful exploitation of the land was the linchpin of a vigorous and effective national defence. As the *Sydney Morning Herald* claimed in 1907, threats would be prevented 'by populating our country, by filling up the waste places, by settling on the land sturdy men of our own race and our own colour, who will hold Australia for themselves and for the Commonwealth'.[2] Australians would find, however, that preserving their security meant stepping beyond the barricades.

The issue of security in a hostile — or potentially hostile — region has been a recurrent theme in Australian foreign policy. Dreams of an Australian sub-empire in the Pacific were not articulated with any real conviction until Billy Hughes became Prime Minister in 1915. Australian interest in the Pacific, hitherto shaped by economic and evangelical motives rather than a belief that their destiny would impinge on Australian sovereignty, was now animated by fears of European and Japanese expansionism. Never prone to self-doubt, Hughes was a curious mix of the sentimental imperialist and aggressive nationalist, dismissive of any challenge to Australian interests, British or otherwise. At the conclusion of the First World War, Hughes, like most Australians, expected to enjoy a portion of the spoils, namely the annexation of German possessions south of the equator. En route to the Paris Peace Conference in 1918, Hughes stopped in New York and called for the creation of an Australasian Monroe Doctrine for the Pacific, based on the American principle enacted in 1823 to keep European powers out of the Western Hemisphere. The idea did not belong to Hughes and had first been expressed in Australia during the 1883 inter-colonial convention, when European colonial acquisitions south of the equator were seen to jeopardise the security and prosperity of the Empire. But Hughes' appeal to American tradition paid off and the local press lapped up his feisty aphorisms. The *New York Times* reported his claim that securing New Guinea was not an act of imperialist expansion, merely an attempt to ensure

Australian sovereignty and security, for 'the possession of islands within striking distance of us in unfriendly hands means that our country must always sleep with the sword half drawn'.[3]

In Paris, Hughes continued in a similar vein. Opening the case for annexation, he unrolled a large map of the region and pointed out to his audience that the islands to the north 'encompassed Australia like a fortress'. Hughes' colourful performance proved something of a spectacle during the sombre conference proceedings. But it was not enough to win the day. With memories of war still fresh, the idea of forceful acquisition of territory had begun to lose its moral and legal legitimacy. Instead, the concept of a territorial 'mandate' administered by a single power on principles laid down by the League of Nations, as opposed to outright sovereign control, was becoming fashionable. The concept of self-determination, typically used in relation to European and Middle-Eastern nationalist movements, was also beginning to be applied to the undeveloped regions of the world. Against this trend the Australian delegation publicly scoffed at the idea of ascertaining the wishes of a people that 'had advanced little beyond the Stone Age'.[4] The permissive mandate Hughes eventually secured required Australia to prohibit slavery, not to supply liquor to local people, not to raise local armies or fortify the territory. But, while Hughes undertook to provide a humane administration, the security benefits were seen in terms of merely denying territory to potentially hostile powers, rather than as an opportunity to garner support from the local inhabitants or bolster their resolve against subversion. Benevolent treatment of the indigenous population was merely an unavoidable price of winning the mandate. Although Hughes failed to annex New Guinea, he had projected Australia's authority beyond its continental borders. And, for the moment, Japan and the rest of Asia were kept safely at bay.

Hughes' suspicion of a future attack emanating from Asia turned out to be disturbingly prophetic. The first serious threat to Australian territory came from the Japanese at the beginning of the Second World War — and it came more quickly and with more violence than anyone had predicted. Asia now loomed larger than ever before in the imagination of all Australians. Japan's seemingly unstoppable conquest of South–East Asia shattered the illusion of Australian inviolability, and confirmed deeply held fears that South–East Asia would be the route to an invasion of the mainland. Geographic isolation — for so long assumed to be a powerful deterrent to invaders — now exacerbated Australian anxiety. Over the course of the war, Australians became more intimately and painfully acquainted with South–East Asia. Australia's first mass engagement with the region, when about 22,000 Australians became prisoners of the Japanese, was as a brutalised and subject people. For the post-war generation of Australians either holding, or destined to hold positions of authority and influence, the mention of Asia evoked a wide range of emotions, from anger to memories of horrific suffering and loss. Even before the end of hostilities, Australian politicians and policy-makers began responding to a new concept of Asia, shaped largely by decolonisation, the emergence of nationalist movements and the rising threat of communism. The responsibility for New Guinea — so hard-won by Hughes — and a shared land border with Dutch New Guinea, now perhaps to become part of Indonesia, further projected Australia's gaze northwards. Interest in Asian opinion about Australia, particularly over the consequences of immigration policies, also began to increase. In general, the cultural, economic and political gulf between Asia and Australia, once seen as a protection from

invasion and decay, now needed to be managed, studied —
even narrowed. This readjustment, of course, did not come
easily or without deep apprehension.

Coming to terms with Australia's isolation from its
strong cultural and military allies was the cause for much
anxiety during the late 1940s when the spectre of
communist expansionism emerged as one of Australia's
fundamental security concerns. The domestic achievements
of Ben Chifley's Labor Government (1945–49) were
considerable. But among the conservatives, the perceived
neglect of defence planning and the weakening British
connection aggravated the concern that Australia was
militarily adrift. Specifically, they saw Labor's foreign policy,
with its faith in the new United Nations (UN) and support
for Asian self-determination, as an attempt to dismantle the
bonds of Empire. Speaking at the First Annual General
Convention of the New South Wales division of the
Liberal Party in 1945, Robert Menzies, then an opposition
backbencher, savaged the logic of Labor's international
liberalism: 'the very arguments used for throwing the Dutch
out of the East Indies are the arguments which will be used
to throw the British out of Malaya, to throw the British out
of Burma, India, for throwing the Australians out of New
Guinea'. Labor's approach to regional affairs, he claimed,
threatened the 'continued existence of the British Empire'
which was 'vital to the peace and the future of the world'.[5]
Some members of the Liberal/Country Party opposition
who, perhaps privately, doubted the strength of the imperial
connection saw the chance to rebuild those ties. In 1949,
Sir Earle Page, the co-founder of the federal Country Party,
berated Labor's volatile and combative foreign minister,
Dr Herbert Vere Evatt, for his support of the Dutch
withdrawal from Indonesia:

> *When we find that the present occupants of*
> *territories which concern us have been told that*
> *they should get out of them for the sake of the*
> *original inhabitants, we wonder whether we are*
> *living in a chapter of* Alice in Wonderland ...
> We should ask ourselves who are our real friends?
> *... Who are those who will support us in our hour*
> *of need? ... The only way we can ensure ... safety*
> *is to build a new British Empire. That Empire is*
> *held together by the great traditions of the past.*[6]

But for many, the bonds of empire had already begun to unravel, the fall of Singapore and the reliance on American forces to defeat the Japanese having been an object lesson in the irrelevance of Britain to Australia's strategic integrity. The Japanese wartime Prime Minister Tojo Hideki accurately assessed Australia's vulnerability and sense of betrayal when, in 1942, he gleefully dubbed Australia 'the orphan of the Pacific'.[7]

The man who brought most of the pressure to bear on the Chifley government and its apparent failure to adequately manage Britain's shifting priorities and prepare for future threats from South–East Asia was Percy Spender. As shadow Minister for External Affairs, he dogged Evatt for three years. With thin lips, a close-cropped moustache and narrow eyes, Spender appeared every bit as fiery and relentless as his political opponents knew him to be. His nickname, the Butcherbird, came from his earlier career in law and his reputation for merciless cross-examination of witnesses. Brilliant as a barrister, Spender took silk at the age of 35 to become one of the country's youngest King's Counsel. He carried his talent for debate and advocacy into federal politics in 1937, when he won the blue-ribbon seat of Warringah on Sydney's north shore. Within 18 months

of his election, Menzies invited Spender to join the United
Australia Party and take up the position of Acting
Treasurer. He later became Treasurer, Minister for Army in
the wartime Cabinet, and a member of the Australian
Advisory War Council. Among the most travelled members
of Cabinet, Spender had visited Japan, Hong Kong and
the Philippines during the late 1920s and 1930s. The
experience left its mark. On one trip to Asia, he recalled
watching a ship being coaled: 'it was almost inhuman to see
these people with baskets of coal upon their backs.
Throwing the coal upon their backs, almost like a treadmill,
going up and down, throwing the coal down the hold,
returning, filling their baskets again with coal and going on
and on, an endless chain of humans'.[8] The picture of poor,
anonymous and vulnerable labourers stayed with Spender
throughout his life. Indeed, what he saw informed his view
that Labor policy-makers had grossly underestimated the
unstable nature of Asian society and its susceptibility to
communism.

Unlike Evatt, Spender had little faith in the UN, and
he came to believe that the Charter was 'manifestly unable
to protect Australian interests' and that, without external
assistance, Australia was unable to guarantee its security.
He attacked Evatt's commitment to liberal internationalism
and cast aspersions on his patriotism. On one occasion
Spender charged Evatt with addressing the parliament as an
'internationalist', not as an Australian. On another,
Spender responded to one of Evatt's numerous speeches
regarding the UN with a rhetorical question: 'The speech of
the right honourable gentleman contained not one word
about matters which are of vital interest to this country.
The events which are taking place not only in Europe but
also in Asia … Where, in his speech, was any reference
made to the Pacific and South–East Asia?' There is little

doubt that Evatt considered the UN to be the principal
instrument for international conflict prevention and
resolution. Evatt hoped that the UN, as an egalitarian
international forum, would ensure that Australia's voice
would not be lost amid the din of Cold War posturing
by the great powers. Yet, despite his belief in self-
determination as the 'best form of security' and the
criticism levelled at him by the opposition, Evatt's
'internationalism' did not abrogate responsibility for
regional security issues. He acknowledged that the mere
existence of a UN Charter did not 'dispose of the need for
national defence forces, and [offered] no absolute guarantee
against armed conflicts and aggression'.[9] Nor did the
existence of the Charter obviate the need to create policies
designed to foster positive foreign relations and collective
security arrangements.

Evatt was perhaps the first to seek a more organic
security policy, outside of the framework of alliance
diplomacy. In 1944 he attempted to strengthen Australian
and New Zealand strategic and territorial interests in the
Pacific with the formation of the Anzac Pact, Australia's
first international defence agreement without the United
Kingdom. Among other things, the agreement envisaged a
'system of world security' based on a zone of defence
'stretching through the arc of islands north and north-east
of Australia to Western Samoa and New Zealand's
possessions in the Cook Islands'. While the defence 'zone'
never materialised, regional security was now seen to
involve much wider responsibilities. Monroe Doctrine–style
isolationism gave way to a tentative regionalism, based on a
wider understanding of defensive planning to encompass
increased economic and social interaction. A statement
issued in January 1944 by the Department of External
Affairs (DEA) announced the new obligations for those

with territorial interests in the area: Australia and other regional powers now had a 'duty to advance the welfare of the native people and to promote their social and economic and political development'. Evatt further developed the idea that political stability and economic and social progress were inexorably linked, and in November 1944 he explained his vision for international peace and regional stability to the House of Representatives:

> *There cannot be freedom from fear unless there is a systematic attempt to achieve the objective of freedom from want. International order cannot continue indefinitely unless the conditions of social unrest are removed. It is urgently necessary to provide machinery for the promotion of human welfare in all parts of the world. But we feel a special responsibility for non-self-governing territories in the region in which we live and in neighbouring regions. We feel that great constructive work can be and should be done by the Governments responsible for territories in the South Seas and in the South–East Asia region to provide for mutual assistance, exchange of information and collaboration in particular problems, such as health, transport, economic development and native welfare.*[10]

The United Kingdom made the first attempt to avert famine and social upheaval following the Second World War. Motivated primarily by the looming withdrawal from India and Burma and the fresh significance this conferred on her remaining possessions, in 1946 Britain appointed Lord Killearn (Sir Miles Lampson), former Ambassador to Egypt, to the new position of Special Commissioner in South–East Asia. Based in Singapore, his job was to coordinate food supply, promote social welfare, organise conferences on regional issues, strengthen political stability and secure economic advantages for the United Kingdom. Through Killearn's endeavours, the Foreign Office hoped, Singapore might become a 'centre for the radiation of British influence' and consolidate her strategic and economic presence.[11] The creation of the UN liaison body Economic Commission for Asia and Far East (ECAFE) in March 1947, however, initially appeared to threaten British regional hegemony. Although resistant to the idea of a regional forum where, as Australia's Commissioner for Malaya in Singapore, Claude Massey, put it, Britain feared they would be 'hopelessly outnumbered by Asiatic representatives', the Foreign Office also hoped that Australia's membership of ECAFE and Killearn's work in Singapore would be sufficiently credible — and conspicuous — to counteract any anti-western or pro-communist sentiment. Killearn made Britain's neo-colonial ambitions abundantly clear when he confessed to Massey that 'the big idea' was to get 'all the interested regions here jointly into consultation with a view to a discussion on the future world lay-out'.[12]

With UK officials preoccupied with getting South–East Asia to look to Britain for 'spiritual leadership', they were surprised when Australia mounted a challenge — even if it was largely rhetorical — as a regional leader. Evatt saw his chance to elevate Australia's regional presence immediately after Britain announced that India was to become independent. On 26 February 1947 he told the parliament that, as Britain's responsibilities declined, Australia's would rise: 'Just as far as the people of South–East Asia cease to be dependent upon the decisions of European Governments, so far do Australia's interests in the councils of South–East Asia increase … The time has now arrived where there should be formed in South–East Asia and the Western Pacific an appropriate regional instrumentality'.[13] The expansionist ethos that governed Australia's national development was central to the achievement of international security. Evatt's plans to set the South Pacific on the road to progress was, in some ways, a judicious transference of the same motivations that drove Australia's quest to develop: if industrious and rapid cultivation of the country could protect Australia from conquest, then surely it could save the backward nations of Asia and the Pacific.

Evatt's subsequent proposal for a regional conference on trade, defence, and cultural relations threatened British hopes to retain the initiative. The Foreign Office despatched Killearn to Canberra to discover the details of Evatt's plan and to remind the haughty colonial of the United Kingdom's existing efforts to foster collaboration via the Special Commissioner in Singapore. Killearn's entreaties, combined with the more pressing question of the Japanese Peace Treaty, resulted in Evatt abandoning his plan for a South–East Asian conference. Nevertheless, Evatt's call for the rubric of regional security to be expanded to include welfare and development marked the convergence of the economic, social and strategic dimensions of Australia's approach to national defence and regional affairs. Although Evatt's plan for Asia faded away, he, along with senior DEA officials, successfully created a consultative regional forum for the Pacific. Australia, France, the Netherlands, New Zealand, the United Kingdom and the United States officially launched the South Pacific Commission on 6 February 1947 to promote development in Pacific Island territories under their administration. Like the Anglo–American Caribbean Commission established in 1942, from which its creators drew considerable inspiration, the veneer of benevolence belied the deeper concern that communist ideology might flow to the islands via the anti-colonial sentiment spreading across the world.

Evatt received diligent support from the secretary of the DEA, Dr John Burton, son of the leading Methodist missionary, the Reverend Dr John Wear Burton. Young, energetic and radical, Burton cut an impressive figure among Canberra's rapidly expanding bureaucratic corps and rose to become Secretary of the DEA at the age of just 32. Although he would not survive long as Secretary following the defeat of the Chifley government, his impact on the direction of Australian foreign policy was considerable. Burton was particularly enthusiastic about extending Australia's diplomatic presence throughout Asia. A recurring theme in DEA discussions on Australia's regional influence was the lack of expert knowledge about Asia and the need for increased diplomatic representation. One of Burton's initiatives to boost Australian awareness of South–East Asia and exert a positive influence on Asia's political elite was the 1948 Macmahon Ball Goodwill Mission to South–East Asia. William Macmahon Ball, a political scientist from the University of Melbourne who had served as the Commonwealth delegate to the Allied Council for Japan between 1946 and 1948, had developed an extensive knowledge of Asia. Charged with investigating the region's aid requirements while making contact with senior Asian diplomats, the six-week tour included 13 major cities in Indonesia, Malaya, Burma, Thailand, China, Indo-China, Singapore and the Philippines. But the timing of the mission was poor, taking place just a few months after 14 Indonesian and Malayan seamen were expelled from Australia in February 1948. On arrival, Macmahon Ball faced a 'storm of protest' against Australian immigration laws and he felt the press interpreted the entire mission as a tawdry effort to make up for Australia's 'insult' to the people of Asia. To make matters worse, Malcolm MacDonald, Commissioner-General for the United Kingdom in South–East Asia, during an informal dinner party with Asian community leaders put Macmahon Ball on the spot by asking him to explain the reasons for the government's actions. With Macmahon Ball clearly under pressure, MacDonald, perhaps seeking political advantage at Australia's expense, added that he thought the incident had done 'irreparable harm' to British and European interests in the region. Macmahon Ball sarcastically thanked MacDonald for expressing himself so bluntly, skipped dessert, and left.

These setbacks certainly damaged Macmahon Ball's higher purpose of exerting a positive and independent influence over Asia's new political elites. But they did not stop him from making constructive observations about the development of Australia's foreign policy towards South–East Asia. 'Burdened by their newfound independence', Macmahon Ball wrote, 'Asian leaders recognised their need for outside economic and technical assistance'. Setting aside Asia's antipathy towards immigration restrictions, its lack of resentment or fear of Australia opened up a unique opportunity to provide 'aid and intellectual leadership'. Asians, he said, did not feel that engagement with Australia would compromise their political or economic independence. The key to cultivating such goodwill lay not necessarily in going through standard diplomatic channels, but in targeting Asia's youth: 'To win the friendship and goodwill of the students and technicians is to win the goodwill of people with great political influence', he reported. 'Goodwill towards these people must become a national habit, built on respect for the racial sensibilities and national aims of our neighbours'.[14] Francis Stuart, the astute political secretary to the Australian Commissioner in Singapore, told Burton that

Australia had misjudged the depth of Asian antipathy to the white Australia policy and that he hoped the goodwill mission finally proved the folly inherent in pretending that foreign relations and immigration policy could be kept apart.[15] Stuart's observations were prescient, for the tension he identified would shape Australia's approach to the region for the next two decades.

A more determined strategy intended to redirect Australia's foreign policy towards Asia took shape in late 1948 when Chifley, as acting Minister for External Affairs, sent a 'Political Appreciation' of the region to the Minister for Defence, John Dedman.[16] Developed by DEA bureaucrats under John Burton, the appreciation outlined a broad long-term plan of strategic and political engagement with South–East Asia. The main features of this strategy were to develop financial and industrial policies to help meet the development needs of the area, to encourage the development of Northern Australia by increasing its population and use of resources, to develop Radio Australia in order to encourage 'genuine nationalist developments', to extend diplomatic ties with the region, to encourage Australian businessmen and other officials to establish commercial links with Asia, and to consult with the United States and stimulate their interest in the problems of South–East Asia.[17] The broad thrust of the DEA's recommendations was that, while these suggestions varied in importance and practicality, they all had an 'important long-term defence aspect [that would be] best considered (though not executed) in a defence context'.[18] Taking up ideas generated by the Macmahon Ball mission, a handful of scholarships were soon offered to foreign students under the South–East Asian Scholarship Scheme, supplementing another small offering made in 1947 through a United Nations Educational, Scientific and Cultural Organisation

(UNESCO) program.[19] By the end of 1948 the major part of a one-off allocation of £A500,000 of clothing, x-ray equipment and medical supplies (taken from £A4 million offered to the United Nations Relief and Rehabilitation Administration [UNRRA]) had left Australian shores. But this supply of war surplus was something of a windfall. In the future the provision of aid would not be so painless because it would be necessary to give away goods destined for Australia's domestic markets. The agricultural supplies, steel, timber, locomotives, tractors and construction equipment desperately needed in Asia were also in strong demand in Australia, the DEA lamented.[20]

While bureaucrats embarked on the onerous task of challenging Australia's history of regional passivity, diplomatic activity in Europe and Asia threatened to overtake Australian planning. Since the formation of ECAFE, regional governments had cautiously inquired about the prospect of a Marshall Plan aid program for Asia. But it was not until October 1948, when Britain's Foreign Secretary Ernest Bevin privately suggested the idea to his department, that a Western government appeared willing to take the idea seriously. However, the Foreign Office did not embrace Bevin's audacious suggestion. Not only might such a plan burden Britain with providing the lion's share of financial aid, it also threatened to upset the complex financial and trading arrangements which had developed since the end of the war. Australia, New Zealand, Malaya, India, Pakistan, Ceylon and the United Kingdom belonged to what became known as the Sterling Area, a fiscal arrangement which served to strengthen the pound and Britain's balance of trade. In order to fund the war effort and purchase desperately needed US supplies, Britain purchased the hard currency from the area in exchange for sterling credits. After the war, countries could then draw on their balances in order to finance their own trade deficits. And at this time, retaining control of Malaya's dollar-earning rubber plantations took on an important economic significance. The prospect of a foreign aid–funded Asian trading bloc threatened to disrupt the trade relations between Britain, Malaya and the United States, and jeopardise Britain's capacity to earn dollars.[21]

Bevin soon came to see that fostering economic growth, girding the region from communists, and protecting British financial and strategic interests required a more robust and inclusive organisation rather than Killearn's piecemeal endeavours, especially at the time when the region appeared increasingly unstable. In 1948 alone, Britain saw communist activity in Burma turn violent, and a state of emergency arose in Malaya after repeated attacks by communist guerrillas on British-owned enterprises and police outposts. Even more worrying for British interests in northern Asia, notably Hong Kong, were the spectacular military advances by Mao Tse-tung's army over Chiang Kai-shek's nationalists. The inevitability of a communist China posed an indirect threat, though no less intimidating, to neighbouring India and Pakistan. But at the Commonwealth Prime Ministers' Conference in October 1948, it was India, not Britain, that reinvigorated its interest in building a non-communist regional association. In a similar vein to his speech at the 1947 Asian Relations Conference in New Delhi — the first meeting of its kind — where he stated that India was the 'natural centre and focal point of the many forces at work in Asia', India's Prime Minister, Jawaharlal Nehru, made only veiled references about the creation of an Asian alliance dedicated to bringing aid into the region.[22] He assured the meeting that Asians had little sympathy for communist ideology: the fortunes of communism would rise or fall on the strength of indigenous political and cultural fortitude, he said, and as long as other forces championed nationalism and the betterment of living standards 'the ground would be cut from under the feet of the communists'. And by flagging the more specific problem of obtaining capital goods and specialist equipment, the lack of which hampered Asia's economic progress, Nehru tactfully prepared the way for future requests of technical and financial aid. Britain was still nervous about Asia's need for financial support and the likely resistance to suggestions that France and the Netherlands join a regional body. In this context, Bevin merely proposed that South–East Asian and Western governments meet periodically to discuss ways of stabilising the political and economic climate. But the prospects for Bevin's recommendation did not look promising, and once again the plan seemed destined to flounder in the fractious regional climate. First, his recommendation was diluted to a proposal for regular discussions on international affairs in general, and not necessarily the affairs of South–East Asia. Second, the unresolved Dutch–Indonesian dispute meant that Indonesia would be unrepresented, a prospect that Killearn's replacement, Malcolm MacDonald, likened to a performance of *Hamlet* without the Prince of Denmark.[23] In fact, regional instability resulted in the proposed discussions being postponed until the Colombo conference of January 1950 — a time when the affairs of Asia could no longer be ignored. From such an inauspicious beginning, the planned meeting turned out to be the kernel from which a regional organisation would grow.

Nascent plans for building a means of providing aid to the developing world gained fresh momentum when the American president, Harry Truman, devoted his inaugural address on 20 January 1949 entirely to foreign policy. He vowed to support the UN, to continue to fund the Marshall

Plan for the reconstruction of Western Europe, to support the creation of the North Atlantic Treaty Organisation (NATO) in order to resist communist aggression, and to bring American scientific and industrial technology to bear on the economic problems of the developing world. With the final proposition, henceforth known as 'Point Four', Truman was careful to offer only limited technical assistance for agricultural expansion, public health and education; it was not a promise to underwrite capital formation in the third world. 'Democracy alone can supply the vitalizing force to stir the peoples of the world into triumphant action', he said, 'not only against their human oppressors, but also against their ancient enemies — hunger, misery, and despair'.[24] Truman's evangelical fervour and apparent willingness to support economic growth in developing countries set the imagination of the world running. But Truman's sonorous mission statement concealed a deeper reluctance to take up the affairs of Asia. In part, those concerns were economic (the burden of aid to Europe was considerable and Asia was, at this point, of secondary strategic importance), but American policy-makers were also unwilling to risk initiating any regional arrangements that might be interpreted as covert economic imperialism.

At the same time that Truman reaped the rewards of his stirring address, Nehru brought together 18 nations in New Delhi to discuss a range of regional issues, including the means to help Indonesia achieve stable independence. Australia, the only Western country to be fully represented, provided some ballast to the proceedings, but most delegates took the opportunity to attack colonialism, demanding that the Dutch transfer power to the Indonesian Republic by 1 January 1950. In a calmer moment, Nehru recommended that delegations 'consult among themselves in order to explore ways and means of establishing suitable machinery, having regard to the areas concerned, of promoting consultation and cooperation within the framework of the United Nations'.[25] Australian–Indian relations were cordial, in part enhanced by Australian facilitation of India's entrance into the international cricketing fraternity. But that did not divert Nehru from his purpose of building an exclusively Asian regional alliance. With a keen eye for the telling symbolic gesture, Nehru postponed the discussion of this resolution until after the Western attendees had returned home. The suggestions adopted by the remaining delegates stopped short of calling for a program of international aid, but a range of activities which could bring Asian governments closer together were proposed. Among other things, the meeting called for a greater exchange of information between Asian governments, periodic meetings to discuss matters of common interest, and increased emphasis on cultural relations, including the exchange of teachers, students and technical advisers. The DEA told Indian officials that, although the plan was 'broadly in accord with the conception of regional association' proposed by Evatt, there was no need to encroach on the UN mandate. Yet the real reason for Australia's ambivalence, however, was fear of interference from the communist powers. Equally cool responses from Burma, Thailand and Indonesia saw the Indian proposal shelved. But India's attempt alerted British and Australian policy-makers to the prospect of a regional initiative created and led by Asians, a prospect that did not bode well for the achievement of Western strategic and economic ambitions. A shared distain for post-colonial domination did not necessarily translate into shared political or economic aspirations. Indeed, in the wake of decolonisation, smaller Asian states grew even more suspicious of the motives of their larger neighbours. A wise assessment came from Australia's High Commissioner in New Delhi, Herbert Gollan. 'In this

period of flux', he wrote, 'no Asian country will take the risk
of keeping entirely aloof from any proposal for an Asian
grouping', but there was no 'great cohesion in the present
show of union'.[26] Asia's smaller states rejected Nehru's
proposed forum, with most reluctant to become associated
with an overtly Western or anti-communist bloc, and
especially one that promised little in the way of aid or
technical assistance. And the blatant anti-colonialism that
underpinned the Delhi conference dashed British hopes for a
regional forum involving the Netherlands or France.

Australian involvement in the creation of a new
regional forum intensified two months after the New Delhi
meetings, when the Australian ambassador to China,
Keith Officer, met with the Indian, US and UK
ambassadors to discuss the consequences of a communist
victory. The Indian ambassador, K.M. Panikkar, claims to
have revived the spirit of the New Delhi conference, by
presenting a paper calling for the establishment of
consultative machinery bringing together Asia and the
West. He argued that 'without immediate and adequate
help in the economic field, the political structure of
South–East Asia would provide no more than a frail barrier
to the expansion of Communism'.[27] The group then
modified Panikkar's proposals and eventually reached, in
the US ambassador's words, 'a tentative consensus of
opinion'.[28] On 7 March 1949 Officer sent Evatt a copy of
the joint memorandum and urged him to take 'more than a
defensive stand' against the advance of communism. The
memorandum synthesised many of the ideas about the
economic and political future of the Asian region
circulating since the Second World War. The achievement
of independence, it claimed, could not solve the problems
at the heart of the pre-modern, underdeveloped economy
and merely paying lip service to Asian self-determination

was not enough to guarantee the emergence of non-communist government. The problem was that transforming an 'oriental' society based on 'anachronistic social bonds and … a starvation economy' into a modern society based on the 'principles of social justice and economic freedom' was inherently revolutionary. The underlying assumption was that a homogenous and generic Asian economy had been denied the slow process of economic evolution which typified European civilisation. Such destabilising forces, therefore, exposed the people to 'new and destructive' ideas.[29]

What then was the solution to the 'immense appeal' of communism, feeding as it did off the turmoil induced by the social and economic transition? The memo was, in fact, far more ambitious than earlier proposals for regional collaboration and suggested the creation of a permanent consultative council, a confederation with 'a planned and integrated economy, which would increase food production through the application of modern technology, embark on a program of industrial expansion, build intra-regional trade networks, develop a 'common system' of liberal-democratic education, and build medical and sanitary facilities to counter the 'enervating effects' of South–East Asia's tropical climate. More than a proposal for the simple correction of Asia's apparent economic stagnation, it called for a cultural and social conversion and the formulation of principles upon which the 'New Society in South–East Asia should be fashioned'.[30] Overlooking the Soviet-style emphasis on planned and integrated economic systems, the Nanking model was reminiscent of the Marshall Plan and underscored the necessity of Western finance. Risking the ire of anti-colonial Asia, the authors suggested that, in order to ensure that development programs were of an anti-communist nature, contributing powers should retain some discretion over the funding and management of aid projects. In Canberra, the Nanking proposals met with a cool response. Burton, although sympathetic to both the thrust of the memorandum and Officer's observations, did not see any value in merely duplicating the UN-managed organisations already in existence, such as ECAFE and the Food and Agricultural Organisation.[31] Officer countered Burton's response by suggesting that the communist influence within these organisations rendered them impotent, mere producers of propaganda and endless discussion. In case his secretary had missed the point, Officer repeated himself: 'What I want is a small very informal machine confined to those who are really prepared to fight Communism of the Soviet variety in the proper way, namely by improving conditions and so providing no field for it'.[32]

The Nanking proposals were never formally implemented, but they at least brought many of the ideas that had been circulating in secret into the open. Commonwealth officials moved closer together on significant issues: the communist strategy had far-reaching regional (perhaps global) consequences; any measures to counter communist expansion required substantial external finance; and, most importantly, Asian governments needed to have considerable discretion and control over that assistance.

Meanwhile, the British Foreign Office made a series of valiant, but unsuccessful, attempts to persuade the US State Department that they should consider providing financial aid to the region. The rhetorical power of Truman's address was not enough to overcome Congressional reluctance to underwrite the reform of the economies of South and South–East Asia. In talks with Britain, the State Department played down the likelihood of American support, dismissed suggestions of a Marshall Plan for Asia as impractical, and hoped that Asian states would tackle the communist problem themselves.[33] American resources were already stretched to cover the Cold War in Europe, and no funds could be spared for Asia. Needless to say, the billions of dollars wasted bolstering Chiang Kai-shek dampened American enthusiasm to embark on another mission to save Asia from communist revolution. These halting attempts to build a regional group faltered also because Western powers, hoping for a tacitly non-communist forum, were still reluctant to enter into a deeper dialogue that inevitably would expose the extent of Asia's technical and capital needs. And without the prospect of aid, there was little incentive for Asian nations to suspend their misgivings about joining a union with their former colonial masters.

Unbeknown to British and Australian officials, American policy-makers were secretly considering the strategic ramifications of a communist Asia and the potential role Western countries such as Australia and New Zealand might serve. An important analysis commissioned by the US State Department proposed that Congressional support for any regional initiative, economic or otherwise, required the dramatisation of the communist threat and the alternative offered by regional collaboration. In order to foster a bulwark against Soviet imperialism, the report recommended US policy should aim to coordinate the discussion of economic and political problems, promote the economic integration of Japan, and facilitate a program of economic and cultural assistance. Significantly, the report suggested that the United States should endeavour to draw regional powers such as 'India, Australia and New Zealand into more direct responsibility for the welfare and stability of the area as a whole'.[34] While British policy-makers concluded that the Commonwealth remained the preferred instrument for achieving regional unity, they too envisaged a pivotal role for the dominions. After conducting investigations into food supply and other counter-measures to communist disturbance, the Foreign Office determined that 'not only are we in the best position to interest the United States in active participation in maintaining the stability of the area, but our relations with the Commonwealth provide a means of influencing and coordinating the policies not only of the Asiatic Dominions, but of Australia and New Zealand, whose strategic interests in the area are, in fact, equal to our own'.[35] Throughout the year bureaucrats on both sides of the Atlantic produced papers and continued negotiations, but the opportunity for the Commonwealth to take the lead went begging.

The British–American talks only recognised Australia to the extent that she supported a much broader vision of regional economic and political hegemony. Men like John Burton, however, envisaged a more active Australian presence — particularly in regard to Indonesia — working in concert with the United States and other international agencies.[36] Aside from disputes between the DEA and the Department of Defence over the emphasis on defence preparations, the notion that development promoted stability was widely endorsed. By seeing poverty as the major cause of socio-political instability in South–East Asia, the Defence Department conceded Burton's main proposition that 'appropriate political and economic measures' should supplement military preparations.[37] In April 1949, just before Mao's troops captured the Chinese capital, the Minister for Defence, John Dedman, threw his department's weight behind the DEA and endorsed the creation of a 'programme of political and economic action' intended to remove the possibility of a 'political and military vacuum' and arrest the spread of communism throughout Asia.[38]

To this end, the DEA recalled its representatives in Japan, China, the Philippines, Thailand, Malaya and India to Canberra in November 1949 for an informal exchange of

views with departmental heads. Also invited to the first two
days of the meeting were M.E. Dening, Assistant Under-
Secretary for Far Eastern Affairs at the Foreign Office, and
Alister McIntosh, Secretary of New Zealand's Department of
External Affairs. With Evatt in the chair, discussions focused
largely on recent political developments and the 'threat of
communism through Asia and the possibility of armed
conflict' involving Australia, while a cooperative arrangement
with South–East Asia 'through some form of regional pact or
association' was formally, although inconclusively, debated.
Delegates discussed the apparent show of unity at New Delhi
earlier in the year and yet another attempt to establish an anti-
communist league, this time from the President of the
Philippines, Elpidio Quirino. All remained concerned that
'mutual suspicion among countries of the region were deep-
seated and must be eradicated before much real political
cooperation could be expected' and New Zealand signaled its
reluctance to become involved in the affairs of Asia.[39]

When the representatives from the United Kingdom
and New Zealand departed, the conference turned to the
specific economic, political and diplomatic challenges to
Australian interests: namely, the lack of awareness among
Australian officials of potential dangers from Asia; the
limited number of skilled diplomats able to represent
Australian interests; the language barrier; Australia's 'bad
reputation' in Japan; the economic problems faced by
South–East Asia; Australia's commercial policy and tariff
restrictions; supply shortages in Australia; and, not least,
the need for greater American assistance.[40] Capturing the
general tenor of the group, Burton's working paper for these
meetings, entitled 'Australia and South–East Asia', stated
that Australia was 'no longer in a position to assume that its
future security and progress [were] assured within the
framework of the British Commonwealth alone'. Building
the 'weak states' of South–East Asia into a 'buffer region

between us and the Asian mainland' required 'a substantial
re-orientation of Australian thought and practice' and a
movement away from the tendency to form alliances with
Western powers.[41]

Burton's ideas reached the highest level in the form
of a tightly argued Cabinet paper, submitted after the
November conference and just before the December 1949
federal election. Evoking the memory of Australia's
vulnerability during the Second World War, the paper
stated that the Japanese advance southwards had 'brought
home to us the extent of our geographical relationship with
Asia and of our geographic isolation from our traditional
points of cultural and economic contact in Europe and
America'. Although active military intervention was
thought unnecessary to prevent the spread of communism,
Burton conceded that an armed response might become
necessary should events change rapidly. But the substantive
changes he proposed were of a deeper and more far-
reaching character. Asia's movement towards autonomy
was 'inevitable and natural', and the changing international
environment demanded nothing less than a 'permanent re-
orientation of Australian outlook and policy'. The Cabinet
paper recommended that Australia's national interests
would be best served by fostering the technological,
economic and social advancement of the region through
increased diplomatic representation, a greater emphasis on
local language and customs, trade promotion, the
relaxation of trade restrictions, closer relations with the
Indonesian military, and an extensive program of technical
education. He also acknowledged that, owing to material
shortages in Australia, any attempt to distribute aid equally
among South–East Asian nations would be counter-
productive. Rather, it would be better to concentrate on
countries, such as Indonesia, where Australia would

achieve the most benefit. The Australian people also needed to ready themselves for Japan's industrial resurgence as a supplier of manufactured goods and importer of raw materials. Significantly, official and public attitudes towards Japan had the potential to nullify Australia's broader policy of increased commercial, political and cultural engagement with South–East Asia. The government, therefore, was obliged to follow a 'conscious policy of educating the public to a greater awareness of the growing interdependence of Australia and South–East Asia'. Burton's appraisal was perhaps the most sharply observed and radical to have been presented before Cabinet. But not everyone was ready to embrace the DEA's recommendations. Indeed, Chifley had only recently denied a British request to provide aid to Burma — the region's greatest food exporter – because he feared the money would be wasted and that it would be impossible to garner popular support for such a decision. Yet, despite this early resistance, the basic thrust of Burton's analysis would go on to form the central pillar of Australia's international aid policy.[42]

The defeat of the Chifley Labor government by the Liberal–Country Party coalition in December 1949 appeared to end the independent trend in Australian foreign policy mapped out by Evatt and Burton. Labor and the Coalition may have shared a deep interest in Australian security, but there was no doubt that a new era in Australian foreign relations had begun. The Cold War polarised world politics into two diametrically opposed camps. For the Menzies government, the spectre of international communism posed the most serious threat to the nation. The United Nations was seen to be manifestly unable to protect Australia from this threat, and establishing an alliance with a great power became a fundamental objective. Australia aligned its foreign policy with the United States by withholding recognition of China, working to keep both China and India out of the Soviet orbit, and seeing that Japan remained militarily weak although industrially strong. Significantly, as the DEA noted, Australia would support the aspirations of independent Asian nations provided they were 'capable of contributing to the economic, political and military strength of the West'.[43] But there was some continuity between Spender's approach to regional affairs and that of his predecessors. They each shared a conviction that Australia needed to guard against its isolation, not just by retreating to the secure embrace of powerful Western allies, but also by helping poor nations to develop and by actively projecting political and cultural influence outside Australia's borders. They each shared the faith that technological, economic and cultural advancement was the natural antidote to the instability that seemed to be creeping across the region.

————

The proclamation of the People's Republic of China on 1 October 1949 quickened Britain's desire to hold a conference to discuss Asian economic and political affairs. On 3 November 1949, British Prime Minister Clement Attlee asked his opposite number in Ceylon, Don Stephen Senanayake, to prepare for a meeting of Commonwealth foreign ministers in January the following year. The conference was, at least superficially, simply another in a series of discussions between Commonwealth representatives that had been taking place since 1944. However, this meeting differed in three significant ways. First, in addition to the issues of European reconstruction and the Japanese Peace Treaty, delegates were to consider the ramifications of the victory of the Chinese Communist Party. Secondly, this was the first time that representatives from the newly independent countries — Pakistan, India and Ceylon —were included on the council and given the opportunity to discuss their views on regional issues. Thirdly, this was the first Commonwealth ministers' meeting convened on Asian soil.

For Australia, the decision to hold the meeting in the Ceylonese capital, Colombo, confirmed a shift in the epicentre of world affairs. Commonwealth forces had been called upon to fight communist insurgents in Malaya, Dutch troops had only recently stopped fighting Indonesian nationalists, and the French were struggling to retain control of Indochina. Most agreed that events in Asia were set to further impinge on Australia's regional future and, as one parliamentarian said, Australia had a 'duty to the awakening giant of Asia that is seeking a place in the world.'[44] But there was still no immediate or obvious means of fulfilling this duty. No forum, political or economic, united Asia, save for the sporadic efforts of UN agencies such as ECAFE, UNESCO, the United Nations International Children's Emergency Fund (UNICEF), and the International Bank for Reconstruction and Development (IBRD). In fact, the Commonwealth remained the main organisational and political link that joined Asia and the West, and that link was tainted with the history of colonialism. If Western powers hoped to foster an independent, stable and non-communist Asia, a new system of cooperation had to be devised. Expectations for the Colombo conference were high. After all, a meeting of this kind had been four years in the making. But exactly how Asia and the West could be brought together remained to be seen. What role Australia might play at this historic conference was similarly unclear.

Footnotes

1   A. Deakin, _Federal story: the inner history of the federal cause 1880–1900_, Melbourne, Melbourne University Press, 1963, p. 179

2   _Sydney Morning Herald_, 3 September 1907

3   R.C. Thompson, _Australian imperialism in the Pacific: the expansionist era, 1820–1920_, Melbourne, Melbourne University Press, 1980, p. 45; _New York Times_, 4 June 1918

4   L.F. Fitzhardinge, _William Morris Hughes: a political biography, vol. 2_, Sydney, Angus and Robertson, 1979, p. 388; W.M. Hughes, _The splendid adventure_, London, Ernest Benn Limited, 1929, pp. 99–100

5   Quoted in C. Hazlehurst, _Menzies observed_, Sydney, George Allen & Unwin, 1979, pp. 289–93

6   _CPD (HoR)_, vol. 201, 16 February 1949, p. 383

7   _Sydney Morning Herald_, 8 January 1949

8   _Conversation with Percy Spender: Hazel de Berg collection_, TRC 353–355, NLA

9   P. Spender, _Politics and a man_, Sydney, Collins, 1972, p. 326; P. Spender, _Exercises in diplomacy: the ANZUS Treaty and the Colombo Plan_, Sydney, Sydney University Press, 1969, pp. 31–2; _CPD (HoR)_, vol. 204, 15 October 1949, p. 964; _CPD (HoR)_, vol. 201, 16 February 1949, p. 354; _CPD (HoR)_, vol. 189, 15 November 1946, p. 338; _CPD (HoR)_, vol. 184, 30 August 1945, p. 5037

10 H.V. Evatt, _Foreign policy of Australia speeches_, Sydney, Angus and Robertson, 1945, pp. 155–56, 165–66; _CPD (HoR)_, vol. 180, 30 November 1944, pp. 2536–37

11 _Straits Times_, 17 May 1946; Quoted in T. Remme, _Britain and regional cooperation in South–East Asia, 1945–49_, London, Routledge, 1995, pp. 52, 86

12 Despatch, Massey to Evatt, 31 March 1947, A1068 ER47/3/8, NAA

13 Quoted in N. Tarling, _The Cambridge history of South–East Asia, vol. 4_, Cambridge, Cambridge University Press, 1999, p. 267; _CPD (HoR)_, vol. 190, 26 February 1947, pp. 164–66

14 Cable, W. Macmahon Ball, Singapore to Burton, 7 June 1948, A4968, 25/35/1, NAA; W. Macmahon Ball, 'Report on a mission to East Asia', 27 July 1948, A1838, 381/1/3/1, NAA

15 Memo, Stuart to Burton, 11 June 1948, A4968, 25/35 Part 1, NAA

16 Memo, Chifley to Dedman, 6 October 1948, A1068, DL47/5/6, NAA

17 Burton to Chifley, 'Political appreciation', 30 September 1948, A1838, 381/3/3/1, NAA

18 Burton to Chifley, 'Political appreciation'

19 Department of External Affairs, _Information handbook no. 2: Australia's aid to developing countries_, Canberra, 1964; C. Waters, 'The Macmahon Ball mission to East Asia, 1948', _Australian Journal of Politics and History_, vol. 40, no. 3, 1994, pp. 351–63

20 'Australian aid to South–East Asia', 8 December 1949, A1838, 532/7, part 1, NAA

21 Remme, _Britain and regional cooperation_, pp. 140–43

22 Asian Relations Conference, *Asian relations: being report of the proceedings and documentation of the first Asian Relations Conference, New Delhi, March–April, 1947*, New Delhi, Asian Relations Organization, 1948, pp. 15–27

23 'Recommendations of the conference of Prime Ministers — October 1948', 25 November 1948, A5799, 4/1949, NAA; Commonwealth Prime Ministers' Meeting, New Delhi, 12 October 1948, A1209, 1957/5826, NAA; Remme, *Britain and regional cooperation*, pp. 148–49

24 Quoted in D. McCullough, *Truman*, New York, Simon and Schuster, 1992, pp. 730–31

25 Girja Shankar Baijpai, Secretary-General of Indian Ministry of External Affairs and Commonwealth relations to H.R. Gollan, High Commissioner in India, 27 January 1949, A5009, A7/3/13, part 2, NAA

26 Despatch, Gollan to Evatt, 3 February 1949, A4231, 1949/New Delhi, NAA

27 K.M. Panikkar, *In two Chinas: memoirs of a diplomat*, London, Allen & Unwin, 1955, p. 55

28 'The Ambassador in China (Stuart) to the Secretary of State', 8 March 1949, *FRUS*, 1949, vol. 7, part 2, pp. 1119–20

29 Despatch, Officer to Evatt, 7 March 1949, A6768, EATS 36, NAA

30 Despatch, Officer to Evatt, 11 March 1949, A4231, 49/Nanking, NAA

31 Memo, Burton to Officer, 29 March 1949, A4145, RC2, NAA

32 Memo, Officer to Burton, 19 April 1949, A1838 490/2, part 5, NAA

33 Memorandum of conversation, by the Director of the Office of Far Eastern Affairs (Butterworth), 12 September 1949, *FRUS*, 1949, vol. 7, part 2, pp. 1197–1204

34 'Outline of Far Eastern and Asian policy for review with the President', 14 November 1949, *FRUS*, 1949, vol. 7, part 2, p. 1214

35 Quoted in Remme, *Britain and regional cooperation*, pp. 165, 192–95

36 'Relations with South–East Asia', 13 November 1949, A1068, DL47/5/6, NAA

37 Memo, Dedman to Holloway, 22 April 1949, A1068, DL47/5/6, NAA

38 Working paper, 'Australia and South–East Asia', 13 November 1949, A621, 753, NAA

39 'Discussions on Asia with representatives of the United Kingdom and New Zealand at Canberra, 10–11 November, 1949', A1838, 535/5/2/2, NAA; 'Summary record of discussions between representatives of the DEA, Commerce and Agriculture and Defence, and Australian representatives in South East Asia, 14 November, 1949', A1838, 532/5/2/2, NAA

40 'Commonwealth policy on South–East Asia', Minute paper, 17 November 1949, A621, 753, NAA; 'Relations with South–East Asia', 13 November 1949, A1086, DL47/5/6, NAA

41 'Australia and South–East Asia: working paper', 13 November 1949, A1086, DL47/5/6, NAA

42 'Australian policy in South–East Asia', December 1949, A1838, 532/5/2/2, NAA; C. Waters, *The empire fractures: Anglo–Australian conflict in the 1940s*, Melbourne, Australian Scholarly Publishing, 1995, pp. 180–83

43 'Note on Australian political objectives and methods in Asia', 1952, A1838, 3004/11 part 1, NAA

44 *CPD (HoR)*, vol. 206, 21 March 1950, p. 973

3. BUILDING A
BRIDGE TO ASIA

In Colombo, on the morning of 9 January 1950, a small crowd gathered to catch a glimpse of representatives arriving for the conference. Delegates posed for a publicity photograph in the gardens opposite the Senate building, unperturbed by a recent theft of explosives and threats to disrupt the meeting. Ceylon's first Prime Minister and conference chairman, the affable Don Stephen Senanayake, moved proudly among the representatives from eight nations and smiled through his magnificent drooping moustache. He knew that the Colombo conference would make headlines and that Ceylon would, at least briefly, be in the world spotlight. To ensure maximum publicity, the British provided confidential daily reports to the US State Department and granted American journalists access to the daily background briefings typically only open to Commonwealth reporters. The popular press in Australia celebrated the 'frank get-together' as a triumph of the egalitarian nature of the Commonwealth with 'all members ... now equal, irrespective of their size, race or creed'.[1] Australia's Percy Spender, who had only been foreign minister for two weeks since the Menzies government's sweeping victory, also mingled among the delegates from Britain, Canada, Ceylon, India, New Zealand, Pakistan, and South Africa. Following the photo session, Senanayake ushered the delegates and their entourages inside. The sixty-year-old Prime Minister of India, Jawaharlal Nehru, jauntily trotted up the stairs, demonstrating his energy to everyone. By contrast, the infirm British Foreign Secretary Ernest Bevin, his strength sapped further by the tropical heat, was carried from the street to the meeting room atop a palanquin (a chair carried on the shoulders of four men). The image served as an apt metaphor for the end of British imperialism and the rise of Asian nationalism. Indeed, although not officially attending, the Americans saw the conference as something of a last hoorah for the British Empire: 'the dying glow of a setting sun', as one US congressman put it.[2]

Once assembled, proceedings moved quickly. In the hot conditions, the congenial opening speeches and discussion were disturbed only by the Senate building's resident crows, who called raucously through the open windows. At regular intervals, Senanayake brought proceedings to a halt with a clap of his hands. Almost immediately, barefooted servants dressed in white sarongs and red sashes padded among the delegates bearing trays of iced water and sweet tea.[3] In welcoming delegates, Senanayake signalled the central purpose of the historic meeting. The obstacles to regional stability, he said, were economic — not political — and nothing less than the peace and future of the world depended on helping Asia support her increasing population.

No one knew quite what to expect from the Australian delegation. Spender's wife, Jean, always said that her husband had a knack for attracting public attention. By virtue of his temperament and professional experience, few men were better qualified to raise international interest in Australia's concerns about the political future of Asia.[4] For Spender, the British Commonwealth Foreign Ministers' Meeting presented a tantalising opportunity to establish Australia as a force in regional affairs; and he made no attempt to disguise the anti-communist sentiment which drove his determination to launch an aid program for South and South–East Asia. Before he left Colombo, Spender told a reporter that he hoped to find a way to support Asians in their bid to 'develop their own democratic institutions and their own economies and thus protect them against those opportunists and subversive elements which take advantage of changing political situations and low living standards'.[5] In his opening address, he returned to one of his favorite themes and told of the 'inescapable fact' of Australia's geographical proximity and the increasingly active role in regional affairs she wanted to play. Delegates, he said, had a responsibility to determine a clear course of action to help stabilise the region and they must not squander the opportunity. 'Could not the old Commonwealth countries contribute part of their resources for the economic development of this area?' Spender asked, gently preparing delegates for his own prescription for regional development, due to be presented the following day.

According to Spender's own recollection, he began formulating a strategy for bringing Western finance to bear on Asia's seemingly intractable economic problems during the long flight from Sydney to Ceylon. Although the comment is characteristic of Spender's brusque style, this was, in fact, probably the first time he had a chance to examine his briefing papers in detail. Of course, they were rich with documents on Asian affairs written by some of the sharpest minds in the Department of External Affairs, which would have been unavailable to him while in opposition. Nevertheless, the 'wide authority' Menzies had granted Spender over how to approach the conference undoubtedly enhanced his sense of propriety.[6] Spender, however, was in for a surprise.

On the afternoon of the second day, Ceylon's unassuming Finance Minister, Junius Richard Jayewardene, stunned everyone, most of all the Australians, when he foreshadowed his own proposal for regional economic development. The essence of Jayewardene's proposal was for Asian governments to draw up ten-year development programs and for the Commonwealth to consider what technical and financial assistance it could provide and guarantee a fixed price for primary exports. A committee of experts would then tour Asia and make recommendations based on what the Commonwealth had made available. Incensed that another delegation appeared to have pipped the Australians, Spender later accused Jayewardene of 'deliberately jumping the gun'.[7] Spender need not have worried. Delegates responded unenthusiastically to Jayewardene's overly ambitious vision. Moreover, the idea of a regulated Commonwealth trading bloc raised more political and economic complexities than it claimed to solve. That evening, Spender and his advisers from the DEA, Arthur Tange and Laurence McIntyre, retired to the colonial splendor of the Galle Face Hotel to finalise the memorandum they had begun writing on the plane. Around this time, it would seem, they also took advice from senior British officials, who were keen for Australia to take the lead and thus deflect any expectation that the United Kingdom was about to offer a more substantial financial contribution. On the morning of 11 January the Australians tabled their freshly-completed document ahead of the Ceylonese delegation, thus ensuring that theirs would be considered first.

Like his Commonwealth colleagues, Spender knew that, without a massive injection of funds, talk of an economic bulwark against communism was futile.[8] As he told Menzies in a telegram from Colombo, his principal objective was to 'show a genuine willingness to meet the serious drift in the political and economic situation in South East Asia, as a basis for an immediate approach to the United States with a view of enlisting their active participation'.[9] The Australian memorandum was structured around the speedy delivery of financial and technical assistance in order to demonstrate the Commonwealth's resolve to fight communism. Drawing heavily on the work of John Burton, the Australian plan located the provision of aid as an international response to the rise of Asian communism: through economic and social development the 'ideological attractions which communism exerts will lose their force'.[10] It called on the Commonwealth to contribute to the UN's Technical Assistance Program, to provide aid to Asia on a bilateral basis, to coordinate the aid delivery with other Commonwealth governments, and for Asian nations to make submissions detailing their development needs, and for the conference to establish a consultative committee to oversee the logistics of delivering aid to the region. The recipients would be Ceylon, India and Pakistan, with non-Commonwealth Asia to be included as soon as possible.

Central to Spender's tactics at Colombo was his conviction that an expensive and open-ended scheme, such as Jayewardene's 'somewhat grandiose proposal' for an

Asian Marshall Plan, would repel the United States. Although delegates had politely dismissed Jayewardene's ideas as unworkable, Spender feared that any obvious lack of consensus among the delegates would jeopardise the entire conference: the Commonwealth would appear fractured and ill-prepared to meet the task of Asian development with conviction. In private, Spender persuaded Jayewardene to support a joint memorandum based primarily on the ideas circulated by Australia. The British, anxious to avoid accusations of post-colonial domination, were content to let Australia take the lead. For his part, Spender tactfully dampened suspicion of economic imperialism by including a clause suggesting that the form of development 'is for Asian countries themselves to determine'.[11] New Zealand agreed to sponsor the proposal, despite private misgivings about Spender, whom the Secretary for the Department of External Affairs, Alister McIntosh, thought 'an absolute little tick', and their doubts about the very idea of an aid program for Asia. 'It is perfectly ridiculous to think that we of the British Commonwealth countries, even with the aid of the United States, can with economic aid effectively stem the tide of Communism', wrote McIntosh; 'for one thing we can't do enough quickly, and for another, what we do is going to be swallowed up and lost in ineffective administration. We haven't a hope in the world'.[12]

Throughout the conference, Spender emphasised the utmost importance of a rapid and enthusiastic response from Western powers. As if on cue, Spender's entreaties about the impending threat of communism and the need for the Commonwealth to move quickly received a timely illustration on the very days delegates were considering his proposals. On 13 January 1950, the Soviet Union's walkout of the UN Security Council, in protest at the failure of the

Security Council to recognise the Chinese communist regime's right to take China's seat on the council, demonstrated Sino–Soviet rapport. However, rising international tension and Spender's determination were not enough to guarantee uncritical support for the proposals. India wanted further research to be conducted before committing to any specific development programs. The British were the most reticent of all, reminding delegates of their government's responsibilities in Africa and the Middle East and of the money already given for the post-war reconstruction in South–East Asia. Nevertheless, publicly, each delegation agreed that communism posed a threat to the region and that economic and social improvement was vital to regional stability. The joint memorandum captured the broad scope of this idea, and showed the right blend of flexibility and precision, which the Ceylonese proposal lacked. Further, the memorandum stressed that the restoration of Asia as an economically productive region would also have commercial benefits for the West. Towards the end of proceedings, representatives voted unanimously in favour of what they now called the 'Spender resolution' — and some even began talking of a 'Spender Plan' for Asia. All agreed to meet for the inaugural meeting of the Commonwealth Consultative Committee in Sydney in four months time. The Ceylonese government capped off the conference by showering upon the delegates a 'glittering series of entertainments', including a rare showing of the sacred relic of Buddha's tooth during an excursion to Kandy, the capital of the hill country — an experience which seemed to fortify the ailing Bevin![13]

Spender was certainly pleased with the outcome of the Colombo conference, but there was little exuberance. He knew how far he had to go. Upon his return to Canberra, he began a campaign to raise domestic and international support for an Asian aid program. Specifically, he continued to woo the United States, hoping to win them over to the Colombo proposals and involve them more explicitly in Australia's regional security. Indeed, giving aid to Asia served the dual purpose of building relations with Asia, but also with the United States. It was a policy validated by Australia's ambassador to the United States, Norman Makin, who, in December 1949, told his newly-elected Minister that efforts should be directed towards making Australia indispensable to America's strategic and economic planning. Although sacrifices would have to be made, rendering 'technical and material assistance to the countries of South–East Asia … would receive the warm approval and goodwill of the US'.[14] Now a decision on the magnitude of Australia's contribution had to be reached quickly in order to demonstrate Australia's commitment to sharing the burden of combating communism in alliance with the Americans.[15] Privately, Spender lobbied Cabinet. Publicly, he adopted a broader strategy that emphasised the growing threat of international communism, regional instability, the inadequacy of the UN, Australian vulnerability, and the necessity of US financial support for Asia.

On 9 March 1950, Spender delivered one of the clearest articulations of conservative foreign policy to the House of Representatives. He told of the growing force of communism and Australia's vulnerability in post-colonial Asia — with Australia drifting within the grasp of communism, without the stability of a resolute and strong ally. The Soviet Union and communist China were to blame for throwing Asia into disarray, casting it and the world into a 'trance of uncertainty, doubt and fear'. Should communism prevail, Spender said, 'and Vietnam come under the heel of Communist China, Malaya is in danger of being out-flanked and it, together with Thailand, Burma and Indonesia, will become the next direct object of further Communist activities'. The burden of regional security now fell to Australia because Britain and America had 'not yet completed their adjustments to the new situation'. Spender deftly juxtaposed another image of Australia as a purposeful and strong Pacific power which, assuming appropriate and resolute action, could assert a stabilising presence in Asia: 'We live side by side with the countries of South and South–East Asia, and we desire to be on good-neighbour terms with them. Above all, it is in our interest to foster commercial and other contacts with them and give them what help we can in maintaining stable and democratic governments in power'. By developing the proposals endorsed at the Colombo conference, Australia would give to the maximum extent of its capacity 'those resources which will help consolidate the governments of South–East Asia on such a basis that no extremism can flourish'.[16]

Unlike Evatt and Burton, Spender had grave doubts about the ability of the UN to protect Australian interests, especially considering that it included representatives from those who were 'working to disrupt the order we believe in'. Instead, to avert the communist threat he hoped to create two mutually supportive instruments of Australian foreign policy: economic diplomacy (encompassing a 'policy of good-neighbourly assistance') and a military alliance with the United States. Using the same sentimental tone employed by Menzies to draw Australia closer to Britain, Spender regularly spoke of the United States as sharing a 'common heritage and way of life'. Importantly, he held little hope for a British 'adjustment in Australia's favour' and he considered the United States to be the natural substitute to help Australia secure both the economic and military aspects of its foreign policy objectives:

*I am sure our friends of the United States will not
misunderstand me when I say that their great
eminence in world affairs to-day not only imposes
corresponding obligations upon them, which it
should be recorded they have most generously been
willing to accept, but it also makes impossible the
solution of such problems as we are discussing
without their active co-operation.*[17]

Few would have missed the point: the era of the
Evatt/Burton analysis of world affairs was over and the
United States, not the UN, was to be the mainstay of
Australia's future survival in South–East Asia and the
Pacific. But the prospect of an Asian aid program served the
left-wing political agenda equally well. Leslie Haylen — a
radical Laborite who led a parliamentary delegation to
Japan in 1948 and caused a furore in Australia by shaking
hands with Emperor Hirohito — thought an aid program
might even realise a new sense of belonging:

*We must cast our eyes on the Asian scene and
endeavour to understand what the Asian is seeking.
We must assist him as far as we can with goods and
services, and cease ... this ridiculous habit of looking
continually to Atlantic Charters, Atlantic pacts, and
other similar regional agreements for our
preservation. On the evidence before us we are on
our own in the Pacific. Asian nation or Pacific
power, what does it matter? We are an outpost of
8,000,000 people dedicated to the task of being good
neighbours to the millions of people to our north. We
can, here and now, build up goodwill and strengthen
the feeling that we are part of the great southern
lands of Asia; that we do 'belong'; that we are not
antagonistic; and that we are not a handful of white*

people who have come to this country to exploit it
and then to get out. Our interests are those of Asia.

An insistent sense of cultural and racial vulnerability, combined with a desire to engage constructively with the region, prompted both sides of the house to support the Spender Plan as one way of maintaining 'democracy in Asia' and 'the future of every Australian man, woman and child'.[18]

While Spender's efforts were sufficient to convince cabinet to allocate £A13 million for Asian development projects, they were not enough to move the US State Department, which remained equivocal but not dismissive. Acting Secretary of State, James Webb, told his Canberra representative to convey the message that, although they declined to attend the Sydney meeting, America's non-attendance did not imply a 'lack of interest in or sympathy ... with the purposes and objectives' of the Colombo proposals.[19] Even better than diplomatic assurances, the DEA took solace in the United States' expanding, if 'imperfectly formulated' policy towards Asia, notably Truman's announcement of substantial economic aid for Indonesia and the French in Indochina.[20] At this point, however, Spender's biggest problem was the caution displayed by the British government.

On Monday 15 May 1950, delegates met at Admiralty House, the Governor-General's Sydney residence, for the first meeting of the Commonwealth Consultative Committee. Before the opening session, delegates had a chance to take in the view across the water, perfectly framed by the Sydney Harbour Bridge, an emblem of Australian industrial and technological prowess. This modern, thriving metropolis was a ready example to the delegates of what 'free men and women' could accomplish, Spender was later to write.[21] Days earlier, delegates had been treated to much of what

Sydney had to offer: sight-seeing, lavish dinners, and a day
at the Randwick races. The largest function was a formal
reception at the Australia Hotel. Spender put his cares aside,
turned on the charm, and together with his wife welcomed
more than 300 guests. At one point Spender cheekily
suggested to a Ceylonese delegate and his pregnant wife that
if their baby was a boy they should name him 'Sydney', if a
girl, 'Canberra'.[22] Outside, the atmosphere was less frivolous
and police clashed with communist demonstrators,
protesting Commonwealth military action in Malaya. In the
confusion, Eleanor Hinder of the British delegation (the
only female delegate) was mistaken for a demonstrator and
was about to be apprehended when another delegate
protested her innocence.

Spender's resolve to launch an aid program for Asia
had intensified since the Colombo meeting. By the time of
the Sydney meeting, he had become consumed with its
importance, no doubt helped along by the press, which
urged representatives towards more than 'a circumspect
elaboration' of the Colombo proposals.[23] By the time of the
Sydney meeting, differences between the Australian and
British approach to regional collaboration that emerged in
Colombo had deepened, in large part owing to their
uncoordinated strategies. Indeed, with the Foreign Office
concerned not to 'frighten the United States Administration
away from cooperation by loose talk of American aid in
staggering amounts', they advised their representatives to
assiduously 'avoid exchanging ideas with the Australian,
United States or other representatives'.[24] As delegates
arrived, Spender wrote to Bevin and explained his concern
that 'the UK government might not be in a position during
the Sydney discussions to accept proposals' that he had in
mind. 'Quite frankly', Spender threatened, if Britain
hesitated to commit funds, he would be 'compelled to

acknowledge publicly that the conference had failed and the Australian Government, for its part, be obliged to indicate that it would now seek to implement a programme of its own in conjunction with whatever other Governments might wish to assist'.[25] All this before the conference had even begun! A stoush between Australia and Britain seemed unavoidable.

Over the weekend Spender suggested to his fellow delegates that they should open the first session to the public to generate maximum interest in the meeting. Reluctantly they agreed, on condition that the speech be non-controversial, and they be given a chance to see an advance copy. Delegates were soon astonished to see that Spender intended to use the open session to publicly reveal the most contentious of his proposals. Protest from the other delegations, particularly the British, saw Spender back down. Nevertheless, the open session went ahead and delegates cordially exchanged the usual platitudes. In contrast to Spender's boiling energy, the British arrived in more sombre and cautious mood. Still reeling from the cost of war, Britain saw the Colombo proposals as an opportunity to address their own economic ills and revitalise the United Kingdom as a force in Asian affairs. A desire to use American finance to offset the massive debts owed to India and Pakistan underpinned the British position: for them there was simply 'no prospect of a satisfactory settlement of the sterling balance problem consistent with a continuous economic development in South and South East Asia unless new money can be found for development … from the United States'. Although the Australians did not see this document, they knew well that Britain had her 'eyes very much on the dollars to be obtained' from the Americans and later dismissed her as being inspired 'more by economic interests than foreign policy'.[26] The DEA never considered the release of sterling debt to India and Pakistan a genuine contribution to regional development, merely an action that they would have taken regardless of the Colombo proposals.[27]

Convinced that the best way to persuade the United States to join was to show an immediate commitment to putting money into Asia, Spender proposed the immediate formation of a technical assistance scheme and an emergency aid pool, which both Commonwealth and non-Commonwealth Asian countries could draw upon. The Australian delegation intended these two schemes to supplement a much longer-term capital aid program. The British opposed both proposals because more planning was required and they would not extend further finance on top of their already heavy debt. Worse still, their arguments helped persuade Asian representatives — initially attracted to the concept — to reject the idea. The argument that long-term economic planning would be more likely to attract a greater portion of American aid impressed the Indian and Ceylonese representatives. The Canadian delegation, also under instructions to avoid extended commitments, simply did not see the value in building an interim program. By the close of the meeting 'the Australian band wagon', reflected the Canadians, 'seemed considerably less crowded than it had been earlier in the afternoon'. Only Pakistan stood by the Australian delegation, primarily because it needed immediate finance to resettle eight million refugees from India.[28]

As self-appointed taskmaster, nothing infuriated Spender more than the apparent lack of commitment on the part of delegates towards the meeting's high purpose. By the afternoon of the first day of the meeting, he could no longer disguise his contempt for Britain's lack of commitment. During a secret session, Spender lambasted those who criticised his proposals and then, according to a British report, 'made a slashing attack on the United Kingdom attitude which he suggested had no regard to the Colombo resolution'. Spender then warned delegates 'that if the Australian resolution was not adopted he would have to report the full facts to his Parliament'. Stunned, the Canadian delegate felt the display was 'more intemperate than any [he had] ever heard except at conferences where Soviets were present'. Another wondered if the Australian minister had somehow imbibed the spirit of his predecessor, Doc Evatt.[29]

For his outburst, Spender earned the tag the 'cocksparrow'. The Australians parried by nicknaming Lord MacDonald, the leader of British party, 'No Commitment Mac'. And before long both delegations were invoking national stereotypes in their now public dispute. Australia played the role of cajoling dominion — the Empire's *enfant terrible* — while Britain played the reprimanding parent. Australia accused Britain of timidity, stand-offishness, and following a 'typically narrow Treasury approach'. The British followed up by suggesting that Australia was 'betraying signs of youthful impatience'.[30] Ted Williams, the British High Commissioner in Canberra, delivered a scathing report card:

> *The most disappointing delegation was the Australian. It was their misfortune … to feel compelled to take the initiative to a degree for which they were inadequately equipped, and it was still more unfortunate that the proposals which they advanced so vigorously … should be revealed on examination as shallow and lacking in substance. Worst of all, these proposals seem to be regarded by the Australian Delegation themselves as closely linked with Mr. Spender's personal prestige … Less*

happily it must be added that Mr. Spender's hopes that his reputation as an international statesman would be firmly established by the Sydney meeting have been completely disappointed. It is to be expected that other Delegations will in reporting to their Governments not fail to comment not only on his arrogant and willful conduct and undignified withdrawals, but also on his patent failure in the ordinary duties of a chairman.[31]

But a crisis in Commonwealth relations was averted when delegates reached an easy consensus over the proposal to provide long-term capital aid. Delegates agreed that each recipient country should produce comprehensive six-year development plans for consideration at the second meeting of the Consultative Committee, scheduled for September 1950. As it stood, the principal donor nations were Australia, New Zealand, the United Kingdom and Canada. Recipient nations included India, Pakistan and Ceylon. Non-Commonwealth Asian countries were soon encouraged to join the program. But the issue of supplying technical assistance would not go away. Later, Spender dropped the original proposal in favour of a fresh memorandum. The Australian delegation suggested a technical assistance program running for three years from 1 July 1950. At a cost of £8 million, Australia, Canada, and the United Kingdom would each contribute one third. After a number of amendments, delegates finally agreed and the British and Canadian delegations reported that they were authorised to contribute. However, that same evening, Spender revived the emergency credit proposal, thereby throwing the conference into disarray. Afterwards, Lord MacDonald explained privately the British objections to the new proposals.[32] Not to be dissuaded, a relentless Spender submitted yet another paper on emergency credits. This time

Robert Mayhew of the Canadian delegation told Spender
that there was insufficient time to discuss his proposals
and they must wait until the September meeting of the
Consultative Committee in London. Before the close of the
conference, Spender withdrew.

In his memoirs, the cocksparrow admitted that he
had not been 'the easiest, nor perhaps the most urbane, of
chairmen'. His greatest sin, however, was to have upset
Washington, who thought Spender was 'heavy-handed and
tactless', intent on establishing 'a foreign policy independent
not only of the UK but of the entire Commonwealth in
those areas where it cannot obtain general agreement'. By
casting aside the 'soft language of diplomacy', as Spender
called it, he almost destroyed the collaborative atmosphere
he thought so crucial to getting the United States involved.
And at the conclusion of the meeting a solid commitment
from the Americans remained outstanding.

The stress of the Sydney conference inflamed
Spender's duodenal ulcer and forced him to convalesce in
Bowral, in the southern highlands of New South Wales.[33]
Given his tenacious approach, Spender may have thought
it entirely appropriate that the program bear his name.
But when the Consultative Committee convened for
the second time, in London between 25 September and
4 October 1950, the 'Colombo Plan' emerged as the
preferred label; talk of the 'Spender Plan' was quietly
forgotten by all but a few.

Before the London meeting, a standing committee
convened in Colombo to establish a Council for Technical
Cooperation and discuss the technical aid bound for India,
Pakistan and Ceylon. On the more difficult issue of the
capital aid program, Commonwealth officials had to reach
important and politically complex decisions about the way
donor nations would provide and coordinate their aid
programs. Although the Commonwealth unceremoniously

rejected Jayewardene's dream of an Asian Marshall Plan, they might have forgiven him for drawing the parallel. After all, as the first major multilateral program of foreign assistance after the Second World War, the Marshall Plan initially appeared to offer a practical model for the delivery of aid to the region. Through the Organisation for European Economic Cooperation (OEEC), the United States spent billions on reconstruction in order to foster economic and spiritual resistance to the attractions of communist ideology.[34] The OEEC had a decentralised governing agency with power residing with national delegations, and it promoted international cooperation, but not economic and political integration. It also had a weak secretariat and a secretary-general with limited authority.[35] Of course, the situation in Asia was radically different. In Sydney, Spender acknowledged the 'great divergence' in economic and social development within Asia and recognised that the physical and human infrastructures of Europe did not exist on the same scale in Asia, and that there was no pre-war precedent against which to measure the goals of reconstruction. In what can best be described as a profound understatement, Spender summed up by saying that 'economic planning for a region so diverse as South and South–East Asia will not be easy. There are no ready-made guidelines'.[36] To make the Consultative Committee mechanism flexible and robust enough to tackle such a task, Commonwealth policy-makers faced numerous obstacles. Not only did the Consultative Committee have to remain a tacitly non-communist avenue for regional cooperation, it had to be free from political qualifications in order to attract Asian countries, and represent nations of varying political persuasions that were at substantially different stages of economic development. Overlay the political and strategic goals Western policy-makers hoped to achieve through the provision of aid, and the challenges facing the Consultative Committee were immense.

In the first flush of excitement to attract additional donors, the DEA planned to persuade Asian governments not to 'raise obstacles to the inclusion of France and the Netherlands'.[37] But the endeavour proved ill-conceived, and France and the Netherlands were quietly sidelined from the Colombo Plan negotiations. In such a sensitive climate, Australia dropped the idea, regarding it as 'premature and impolitic'. With French troops still engaged in Indo-China and the imbroglio over West New Guinea far from over, the inclusion of these powers had the potential to jeopardise the entire program. Later, the DEA determined that the inclusion of France and the Netherlands would alienate Burma, Indonesia and Thailand, leaving a scheme 'preponderantly for Commonwealth–Asian and "Western" governments, which was not and is not the intention of the Plan'. Further, pressure for their admission would 'provide ammunition for communist propaganda ("new form of colonialism") against the Plan'.[38]

In Sydney the Consultative Committee had proved itself a robust, if somewhat unwieldy, forum for discussing regional issues. But why was it necessary to duplicate established UN mechanisms, such as ECAFE, which already funded Asian development programs? Or, as Canada's Minister for External Affairs, Lester Pearson, explained when he returned home after the Colombo meeting to address parliament: did the world need a new committee to bring aid to Asia 'merely because it looks like an attractive piece of international furniture for an already cluttered-up home'?[39] While the exact nature of the Consultative Committee was determined in private discussions between Australian, British, and American officials, parliamentary discussion presented Spender with an opportunity to garner government and opposition support for the new venture. Spender used the debate to reinforce his conviction that the communist threat required a rapid response, and, once again, he attacked the excesses and inefficiencies of the UN multilateral aid agencies. More to the point, he deemed ECAFE an inappropriate mechanism for the delivery of aid because the Soviet Union and China were both members and Canada and Ceylon were not — a clear violation of the Commonwealth's anti-communist agenda.[40] With the Consultative Committee framed as an independent (i.e. non-UN) and tacitly non-communist development forum, Australia had a more direct aid relationship with Asia. The informal structure established a congenial and non-threatening forum outside the communist gaze and, as Spender suggested, filled a 'conspicuous gap in an area of profound interest to Australia'.[41] Most importantly, Australia's limited aid budget would not be subsumed under the mantle of another UN program, thus giving Australia the freedom to use aid for specific political, strategic, and diplomatic objectives. British thinking ran on similar lines. Not only did the forum give Western powers the chance to bring 'discrete [*sic*] pressure to bear on the underdeveloped countries to tackle the problems of development planning in a realistic and energetic way', it provided a venue where Asian countries could discuss development issues 'frankly and without publicity (or polemical interference from the Russians, who are members of ECAFE)'.[42] Although communist powers expressed little interest in joining the Colombo Plan, which they considered an imperialist ruse, in 1952 the Consultative Committee invited ECAFE representatives to observe the annual conference. The decision amounted to a tactful compromise because Western powers considered it decidedly easier to manage the Russians and Chinese within the confines of ECAFE, than risk having them joining the Colombo Plan and compromise its non-communist exclusivity.[43]

Australian parliamentarians and bureaucrats hoped that the United States would broaden its cold war economic and military strategies to include Asia. The outbreak of the Korean War on 25 June 1950, by amplifying fears of a wider regional conflict, lent greater urgency to Commonwealth plans to apply financial and technical assistance as a containment strategy. And Australia's speedy despatch of force to the Korean peninsula served as a tangible expression of the commitment to fighting communism and its support for US foreign policy, as did withholding recognition of communist China, and granting recognition of Vietnam's anti-communist leader, Bao Dai. These decisions would eventually help secure the second arm of Spender's regional security strategy, namely the ANZUS (Australia, New Zealand, and United States) Treaty, officially endorsed in February 1951. But Spender also hoped that the United States would now be far more predisposed to joining the new aid program. Behind the scenes, US officials began talking more freely about the possibility and implications of funding: that US foreign policy should rely on something more than military might in order to contain Asian communism, and that cooperation would build a link between east and west 'more powerful than guns and more precious than gold'.[44]

Washington's decision to appoint a liaison officer to the London meeting of the Consultative Committee was the clearest indication yet of America's changed attitude towards Asian development. Yet, British and Australian representatives knew there was no guarantee of US endorsement and that the results of this meeting would be more important than those of the previous two.[45] The first job faced by delegates was to assess the development questionnaires (similar to those used by the OEEC) distributed after the Sydney conference on the suggestion of the British official Robert 'Otto' Clark.[46] The economic and technical blueprints submitted to the meeting, however, proved to be little more than an attempt to give the impression that donor nations were making a genuine attempt to quantify Asia's economic needs, while providing a convenient means of arriving at a total figure with which to approach the United States. Revealing attitudes underwritten by no small amount of paternalistic condescension, most thought Asian governments ill-equipped to assess their own developmental needs. In August 1950, James Plimsoll, Australia's representative to the UN, reported to Burton's replacement at the DEA, Alan Watt. A senior official from the Economic Cooperation Administration explained that he had little 'faith in questionnaires' because 'most under-developed countries [were] unfitted to estimate their needs accurately or sensibly'. He also suggested that the Commonwealth and the United States should determine the total amount of assistance to be allocated to Asia and leave decisions on 'the nature of that assistance' to their representatives 'on the spot'.[47] The fact that the Commonwealth had to postpone the London meeting by two weeks after it became obvious that Asian non-Commonwealth governments were struggling to complete the questionnaires on time reinforced the apparent ineptitude of aid recipients. In any event, the simple attendance of non-Commonwealth Asia was more important than completion of the six-year development plans and, regardless of what they specified, there was no time for 'substantial modification' of the programs already planned by the UK Government.[48] Malcolm MacDonald, the UK Commissioner-General in Singapore, reasoned that by at least appearing to be responsive to these blueprints, even if they proved irrelevant, donor nations avoided 'the psychological error of arousing suspicion amongst these sensitive peoples'.[49] Despite the extension of time, the first report of the Consultative Committee included Commonwealth Asia only. Cambodia, Thailand, Laos, and Vietnam each attended the London meeting without lodging formal requests for assistance. Burma and Indonesia, still wary of post-colonial domination, attended as observers only.

The economic blueprints served a more useful tactical purpose in persuading the United States that joining the Colombo Plan would not bind them indefinitely to underwriting Asia's journey to modernity. During an informal meeting between Treasury, the Foreign Office and the US Department of State, Clarke reported that in drawing up their economic blueprints since the Sydney meeting, Asian governments had 'scaled down the size of the development programs to a point considerably below what we would originally have desired to undertake ... [and] they have recognised that the limiting factor is the amount of external financial assistance likely to be available'.[50] By suggesting that Asian governments had exercised restraint and did not see the offer of aid as an opportunity to profiteer, British officials sought to allay American fears of an expensive, politically-charged and long-term assistance program. Nevertheless, Commonwealth donor nations could only provide £362 million of the £1,085 million required and now waited, as Spender put it, for the United States to 'fill the political and economic gap.'[51]

The major concern for the Commonwealth was that any public presumption of American finance might offend Washington and jeopardise the entire program. Indeed, Spender feared the United States saw the entire conference as a ham-fisted attempt by the Commonwealth to 'impose a commitment upon the United States in the form of a report already prepared for publication'.[52] The Americans suggested that the Commonwealth aid scheme should not appear to be dependent on US aid; that it should emphasise discrete 'project based' development rather than continuous financial support; that it not imply the US aid would be used to solve the United Kingdom's currency difficulties; and, finally, that the report should not mention a 'gap' to be filled by a third party. Tiptoeing around the US sensitivity to 'the gap' prompted the plain-speaking Tange to report that '[n]evertheless the fact of the matter is that there is such a gap and, unless it is filled the plan could not be implemented without drastic modification'.[53] With US aid integral to the successful launch of the program, the London meeting was intended to suit an American vision for Asian economic development. The report concluded with the inevitably ambiguous statement that the Consultative Committee 'could review progress … draw up periodic reports, and … serve as a forum for the discussion of developmental problems'; yet the precise 'form of such an organisation cannot be determined until it is clear what the sources of external finance will be'.[54]

Just as Commonwealth policy-makers worked to get the United States involved, they nevertheless worried that the sheer volume of US aid, in addition to the concessions made to secure that aid, had the potential to distort the Colombo Plan's economic and developmental objectives. In particular, concerns were raised about American insistence on tying the bulk of their aid contribution to the purchase of US supplies, which would effectively stem the expected flow of dollars that might otherwise be spent on British and Australian goods. Project aid of this kind would not meet India's need for food imports that could be sold on to finance their own development plans with minimal inflation. Large-scale infrastructure projects, and the inevitable bevy of Western expertise that came with them, were also more liable to bring accusations of post-colonial interference. Compromise was reached on most of these issues; in operation, the Colombo Plan involved a range of aid programs, from externally-funded 'tied' infrastructure projects and 'locally-funded' development, through the sale of donated commodities, to collaborative projects between local technicians and workers, and international staff. In general, American policy-makers insisted on a large measure of independence from the Commonwealth organisation in order to meet their own strategic and economic objectives, and maintain congressional approval. The United States eventually agreed to join the Colombo Plan in November 1950 (they were officially admitted in February 1951), on condition the scheme remained informal, exploratory, advisory and consultative.[55] It was indicative of the control the Americans hoped to retain over their aid allocations that they demanded that word 'Commonwealth' be omitted from the Consultative Committee's official title — the final price of US involvement.[56]

It is important not to overstate the degree to which Australian (and British) leaders danced to Washington's tune. At all times, Australia pursued an aggressively self-interested policy, based on a distinctly realist interpretation of its own political and strategic imperatives. Indeed, subservience to the United States sharpened Spender's sense of what the Colombo Plan meant for Australia's own political, military and social objectives. He had a strong sense of the Colombo Plan's significance beyond its role in securing American finance. In addition to helping cement the ANZUS Treaty, the scheme was to have the wide-reaching — if ambiguous — goal of neutralising anti-Western sentiment directed towards Australia. He cabled Menzies from London, explaining that Australia should use the influence of the Commonwealth 'as a cohesive force progressively to bind Asia to the West in a way which has so far been impossible by direct political pressure in a region whose rationalism is founded on reaction against the West'. Where the United Kingdom was anxious to 'be quit of responsibilities' in Asia, Australia should be ready to take charge: 'deliberate Australian isolation from Asia while we are achieving our small population increases seems to me to lose us the opportunity of using foreign policy effectively in our long term defence'. Again, the vulnerable outpost mentality, which dominated so much of Australian foreign policy, reared its head. At this stage, Spender prescribed very little in the way of a constructive engagement strategy for Australia. Rather, he saw the Colombo Plan as an instrument deployed as 'part of a foreign policy designed to deny this important part of the world to Soviet Russian influence'.[57]

With his plan for emergency credits and a technical aid pool subsumed beneath the Colombo Plan's twin prongs of a capital and technical aid program, Spender was forced to revise the total amount of Australia's contribution to the plan. Of course, he took the opportunity to try to secure even more. The stakes could not have been higher, he told Menzies from London, with an early indication of Australia's generous support 'essential if we are to carry to success the initiative we have taken'. He suggested that wool export earnings supported an initial contribution of around £A10 million. Although he did not spell it out, the implication was that this level of funding would be sustained over the six-year life of the scheme. This £A60 million ambit claim was sternly rebuffed, first by Menzies, who thought the idea 'quite impracticable' in view of Australia's heavy defence commitments and the future rehabilitation of Korea, and later by Cabinet. Instead, Menzies restricted Spender to a total of less than £A25 million and advised that the grand gesture of £A10 million in the first year set a dangerously unrealistic precedent. Although conciliatory in defeat, Spender said that a first contribution of just £A3 or 4 million would be 'conspicuous in its inadequacy', and he pressed for permission to make a much higher first offer, with the proviso that subsequent allocations would be considerably reduced. Nevertheless, just as Australia rebuked the tight-fisted British, other delegates looked askance at Australia's lack of charity. The Canadians, for example, privately suspected that Australia overstated the financial hardships she would incur through her involvement with the aid scheme. In late 1950, the economies of Asia and Australia received a sudden, if short-lived, boost from US spending and stockpiling programs induced by the Korean War. With good prices for wool and rising sterling levels, Lester Pearson explained to his finance minister , 'the Australians are not going to have to pull in their belts this year in order to meet their contributions to the Colombo Plan'. In December, with America having just agreed to join the Colombo Plan, Cabinet approved Spender's recommendations, adding that the terms in which the formal announcement would be expressed would first need approval from the Prime Minister and that 'care must be taken to avoid raising the expectations on the part of the proposed recipients'.[58]

In the estimation of the British Chancellor of the Exchequer and conference chairman, Hugh Gaitskell, the London meeting of the Consultative Committee was characterised by a 'striking sense of common purpose', assisted by the fact that Spender adopted a lower profile and was in a 'much more constructive mood than at Sydney'.[59] Some of the enmity present in Sydney re-emerged in London, albeit in muted form, when the Australian delegation chided the United Kingdom for rushing

discussions which did not concern British interests and for
their otherwise 'lukewarm' attitude towards the inclusion of
non-Commonwealth Asia. Australia 'found it necessary to
insist on more emphasis on the "humanitarian" approach' in
order to make it easier to bring other Asian countries into
the program. Gaitskell conceded the point, but saved his
disapproval with the Australian delegation — and, of
course, its leader — for his diary. Spender, he wrote, was 'like
a little terrier, self-important, talks a good deal … He has no
inhibitions about raising awkward subjects and is what you
call fairly crude … but then so are most Australians'.[60]

Since 1945, Australian policy-makers and politicians
knew that many Asian governments feared that a
commitment to a Western aid program entailed strategic
and military entanglements with the anti-communist bloc.
Nevertheless, some Australian politicians leapt on the
emerging mechanism as an opportunity to restore the
prestige and 'historic destiny' of the English-speaking world.
The conservative Alexander Downer, for example,
suggested that the Consultative Committee would blossom
forth into a 'permanent Empire Secretariat' responsible for
law and order, and offered the chance to 'adopt a more
forthright attitude' over territorial disputes, such as
Indonesian designs for West New Guinea. 'In our desire to
help the peoples of South and South–East Asia', he
continued, 'we should set out not only to feed them but also
to lead them'.[61] Downer's muscular approach was, in fact, a
neat caricature of what Australia hoped its aid program
might achieve under the best possible conditions. However,
the Australians would need to exercise a little more tact
and diplomacy, even by Spender's standards, in their efforts
to entice Asian leaders into the Colombo Plan.

Australian and British policy-makers were concerned
to expand the Consultative Committee beyond a kind of

confederacy of Commonwealth nations, but without appearing to dominate or compromise Asian economic and political sovereignty. Spender told Menzies during the Sydney conference that, with Asian leaders wary of economic imperialism, it was crucial 'not to appear to infringe the sovereign rights of states which had acquired their independence'.[62] For should independent Asia fail to join the scheme, the Consultative Committee's symbolic role as a unifying bridge between post-colonial Asia and the West would be jeopardised, and in the DEA's estimation, it might then be 'regarded as a purely British or Commonwealth "show"'.[63] Fear of offending Indonesia's sensibilities and thus pushing them away from Western influence, for example, tempered Australia's impatience with the tortuous negotiation process. Australian officials juggled their rising frustration with Indonesia's neutral foreign policy — which Hugh Gilchrist, the First Secretary of the embassy in Djakarta, derided as a position of 'superficial neutrality between the Soviet and anti-Soviet blocs' — and their unease at forcing Indonesia to make a commitment to the Colombo Plan.[64] Asian assertiveness had direct ramifications for Australian efforts to engage with the region, and the increasingly assertive behaviour of many Asian governments, with their apparent solidarity against the Western and Eastern political blocs, made Australian and British representatives nervous. John Hood, Australia's Ambassador to Indonesia, told Casey that the 'sense of solidarity which appears to be growing among South–East Asian peoples' meant that 'any attempt to bustle them into an anti-communist camp may well have the effect of uniting them in an angry reaction against all Western influence'.[65] After much diplomatic wrangling, Indonesia's decision to join the Consultative Committee in late 1952 proved an important step in the development of Australian–Indonesian relations. In the estimation of the

British Ambassador to Indonesia, Derwent Kermode, the Colombo Plan's mantra of 'aid without strings' proved to be 'a useful weapon in the prime task of breaking down the walls of suspicion and distrust of the West with which many Indonesians still surround themselves'.[66]

The very nature of the Consultative Committee as a malleable and non-coercive forum helped reassure tentative governments that joining the new confederation came without strings, military or otherwise.[67] Other regional development forums oriented toward bilateral cooperation, such as the South Pacific Commission (SPC) — which had no formal connection to the UN and was mandated only to correlate and disseminate information concerning Pacific countries, to make recommendations for the promotion of economic and social development, and to facilitate the discussion of problems of mutual concern — provided a useful template.[68] Publicly, the Consultative Committee echoed the spirit of the SPC. Like the SPC, the Consultative Committee had no supra-national powers, took no collective decisions save for voting in new members and deciding the location of the annual meeting, and only made recommendations to participating governments. As donors and recipients negotiated their aid projects on a bilateral basis through standard diplomatic channels, the Consultative Committee simply became a public discussion forum and clearing-house for the admission of new members and the consolidation of national development reviews in the annual report. Not only was this an appropriate and workable forum considering the various agenda the committee was forced to bear, but it proved sufficiently benign to attract most of South–East Asia over the next four years: Indo-China (1951), Burma and Nepal (1952), Indonesia (1953), Thailand and the Philippines (1954). Japan also joined in 1954, but as an aid donor.

Throughout the Commonwealth in the 1950s, the words
'Colombo Plan' became synonymous with aid initiatives for
South and South–East Asia. The diverse nature of projects
financed under the scheme and their wide geographic
distribution lent credence to the image of the plan as a
systematic and integrated approach to regional
development and cooperation. Donor governments used
the relaxed nature of the proceedings to further political
and economic ends. On one level, the annual meeting
offered an ideal opportunity for the promotion of Western
political objectives. As one Foreign Office appraisal
claimed, 'the meeting of the Consultative Committee is the
major event of the year so far as the Colombo Plan is
concerned. It is an occasion of worldwide interest and the
fullest possible use should be made of the publicity
opportunities'.[69] The Colombo Plan forum also provided an
attractive package for Australian generosity and helped
disguise the limited nature of the early donations. The DEA
quietly confessed that Australia's early effort, which
consisted primarily of a donation of wheat and flour to
India and Ceylon, would have been sent 'whether there had
been a Colombo Plan or not'.[70] These contributions were
sold to pay for major infrastructure programs, such as
railways, roads, dams and hydro-electric power plants.
Beyond this, Australia typically directed its capital aid
contributions towards the creation of more efficient,
mechanised agricultural production. For example, of the
£A10 million in capital assistance provided by Australia to
Pakistan between 1950 and 1957, 62 per cent went towards
irrigation projects, and a further 13 per cent was devoted to
the supply of tractors and refrigeration plants. Just 2 per
cent went to increasing power generation capacity.[71] But
the Colombo Plan was not a coherent program for regional
development. It featured no centralised or multilateral

institutions, no blueprint for integrated economic regionalism, and it had no substantive decision-making power. The 'whole enterprise', wrote Canadian academic William Harrison, 'was something of a misnomer ... a co-operative and co-ordinated study of a number of economic situations, too varying as to stages and patterns of growth, and too immense in the aggregate, to be considered amenable to any centrally planned and directed scheme of development'.[72]

Talk of a military defence strategy was taboo during the formation of the Colombo Plan. Spender and other Commonwealth officials tactfully avoided the thorny issue of collective military defence by proposing a course towards regional integration through economic cooperation.[73] It is hardly surprising the Colombo Plan emerged as a nebulous and relatively benign regional forum. Arguably, Commonwealth policy-makers could not have achieved these complex, intertwined objectives within multilateral agencies under UN control. Yet, loaded as it was with political and military objectives, the welfare of Asian people now assumed a greater significance than ever before. This occurred, not because of a groundswell of humanitarian sentiment, but because their well-being was now seen to impinge on the post-war order imagined by Western powers.

To some extent, the Colombo Plan was a façade, a device intended to lure independent Asia into an alliance with the Western bloc. Its congenial unity was calculated to entice non-Commonwealth Asia, secure the material might of the United States, and marginalise the Soviet Union. On 1 July 1951, the Colombo Plan finally lurched into existence with its public symbolism intact. As Tange's appraisal confirmed, the result was tantamount to a diplomatic sleight-of-hand. The Colombo Conference, he wrote, 'proved an opportunity for creating a piece of Commonwealth machinery devoted specifically to a purpose which, in the minds of the public in the Commonwealth, was straight-forward and uncomplicated by any doubtful political motives'.[74] From Australia's perspective, Asia's economic progress, cold war anxiety, and a deep concern about the consequences of decolonisation for political stability, all coalesced beneath a malleable regional forum, ostensibly dedicated to economic progress. The Menzies government hoped that relations augmented under the Colombo Plan would rejuvenate the Commonwealth bond between Australia and the governments of South Asia and help to install Australia as a regional authority free to pursue its interests alongside a compliant Asian elite.

Although Spender offended the sensibilities of Western allies, he infused the right degree of urgency and desperation into the proceedings in order to get Australia — and otherwise unenthusiastic Commonwealth powers — to commit finance and technical resources to the struggle against communism. By virtue of his rumbustious diplomacy, Spender galvanised Australia's role in the formation of the Colombo Plan and as a force in regional affairs. Yet early reports from among Australia's more idealistic diplomats revealed a degree of doubt about the capacity of an aid program to stabilise the region and bolster Australia's regional profile. In 1950 Francis Stuart, now Official Secretary at the Australian High Commission in New Delhi, wrote of a widespread 'public curiosity' about Australia and the 'remarkable extent to which Australia's existence as something of a power in the world is known and accepted'. However, in the longer term he was less sure: the 'conduct of South East Asian relations with Australia is likely to present something of a continuing dilemma to South East Asia's leaders; events compel them to co-operate with us, but we must not believe that their hearts are really in it.'[75] But for now — with the question of just how the Colombo Plan might achieve its breathtakingly ambitious goals still unanswered — the optimists could ignore the doubters.

Footnotes

1   T. Remme, *Britain and regional cooperation in South–East Asia, 1945–49*, London, Routledge, 1995, p. 208; *Age*, 7 January 1950; *Sydney Morning Herald*, 10 January 1950

2   Charles Bohlen, 'Minister to American Embassy in Paris: seventh meeting of the policy planning staff in the State Department, 24 January 1950', *FRUS*, 1950, vol. 3, pp. 620–21

3   D.V. LePan, *Bright glass of memory*, Toronto, McGraw-Hill Ryerson, 1979, pp. 170–71

4   J. Spender, *Ambassador's wife*, Sydney, Angus and Robertson, 1968, p. 1

5   *Sun* (Sydney), 3 January 1950

6   P. Spender, *Exercises in diplomacy: the ANZUS Treaty and the Colombo Plan*, Sydney, Sydney University Press, 1969, pp. 194–214

7   D. Wolfstone, 'The Colombo Plan ten years after', *Far Eastern Economic Review*, 3 August 1961, p. 219

8   Spender, *Exercises in diplomacy*, pp. 197, 271–72

9   Cable, Spender to Menzies, 11 January 1950, A1838 item 532/7 part 1, NAA

10 'Economic policy in South and South–East Asia: memorandum by the Australian delegation', 11 January 1950, A1838, 381/3/1/3 part 1a, NAA

11 Cable, Spender to DEA, 14 January 1950, A1838, 532/7 part 1, NAA

12 I. Gibbons, ed., *Undiplomatic dialogue: letters between Carl Berendsen and Alister McIntosh, 1943–52*, Auckland, Auckland University Press in association with the Ministry of Foreign Affairs and Trade, 1993, pp. 226, 202–05

13 Gibbons, *Undiplomatic dialogue*, p. 202

14 Despatch, Makin to Spender, 23 December 1949, A4231, 1949/Washington, NAA

15 'South–East Asia preparations for the Consultative Committee', A1838, 708/9/2, NAA

16 *CPD (HoR)*, vol. 6, 9 March 1950, pp. 623–39

17 *CPD (HoR)*, vol. 6, 9 March 1950, pp. 623–39

18 *CPD (HoR)*, vol. 206, 21 March 1950, p. 973

19 'The Acting Secretary of State to the Embassy in Australia', 18 March 1950, *FRUS*, 1950, vol. 6, p. 63

20 R.N. Birch, 'Economic assistance in South–East Asia', 10 February 1950, A1830, TS708/9/2 part 1, NAA

21 Spender, *Exercises in diplomacy*, p. 244
22 *Sydney Morning Herald*, 14 May 1950; R. Bodinagoda, interview with author, 8 September 1999, Colombo
23 *Sydney Morning Herald*, 12 May 1950
24 Cable, Foreign Office to Commissioner General for United Kingdom in South–East Asia, Singapore, 10 March 1950, FO 371/84553, PRO, UK
25 Cable, Spender to Harrison, 10 May 1950, A1838, 708/9/2 part 2, NAA
26 R. Butler & M.E. Pelly (eds.), *Documents on British Policy overseas, series 2: the London conferences — Anglo–American relations and Cold War strategy, January–June 1950*, vol. 2, London, HMSO, 1987, p. 158; R. Hyam (ed.), *British documents on the end of empire, vol. 2: the Labour government and the end of empire 1945–1951, part 2: economics and international relations*, London, HMSO, 1992, p. 142; Cable, J.F. Nimmo, London, to Fred Wheeler, Treasury, Canberra, 15 June 1950, A1838, 708/12/1 part 1, NAA; A. Tange, 'Political objectives of the Colombo Plan — working paper', 19 March 1952, A1838, 3004/11 part 1, NAA
27 Tange, 'Political objectives of the Colombo Plan – working paper'
28 'Proposal of Australian Government for establishment of a Commonwealth fund', 3 May 1950, CP529, 16/A/5, NAA; LePan, *Bright glass of memory*, p. 196; 'UK delegation to Consultative Committee, Sydney, to the Commonwealth Relations Office, London', 16 May 1950, FO 371/84546, PRO, UK; *Documents on Canadian external relations*, vol. 16, Ottawa, Queen's Printer, 1999, p. 1214
29 'UK delegation to Consultative Committee, Sydney, to the Commonwealth Relations Office, London'; LePan, *Bright glass of memory*, p. 197; *Documents on Canadian external relations*, vol. 16, p. 1214
30 *Sydney Morning Herald*, 17 May 1950
31 Williams, UK High Commission, Canberra to Secretary of State for Commonwealth Relations, 29 June 1950, FO 371/84548, PRO, UK
32 Spender, *Exercises in diplomacy*, p. 262. For the full text of the final communiqué, see *Current Notes on International Affairs*, vol. 21, 1950, pp. 350–51
33 D. Lowe, 'Percy Spender and the Colombo Plan 1950', *Australian Journal of Politics and History*, vol. 40, no. 2, 1994, p. 171; Spender, *Exercises in diplomacy*, p. 262; A. Tange, Monologue, TRC 2447, tape 3, NLA
34 M.J. Hogan, *The Marshall Plan: America, Britain, and the reconstruction of Western Europe, 1947–1952*, Cambridge, Cambridge University Press, 1987, pp. 45, 142–44, 204–07
35 L. Gordon, 'The Organisation for European Economic Cooperation', *International Cooperation*, vol. 10, no. 1, 1956, pp. 1–11; L. Gordon, 'Economic regionalism reconsidered', *World Politics*, vol. 13, no. 2, 1961, pp. 231–53
36 'Statement to be made by Hon. Spender KC – Australian Minister for External Affairs and leader of the Australian delegation at opening of the Commonwealth Consultative Committee, May 15, 1950', CP529, 16/A/4/2, NAA

37 'Proposal of Australian government for establishment of a Commonwealth fund', 3 May 1950, CP529, 16/A/5, NAA

38 Cable, DEA, Canberra to High Commissioner, London, Karachi, Ottawa, 8 February 1951, A1838, 851/18/8 part 3, NAA

39 L.B. Pearson, 'The Colombo conference', *External Affairs of Canada*, vol. 2, no. 3, March 1950, p. 82

40 *CPD (HoR)*, vol. 208, 8 June 1950, pp. 4013–27; L.P. Singh, *The politics of economic cooperation in Asia: a study of Asian international organizations*, Columbia, University of Missouri Press, 1966, pp. 181–82

41 *CPD (HoR)*, vol. 208, 8 June 1950, p. 4013

42 'Brief for Lord Reading's visit to Rangoon – ECAFE and the Colombo Plan', undated (*circa* January 1951), FO 371/101248, PRO, UK; S.P. Bray, 'Report of the Australian delegation to the committee on industry and trade of the Economic Commission for Asia and the Far East, second session, Bangkok, 9 to 17 May 1950', June 1950, A9879, 9121/7, NAA; 'Report of the meeting of the British Commonwealth Consultative Committee, Sydney May 15 to 20, 1950', A1838, 708/12/1 part 1, NAA

43 'Brief for Australian delegation', British Commonwealth Consultative Committee on aid to South and South–East Asia, Sydney, May 1950, CP529, 16/A/4/1, NAA

44 Telegram, Satterthwaite, US Embassy, Colombo, to Secretary of State, Washington, 11 November 1950, RG 59, 846E.00 TA/11-1150, USNA

45 R.H. Scott to M.E. Dening, UK Embassy Washington, 8 September 1950, FO 371/84584, PRO, UK

46 Spender, *Exercises in diplomacy*, p. 264; LePan, *Bright glass of memory*, p. 209

47 Memo, J. Plimsoll to A. Watt, 'Economic development of South East Asia', 11 August 1950, A5460, 301/5, NAA

48 Cable, Secretary of State for Commonwealth Relations, London to DEA and various posts, 2 August 1950, A1838, 708/12/1 part 2, NAA

49 Cable, Commissioner-General, Singapore to Commonwealth Relations Office, 'Follow-up of Sydney conference', 5 August 1950, A5460, 301/5, NAA

50 'Record of informal United States–United Kingdom discussion, London', 22 September 1950, *FRUS*, 1950, vol. 5, pp. 212–15

51 Cable, Spender, London to Menzies, 27 September 1950, A3320, 3/4/2/1 part 2, NAA

52 Letter, Spender to Bevin, 8 September 1950, A1838, 708/9/2 part 2, NAA

53 A. Tange, 'Points about Colombo Plan of interest to Australia', 15 December 1950, A5460, 301/5, NAA

54 Commonwealth Consultative Committee, *The Colombo Plan for cooperative economic development in South and South–East Asia: report by the Consultative Committee, September–October 1950*, London, His Majesty's Stationery Office, 1950, p. 63. See also: Cable, Secretary of State for Commonwealth Relations, London to DEA, Canberra, 19 December 1950, A6364, LC1950/015, NAA

55 Telegram, 'Secretary of State (Acheson) to US Embassy, London', 22 November 1950, *FRUS*, 1950, vol. 6, pp. 160–61

56 Tange, 'Political objectives of the Colombo Plan – working paper'

57 Cable, Spender to Menzies, 28 September 1950, A4534, 44/13 part 3, NAA

58 Cable, Spender to Menzies, 28 September 1950; Cable, Menzies to Spender, 1
    October 1950, A9879, 2202/E1 part 1, NAA; Cable, Spender to Menzies, 2
    October 1950, A9879, 2202/E1 part 1, NAA; *Documents on Canadian external
    relations*, vol. 17, Ottawa, Queen's Printer, 1999, p. 1044; Cabinet submission
    37a, December 1950, A4940, C353, NAA

59 Hyam, *British documents on the end of empire*, p. 142

60 'Departmental notes on the London meeting of the Commonwealth
    Consultative Committee, September 6 to October 4, 1950', A5460, 301/5,
    NAA; P. Williams, ed., *The diary of Hugh Gaitskell*, 1945–1956, London,
    Cape, 1983, pp. 200–01

61 *CPD (HoR)*, vol. 208, 8 June 1950, pp. 4029–31

62 Cable, Spender to Menzies, 25 May 1950, A1838, 381/3/1/3 part 4, NAA;
    'British Commonwealth Consultative Committee meeting in Sydney: some
    general conclusions', 24 May 1950, A1838, 381/3/1/3 part 4, NAA

63 W.T. Doig, 'Notes for the Minister: proposed discussion with Dr. Subardjo on
    the Colombo Plan', 19 September 1951, A1838, 3004/11 part 1, NAA

64 Despatch, Gilchrist to DEA, 21 April 1952, A4231, 1952/Djakarta, NAA

65 Despatch, Hood to Casey, 13 July 1950, A4231, 1950/Djakarta, NAA

66 Cable, D.W. Kermode, British Embassy, Djakarta, to Anthony Eden, Foreign
    Office, 20 November 1952, FO371/101245, PRO, UK

67 Summary Record, 'Consultative Committee: seventh plenary session, Friday
    19 May 1950', A5460, 301/5, NAA

68 N.J. Padelford, 'Regional cooperation in the South Pacific: twelve years of the
    South Pacific Commission', *International Organization*, vol. 13, no. 3, 1959,
    pp. 383–84

69 'Colombo Plan Consultative Committee meeting, Singapore, September
    1955: UK delegation paper', 16 September 1955, DO 35-5726, PRO, UK

70 J.W. Cumes, 'The Colombo Plan: present status of the Australian effort', 8
    January 1952, A1838, 2020/1/12 part 1, NAA

71 Government of Pakistan, *Foreign aid review committee*, Ministry of Economic
    Affairs, Karachi, July 1957, A1838, 2020/1/11, NAA

72 W.E.C. Harrison, *Canada in world affairs*, 1949–1950, Toronto, Oxford
    University Press, 1957, p. 231

73 J.R.E. Carr-Gregg, 'The Colombo Plan: a Commonwealth program for
    Southeast Asia', International Conciliation, no. 467, January 1951, pp. 16–21

74 Tange, 'Political objectives of the Colombo Plan — working paper'

75 Letter, F. Stuart to A. Watt, 28 August 1950, A1838, 3004/ 11 part 1, NAA

4. THE SEED
OF FREEDOM

'Hungry people are dangerous people', exclaimed the Melbourne correspondent for the *Eastern World* journal, 'the East keeps clamouring for rice and more rice and the bullock cart and the wooden plough are poor instruments in breaking up virgin land quickly enough to supply the need — only the bulldozer and the tractor plough can hope to win in this race for food'.[1] The remedy for socio-political instability in Asia seemed profoundly simple: if the people were hungry and restive then feed them, or at least provide the technology for them to do so themselves. 'The key to the political problem of South–East Asia is food', said Kim Beazley (Snr) during a parliamentary debate.[2] But how could an aid program such as the Colombo Plan remedy a problem of such magnitude? And what exactly was Australia's obligation to the starving millions to the north?

Humanitarian duty to poor Asians was a relatively minor feature of Spender's effort to garner support for the Colombo Plan. His preoccupation with geo-political security meant that, if anything, he deflected suggestions that charity formed the basis of Australia's aid program. The provision of aid, he said in parliament, is 'not a policy of mere humanitarianism; it is also a policy of serious self-interest'.[3] Striking a harder line, Department of External Affairs officials did not consider 'appalling poverty … sufficient grounds for a government program'.[4]

The earlier concern with establishing the Colombo Plan and attracting the interest of the United States also precluded any serious political analysis. Only after the program had been in operation for a year did the DEA begin to appraise the various objectives Australia's foreign aid program was to achieve. Working in secret, DEA officials determined basic policy objectives that were animated by a deep unease about living beside a region they saw as poverty-stricken, unstable, vulnerable to communist takeover, and lacking the steadying hand of colonial rule. Through the Colombo Plan, they aimed to influence Asia's economic and political future and secure Australia's place in the region.

By 1950, the idea that aid would buttress South–East Asia against communist ideology thus strengthening the 'spine of resistance from Delhi to Djakarta', as one parliamentarian put it, was already widely publicised by the Australian media.[5] In the minds of DEA policy-makers, this was the Colombo Plan's fundamental *raison d'être*. The aid program, they wrote:

> *may be justified as a counter to communism in fairly simple terms. On the assumption that low living standards — or even more so, declining living standards — provide communism's most*

> *fertile ground, effective action to raise living standards or at least prevent present standards from falling, will weaken the appeal which communist agitators are able to make.*

Equal to these anti-communist ambitions was a more secretive agenda to use aid to 'modify any resentment arising from differences between Australian and Asian living standards' and 'strengthen or develop amicable political relations' by using economic and social instruments to assert political and cultural pressure on Asian people and their leaders. Specifically, aid should 'not interfere with the established governments or existing constitutions or political institutions and procedures', and while there was 'a tacit understanding that no assistance will be given to communist governments', potential aid recipients have been 'encouraged to believe that they need no political qualification for assistance'. Furthermore, the DEA, like most people at the time, felt uneasy about the existence of great poverty next to great wealth. In a politically unstable climate, they believed that the 'proximity between Australia, with its high living standards, and Asia, with its extreme poverty, easily arouses resentment'. Economic aid was one way in which Australia could make a gesture towards Asia and take the 'edge off Asian resentment'. In order to achieve these covert objectives while maintaining the Colombo Plan as a symbol of non-political union between Asia and the West, a public image distinct from private understandings became essential. 'In any public discussion', Tange recommended, 'it is desirable to avoid any reference to the political and strategic objectives of the plan, or at least to make references only in the most cautious terms'.[6]

A cohort of DEA staffers, however, expressed a moderate and less interventionist approach. W.T. Doig from the Economic and Technical Branch, which managed the

Colombo Plan, explained his views directly to Spender. Australians, he said, ignored the history and culture of Asia:

> *We understand them possibly as much as they understand us — only a little. The political objectives therefore of our policy should be not to secure complete and full understanding immediately or quickly; not to expect in return for economic and technical aid, an identity of viewpoint with our own on all current and international issues.*

Doig suggested that the Colombo Plan would better serve Australia's long-term regional interests if it played a more organic role by providing a framework for continuing relations, as opposed to the mere provision of assistance, which would facilitate further regional cooperation and develop 'greater understandings of attitudes, prejudices, fears, motives, customs, etc, between East and West'. Specifically, the Plan should not take a coercive approach but aim to 'convince Asian countries that we do not expect them to adopt our systems, our ways of life, our customs, or our religion, and that we are on their side against Soviet imperialism'.[7] Only later would the DEA incorporate Doig's idea into the Colombo Plan and, more broadly, into Australian foreign policy. In the early 1950s, the urgency of the international situation called for a more forthright approach.

However, the ability of Western aid to increase agricultural and industrial production and thus affect the political future of Asia was always questionable. Both the government and the DEA knew that the Colombo Plan's failure to deliver quantifiable change would contradict the basic principle on which the program rested. 'The ordinary Asian is likely to suffer considerable disillusionment, if he has heard about the plan, when he sees what little it achieves, in terms of Asian needs, and how thin the chances are that it will bring about … real development and capital investment, as opposed to an occasional first aid operation'. The DEA advocated caution. If no tangible evidence of progress could be identified then 'emphasis on developmental aspects for propaganda purposes [was] likely therefore to return to plague the inventor'. Of course, simply establishing contact and providing financial aid did not guarantee a positive rapport with a recipient nation. Indeed, if the funds were misdirected or mismanaged, aid might have little impact or contribute to a deterioration of relations. By the same token, the domestic political arena of a recipient nation had to be examined closely. Contrary to public assurances, certain 'political qualifications' were required:

> It would be logical to increase economic aid to those countries where the threat of communist disruption was especially acute. [However] without any control of the domestic policy of recipient governments, the benefit of any external aid could be completely offset if the recipient government's domestic policies were reactionary or unimaginative. Even though 'average' per capita income in the underdeveloped countries may be rising, with national income increasing at a greater rate than population, effective internal policies of income distribution are essential to ensure that the benefit is passed on to those sections of the population most susceptible to communist propaganda.[8]

Goods entering Asian countries under the Colombo Plan certainly raised the prospect of securing longer-term commercial markets for Australian exports, but over the decade it became more important not to 'supply foodstuffs where the effect of the gift would be to replace normal commercial sales'.[9] Rather, the DEA hoped that economic cooperation would help to ameliorate any political animosity that may have developed towards Asian countries, especially non-Commonwealth nations. Even more ambitiously, it was asserted that cooperation and aid might transform an attitude of 'virtual neutrality ... into something more positive', reducing the strategic significance of certain countries.[10] For example, the ambivalence of Indonesian officials towards the Colombo Plan would have been less of a concern to DEA officials if Australia established links with countries north of Indonesia. At the time, the department considered Indonesia, Indo-China, Thailand, the Philippines, and Burma the most likely to be drawn into closer diplomatic relations through an economic alliance. Over the decade, while Australian diplomats warned that relations with the region would be determined by much weightier issues than foreign aid, some recognised the Colombo Plan's capacity to preserve 'latent goodwill' and serve as 'an antidote to unfavourable publicity', particularly over difficult issues such as West New Guinea and immigration policy.[11]

The primary weakness of the Colombo Plan lay in the untested assumption that economic assistance and development would 'moderate political conflict'. Consequently, the DEA followed a careful — if crude — process to distribute aid to maximise the short-term political and social benefits for Australia. The development plans drawn up by member nations at the Consultative Committee's request had limited bearing on this process. Australia allocated aid according to four criteria: political objectives, commercial interest, relative needs based on per capita income, and the amount of aid provided by other countries. The DEA then divided aid recipients into three categories, based on their potential for sustaining a positive political rapport with Australia. The first category comprised those countries with close political associations with Australia, 'where economic aid is expected only to confirm and improve the existing position, rather than help build a new political relationship'. This category included India, Pakistan, Ceylon, and British territories in South–East Asia. The second group comprised countries considered 'neutral' who might develop into 'allies' through economic aid; it included Thailand, the Philippines, and Burma. The final group comprised nations where the political situation had 'passed beyond the stage of forestalling unrest through extension of economic aid', and required military intervention. This was the case for Indo-China, where the extension of assistance was likely to be 'almost wholly wasted' and any token offering would make only a 'fleeting political impression'.[12] It was futile, as one diplomat put it, to 'fatten a country which will soon pass into Communist hands'.[13] However, this assessment altered as the strategic importance of Cambodia, Laos, and South Vietnam became apparent.

Just as the US State Department considered South Asia of 'determinative importance' to its military plans, Australian strategic assessments drew attention to the significance of the sub-continent.[14] Congenial relations with both India and Ceylon were important components of defence planning, with access to Ceylon's naval and air bases of particular significance. Ceylon's primary military value was as an 'air funnel', which allowed more effective protection of Indian Ocean sea lanes than bases in Malaya or on the east coast of Africa could offer. Also, in the event of nuclear conflict, Ceylon might operate as a guidance station for Polaris nuclear missiles launched from submarines in the Indian Ocean.[15] By and large, the government still endorsed Secretary of Defence Frederick Shedden's view that one of Australia's strategic objectives in South Asia was to establish 'satisfactory political relations with the future independent Government of Ceylon with a view to retain Ceylon as a co-operative member of the British Commonwealth'.[16] Of the initial bounty of £A31.25 million, Australia gave over £A19 million to Ceylon, India, and Pakistan; setting aside the remainder in anticipation that non-Commonwealth Asia would sign on.[17] Not only did this reinforce Commonwealth relations and enhance Australia's status as a good neighbour, it signalled to the rest of Asia the benefits they might gain once they elected to join the Consultative Committee.

By the mid- to late-1950s, as Australia's strategic interests shifted to South–East Asia, so too did the emphasis of overseas aid. Although the government's intention to bring most of Asia into the Colombo Plan 'family' tended to disperse Australia's already limited aid budget, by the 1960s South–East Asian countries (Indonesia, Malaya, Cambodia, Laos, Vietnam, Burma, Thailand, and Singapore) had received over 60 per cent of all Australia's Colombo Plan allocations.[18] At the same time, as the region started to show signs of economic growth, aid to Malaya increased from approximately 10 per cent of the total budget in 1956 to around 30 per cent in 1970.[19] During the Plan's first twenty years, Malaya and Indonesia consistently received the highest amounts of educational and technical assistance. The number of Australian staff responsible for the administration of Colombo Plan projects also reflected the significance of Malaya. By 1965, three officers in Kuala Lumpur and one in Singapore oversaw Australia's aid projects, as opposed to India and Pakistan, where only one officer was responsible for administering the Colombo Plan.

Notwithstanding the DEA's admission that Australian aid contributions to Asia were 'little better than trifling', the Colombo Plan represented a revolution in the pattern of Australian overseas aid spending.[20] The Australian government had regularly supported aid organisations run by the UN, such as UNRRA, IRO, UNKRA, UNICEF, UNRWAPR, UNEPTA and IBRD,[21] but an ongoing bilateral aid relationship with Asia did not exist. From 1950 on, Australia shifted the focus of its aid contributions towards the Colombo Plan and gradually reduced its multilateral commitments to the UN. Of course, assistance to Papua New Guinea remained the government's overriding aid priority. In 1950, when Spender managed to wrest around £A5 million a year from Treasury for the Colombo Plan, Australia was already spending over £A10 million per year in Papua New Guinea. Further, in contrast to Colombo Plan allocations, which remained relatively stable, aid to Papua New Guinea increased rapidly from the mid-1950s, from £A10 million per annum in 1956/57 to over £A36 million in 1965/66.[22] Australia's aid program alone was clearly unable to remedy the major economic problems endemic to many of the recipient nations. The total amount of aid provided by other donor nations was substantial, boosted massively by over $US1.4 billion from America under its Mutual Security Program.[23] Even so, the Colombo Plan's six-year total budget of $US2 billion paled in comparison with the $US13 billion channelled into Europe through the Marshall Plan between 1947 and 1952.

At face value, the Commonwealth's reluctance to make a greater commitment to the Colombo Plan illustrated a lack of faith in the ability of aid to effect real change in Asia. In Australia, for example, the Colombo Plan's annual budget of around £A5 million stood in stark contrast to the yearly expenditure on defence which exceeded £A170 million for most of the 1950s.[23] However, like all foreign-aid programs of the post-war era, the

Table 1: Colombo Plan Assistance provided by major donor nations between 1950 and 1964/65[24]

	Capital assistance (£A '000)	Technical assistance (£A '000)	Number of students accepted	Number of experts sent on assignments
Australia	38,476.6	17,290.5	5,908	679
United Kingdom*	520,206.7	17,876.0	6,256	731
Canada	269,647.1	9,479.4	2,997	427
New Zealand	9,389.3	5,057.0	1,763	244
United States	8,292,273.2	220,048.2	15,709	3,567
Japan	71,011.9	3,842.5	1,887	610
TOTAL	**9,201,004.8**	**273,593.6**	**34,520**	**6,258**

* UK figures exclude the release of sterling balances up to 1958 under arrangements with India, Pakistan, and Ceylon (£Str252 million)

Colombo Plan was predicated on a series of assumptions central to Western concepts of economic growth. In Western thought the concept of development has been (and is) so deeply ingrained that it is assumed to act as a law of nature, and during the 1950s, the term 'development' was used interchangeably with 'progress', 'evolution', 'change', and 'growth'. Following the Second World War, European and American economic theorists turned their attention to the problems of the underdeveloped world. Key individuals who contributed towards a modernist development theory based on the application of Keynesian principles included P. Rodan-Rodenstein, Roy Harrod, William Arthur Lewis, Ragnar Nurkse, and Walt Rostow.[26]

Driven by a tremendous sense of optimism, these planners — along with their devotees around the world — hoped that the application of advances in technology and the social sciences to the developing world would rapidly bridge the gap between rich and poor countries. 'Backward economies', later known by the more polite synonym 'underdeveloped', were characterised by rural overpopulation, inefficient agricultural practices, inadequate technical equipment, lack of scientific knowledge, and an inability to generate capital. The path to modernity, they argued, involved a number of common factors, including the accumulation of capital, increased use of technology, industrialisation, sophisticated administrative structures, large-scale development projects, and external aid. Extensive state intervention was initially required to overcome the long years of stagnation, but once started, future growth would be self-sustaining. As W. Lewis put it in 1950: 'Once the snowball starts to move downhill, it will move of its own momentum, and will get bigger and bigger as it goes along … You have … to begin by rolling your snowball up the mountain. Once you get there, the rest is easy'.[27] In another incarnation, Western technology was believed to yield almost magical results. New Zealand's Minister for External Affairs, Frederick Doidge, claimed dramatically: 'We could almost wipe out hunger overnight if we could only get the people of these primitive lands to use scythes instead of sickles, and steel ploughs instead of wooden ploughs'.[28] The point to note is that the idea of self-sustaining economic development was not a convenient rationalisation for offering limited assistance. The quantity and type of aid provided, while important, was less significant than the process it was intended to start.

The idea that development was an unstoppable, linear process was popularised in 1960 in economic historian Walt Rostow's classic text *Stages of economic growth*. Rostow argued that every economy passed through a sequence of stages leading from 'traditional society' to 'high mass consumption'. The critical phase, he suggested, was the one that achieved 'preconditions for take-off', where a massive mobilisation of capital would stimulate structural reform and then launch a process of self-sustaining investment and growth. In a passage replete with Darwinian overtones, Rostow envisaged a state of affairs where 'traditional' culture would disappear beneath the advance of modern civilization, with a 'modern alternative ... constructed out of the old culture'. Supplementing the economic revival would be the formation of a new elite, driven by an entrepreneurial spirit.[29] The power of Rostow's book lay in its simplicity and in the way he pushed his analysis as a practical alternative to Marxism. The subtitle, *a non-communist manifesto*, left no doubt as to his political proclivities. Economists debated the merits of Rostow's model for decades, but the basic tenets of his theory and those of this contemporaries, particularly the emphasis on industrialisation, the necessity for state-initiated development planning, and a development model based on Western experience, remained influential well beyond the 1950s.[30] Cold war anxiety and the need to show no weakness in the face of communism also encouraged the suppression of more critical or even pessimistic analyses.

In this context, these theories soon became more than the fruits of benign intellectual pursuit. Development was an opportunity to carry Asia towards an idealised notion of industrial civilisation. Theorists deemed the archetypal modern society to be composed of key economic, social, and psychological ingredients, such as mass consumerism, high savings and investment, urbanization, high literacy, and a strong work ethic. Successful development required a holistic approach to reforming the underdeveloped economy. H. Laugier, Assistant Secretary General of the UN's Department of Social Affairs, put it succinctly when he wrote that 'human progress depends on the development and application to the greatest possible extent of scientific research' and where a country's 'physical, intellectual, and moral development lags behind the general pace of civilisation, immediate concrete measures' must be taken to 'help them along the path of human progress'.[31] An assessment of the Colombo Plan written in *Australian Outlook* explained that to achieve such progress 'required grafting onto Asian societies ... the best in capitalist thinking and attitudes, as well as techniques'.[32] For this reason, the proponents of development emphasised the importance of education and the mass media in helping to disseminate the Western cultural and attitudinal qualities they thought essential to the achievement of modernity. For example, in December 1952, when Indonesia finally yielded to entreaties to join the Colombo Plan, Australia agreed to provide six mobile cinema vans, textbooks, educational films and equipment for two vocational training centres, in addition to over £A1 million worth of buses, marine engines and agricultural vehicles.[33] Notably, by the mid-1950s Australia had offered over a quarter (500) of its Colombo Plan scholarships to Indonesia.

Before Rostow's ideas achieved prominence, the National Security Council (the American President's high-powered forum for considering national security and foreign policy issues) articulated a similar, although less colourful, development philosophy. Its view was that the Colombo Plan would not 'of itself bring about significant increases in living standards.' Rather, they hoped that after a few years recipient countries 'would have established an environment that would encourage a maximum utilization of domestic savings and a reasonable flow of outside investment capital for further development activities'.[34] Development theorists like Rostow confirmed the basic thrust of Western economic diplomacy and lent it academic credibility. For this reason, their ideas achieved rare prominence among bureaucrats and politicians responsible for foreign affairs decision-making. Rostow himself went on to become Special Assistant for National Security Affairs for President John F. Kennedy and President Lyndon Johnson.

Australian planners embraced modernisation theory in the post-war years, not least because Australia saw itself as a developing nation, requiring external capital and economic stimulation. Under the guidance of the Department of Postwar Reconstruction (DPR) and its influential head, Herbert ('Nugget') Coombs, Keynesian economics reigned supreme and few doubted the active role the state should play in governing economic growth. Coombs' vision for Australia embodied the same faith in science and technology as the 'take-off'–styled boosters.[35] 'Modern technology', he wrote in his memoirs, 'could be placed at the disposal of communities — not as a framework constraining and determining their lifestyles but as a force capable of liberating their imagination and giving scope to their creative energies'.[36] Here, Coombs was referring to Australia's rapid industrial expansion, but the same interventionist ethos he espoused applied equally to the less developed economies in Asia. Australia, of course, had practical experience in stimulating economic growth in undeveloped countries. Paul Hasluck, Minister for Territories between 1951 and 1963, saw Papua New Guinea as a 'society still awaiting the full effects both of the techniques and mechanical strength of Western civilisation, the blessings of Western medicine and society, the ferment of ideas of civilised man'. Australia, he said, had a duty to create both a 'community and an economy' whereby 'primitive beliefs and codes' gradually gave way to a 'new order'.[37] Rostow himself could not have been clearer.

More directly, Australian experts working in Asia under the Colombo Plan often reinforced the key assumptions about Asian society which underpinned the program, namely that apathy, conservatism, and laziness left them destined to languish as a poor and vulnerable race. Agricultural economist T.B. Paltridge, for example, undertook a two-year assignment in Ceylon in the mid-1950s to establish a Division of Agronomy at the Coconut Research Institute and locate pasture suitable for coconut plantations. Paltridge received full cooperation from local Ceylonese staff, the equipment he ordered arrived from Australia promptly, and he successfully helped establish the facilities to undertake soil analysis; nevertheless, he devoted most of his report to the Ceylonese attitude to Colombo Plan aid and the nature of Ceylonese society. He encountered a curious resistance to change and a 'peculiar lack of incentive' at all levels of society. The people, he wrote, believed that 'international aid is their right; rather than a gesture of goodwill'. Over time, Paltridge mused, 'the Ceylonese have gradually become a subservient and ineffective people'. He wondered if this was because of a lack of leadership, malnutrition, climatic conditions, disease, or even genetics. Paltridge proposed that Australia launch an investigation into the factors causing the loss of vigour and initiative, although he warranted that such a study would be difficult to implement. 'On the other hand', he concluded, 'if we could pinpoint some real and basic problem of that nature and if we could remove the fundamental cause of lassitude among these peoples, then it might be possible to encourage the greatest revival and development in human history'.[38]

The London report of the Consultative Committee, which set out the Colombo Plan's basic aid philosophy, encapsulated the very essence of modernist development

theory, which was sweeping the world. The report stated
that the particular strength of the program was its ability to
lay 'sound foundations for further development' and thus
promote a domestic economy able to 'sustain its own
investment programme'. The Colombo Plan would 'involve
the application of modern technology and skills to the
under-developed and traditional economies of the countries
of South and South–East Asia'. Administrators, scientists,
and technicians from overseas can help Asians 'equipping
themselves to use the recent advances in science and
technology which, applied to the tasks of peace, can bring
incalculable material benefits to all in South and
South–East Asia'. Furthermore, rising standards of living
would increase the 'vigour and productivity' of the people
and 'eventually exercise a steadying influence' on
population growth, seen by many as the fundamental
reason for Asian poverty.[39] The Consultative Committee
report rang with evangelical fervour: 'they must be liberated
so that they can contribute towards the self-realisation of
individuals, towards the fulfilment of national aspirations'.
Development 'by its own momentum [would] ultimately
bring about a solution' and lead the poor nations of Asia —
phoenix-like — out of the ashes of underdevelopment.[40]
Significantly, administrators from recipient nations
themselves agreed with this logic and recognised that
although the funds made available were low, a cohesive
basis for growth had been set in place.[41]

At its heart, then, the Colombo Plan aimed to oversee
Asia's embrace of Westernisation and build the foundations
for a self-sustaining, modern economy. It presented Asian
underdevelopment as a problem requiring a non-political,
scientific solution that encompassed social reform.
Discussion of fiscal policy, health reform, and lack of
technology and expertise, however, masked the overarching

assumption that cultural and social factors, not just economic ones, had retarded development and exposed these nations to the lure of revolution. In official circles, Asians were considered psychologically susceptible, by virtue of their physical poverty, to communist blandishments. Poverty, as the Consultative Committee put it, had circumscribed their bodies and their minds. The cock-sure Percy Spender seized the opportunity to step into the breach. Rejecting any suggestion that a non-interventionist approach would foster greater appreciation from the people of Asia, Spender believed it was insufficient for the West to present passively the advantages of liberalism, individualism, and democracy. In a long article for the respected US journal *Foreign Affairs* in January 1951, he made the point that communism was an idea 'foreign' to Asian people and acted as an instrument of 'internal intervention', working 'with and among the people … on the minds and political life of the community'. Aid donors needed to look beyond the 'realm of material welfare' towards 'abstract ideas' if they were to confront communist subversion. The West, he said was 'entering the struggle for the purpose of winning the mind of Asia'. Australia's religious fraternity also joined the fray. In 1953, the distinguished Archbishop Howard Mowll claimed that undernourishment had left the Asian mind as a kind of *tabula rasa*, open and willing to receive. The solution was a 'spiritual Colombo Plan', because the people of Asia were like 'soft wax, ready to receive impressions which, if imparted before the wax got cold, would be retained as their future character'.[42]

Asia's apparent vulnerability and the regenerative power of development reinforced the Colombo Plan as the natural and necessary interface between the problem of Asian underdevelopment and the arrest of communist subversion. By feeding the belief that communism could not take hold in the face of unbridled economic expansion, development programs such as the Colombo Plan became instruments of international relations and legitimised Western intervention in the underdeveloped world. Bolstering Asia through economic support represented only one facet of the Colombo Plan's underlying political strategy. Competing directly for intellectual and ideological influence also became an increasingly prominent feature of Australia's aid initiative. The first wave of Colombo Plan scholars presented an exciting chance to directly engage Asians and instil in them the virtues of Australian culture and democracy. To this end, the DEA also considered the scholarship program to have long-term and 'self-sustaining' political benefits: it created 'the body of people in Asian countries which is gradually built up with an intimate knowledge of Australia and, it may be hoped, some affection for this country', but also provided a 'balm' to those who resented Australia's immigration restrictions. Similarly, the DEA reasoned that the scholarship program and supply of expert personnel and technical equipment would encourage understanding and acceptance of Western values more effectively than capital aid. Officials thought the personal interaction between Australian technicians and Asians would provide some compensation for the fact that their reports would be quickly superseded if, in fact, they did not 'gather dust from the start', and that Asians would soon forget where the technical equipment had come from.[43] Reflecting these priorities, the DEA initially devoted 70 per cent of the technical aid budget to training and scholarships, 20 per cent to equipment, and just 10 per cent to the supply of technicians.

By the second year of operation, the DEA's concerns about the effectiveness of the program began to materialise. In what would become a depressingly familiar formula, the

Consultative Committee's annual report stated that economic advances were slight and outpaced by increases in population. When the afterglow of Korean War stockpiling faded and the price of primary commodities tumbled, the Consultative Committee could only lament Asia's vulnerability to the vicissitudes of the world market.[44] While Colombo Plan donors now reported Asia's economic future in 'less airy and less optimistic terms', they offset their pessimistic assessments with the promise of future growth, lest they quash the hopes of the underdeveloped world or the spirit of the Colombo Plan. The publicity wing of the Colombo Plan Bureau, opened in 1954, was particularly careful not to raise the hopes for an economic miracle in spite of any Herculean efforts from Asian workers: the hard road was inevitable, one promotional pamphlet told, because 'the process of economic development is slow and must go on for years as it did in the West'.[45] In an Orwellian twist, as genuine economic improvement seemed unlikely, the Australian government began to emphasise more forcefully the humanitarian dimensions of the Colombo Plan and its capacity to foster international goodwill.

The man charged with the task of incorporating the Colombo Plan into the wider ambit of Australian foreign policy was Spender's successor as foreign minister, Richard Casey. Spender had resigned after the signing of the ANZUS treaty in early 1951 to take up the distinguished position of ambassador to the United States. (Gossip suggested that Menzies saw Spender as a potential rival and so made him the handsome offer.[46]) Nevertheless, Casey's appointment to the portfolio, which he would hold until 1960, marked an important change in the tenor and scope of Australia's diplomatic relations. No less hawkish than his predecessor, Casey was, however, a more measured and congenial character — far more adept at building diplomatic rapport with regional neighbours. His dapper dress-sense, impeccable deportment, and legendary dislike of economics confirmed the opinion of his detractors that he lacked depth, but his outstanding personal relationships with influential people throughout the world proved adequate compensation. To his friends he was an urbane, well-travelled and well-read gentleman with a 'modulated resonant voice'.[47] To others, this impeccably dressed engineer-cum-politician, with literary pretensions and a passion for flying his own aircraft, stood aloof from the Australian political scene. The UK Chancellor of the Exchequer, Hugh Gaitskell, found him 'curiously English and un-Australian'.[48] Certainly, Asian leaders came to prefer his urbane and quiet manner to Spender's brash effervescence.[49]

Few Cabinet members rivalled the diversity and breadth of 61-year-old Casey's career. An engineer by training, he came from a wealthy and well-connected family. During the First World War he served in Egypt, at Gallipoli, and on the Somme, earning the Distinguished Service Order and the Military Cross. In 1924, Prime Minister Stanley Bruce appointed him Commonwealth Liaison Officer in London. Returning to Australia in 1931, he joined the United Australia Party and won the federal seat of Corio. A dutiful and diligent parliamentarian, Casey served in a variety of ministerial positions, but his ambitions of becoming Prime Minister were thwarted in 1939 following a failed leadership challenge. A humbled Casey accepted Menzies's offer to head the Australian Legation in Washington. In America, he was quietly impressive, enhancing his reputation and gaining important experience in the ways of diplomacy. His reputation as a capable diplomat reached Winston Churchill, who offered

him the position of British Minister of State resident in the
Middle East. In 1943 he accepted another imperial posting,
this time the governorship of Bengal. Three years in this
difficult position brought him into close contact with Asian
leaders and, importantly, anti-colonial feeling. In 1949 he
re-entered parliament, but with Menzies now firmly at the
helm of the Liberal Party, any lingering hopes Casey had of
leading the party were dashed.[50]

Casey's interest in the region grew rapidly from the
time he took over the External Affairs portfolio in April 1951
and made his first overseas trip to Asia as minister. He opened
new diplomatic posts in Saigon and Rangoon, and raised the
consulate-general post in Bangkok to legation status.
Throughout his career, Casey extolled the virtues of cultural
exchange facilitated by the Colombo Plan's scholarship
program. He was also among the first to identify the scheme's
potential to change the way Australians thought about
themselves, as well as the way they thought about Asia. 'We
need to understand and be understood by the countries of
South and South–East Asia', he told the Australian Institute
of International Affairs on 25 September 1952. For Asian
students 'to see Australia at an impressionable stage of their
lives and to exchange views at our universities and with our
officials should do a great deal to break down prejudices and
misunderstandings on both sides'.[51]

Casey prided himself on his belief in the importance
of personal diplomacy. His addiction to the press release,
and what he called the 'human and personal element' of
inter-governmental exchange, naturally spilled over into
his approach to the Colombo Plan. Casey pushed the idea
of aggressively promoting public awareness of Australia's
aid programs, telling his Cabinet colleagues that Australia
must seek to generate 'intensive publicity'.[52] He made a
particular point of using Colombo Plan funds on short-

term, identifiably Australian projects. In 1953, he directed the Assistant Secretary of the DEA, James Plimsoll, to pay close attention to publicity and avoid having Australia's contributions 'sunk', or become unidentifiable, in large projects. Casey requested that attention 'be given to a series of plaques of different sizes and applicable to various types of equipment ... If this is done in a not too obtrusive way, it would go some way towards having a permanent record that they [Asians] would be aware of, of the fact that Australia had provided equipment'.[53] Here Casey set an enduring precedent. His goal was to give Australia a visible presence in Asia and secure long-lasting political dividends; the effectiveness of the projects themselves were only important to the extent they served this objective. Cooperation with the media also helped ensure popular support for the plan, which in turn, helped Casey generate interest from an indifferent Cabinet. Rather than vague forecasts of economic development, he could point to improvements in Australia's international reputation, something of more immediate concern to his worried colleagues.

Sober appreciations about the effectiveness of development projects, the need to obtain political benefits (both domestic and international), and a desire to promote Western values — all meant that publicity and propaganda would never be tangential to the Colombo Plan. All the major donors shared these concerns. The British Foreign Office reasoned that publicity would help disguise the low levels of assistance and convince left-wing detractors that the 'development of South and South–East Asia has not been sacrificed to the rearmament drive'.[54] For the US State Department, the publicity attached to aid projects should foster an 'understanding of the nature of Soviet Communism and encourage attitudes hostile to it'.[55] Of course, donors attempted to counter accusations that the Colombo Plan amounted to little more than a public relations exercise — ironically, with more publicity. Indeed, Spender wrote in the introduction to *New hope for Asia* (1951), the first major publication designed to promote and popularise the Colombo Plan, that the scheme was 'a concrete, material answer' to Asia's development problems; 'it gives new hope for Asian peoples, not the faint hope inspired by shallow propaganda'.[56] Another underlying message was that Western aid was an expression of genuine and dispassionate concern for Asian progress, and in no way like the empty promises made by Soviet and Chinese communists.

In the bilateral climate, so integral to the Colombo Plan philosophy, the Australian government soon discovered that the political and publicity value of an aid project depended on a host of other factors, such as aid relationships with other donors, the attitude of the recipient government, and the general economic conditions. For example, the main factor influencing Indonesia's decision to eventually accept aid under the Colombo Plan was the country's rapidly deteriorating economy. As US aid priorities shifted towards India and Indo-China — regions the US State Department considered strategically more significant and vulnerable to communism — non-military aid to Indonesia fell from $US13 million per annum in 1951 to just $US3 million in 1953. Large quantities of US aid, which had hitherto deflected interest in the more limited Colombo Plan, were now being offered to India and Indo-China. Indonesia's misfortune favoured Australia. Australia was poised to assume the role of magnanimous aid donor as economic conditions worsened and goodwill toward the United States evaporated.[57] Australia's Minister and Chargé d'Affaires in Djakarta, John Kevin, explained the benefits of this 'flying start':

One would suppose that there are few countries in Asia where the volume of Australian aid has a prospect of approximating that currently granted by the United States; and it is more valuable from our viewpoint that the exception should be Indonesia, where we have so important a political, economic and strategic interest and where the injection of Australian help comes at so opportune a time.[58]

Differentiating Australian aid from the American largesse became increasingly important, not merely to attract the attention of Indonesia and other non-Commonwealth nations, but also to improve Australia's nascent regional profile. A persistent problem for Australia, Casey told Menzies in 1954, was that of 'combating the belief that is held in some quarters that we are an American "satellite"'.[59] The pursuit of US military protection and support, especially over West New Guinea, may have been central to foreign policy, but it was not to come at the expense of Australia's regional identity. In April 1953, Australia stymied an Indonesian attempt to reshape the Colombo Plan's technical cooperation committee by having monthly instead of annual meetings. Australian representatives in Djakarta thought the idea sound and likely to facilitate contact between individuals interested in making aid projects more efficient, but they determined it was 'undesirable for any other body to develop too prominent a local role in relation to the Colombo Plan in which we feel our special identity should be obscured'.[60] Projecting Australia's identity into the region had become a defining feature of the Colombo Plan and was already having important consequences for the political and economic goals the scheme was intended to fulfil. This was also the case in Indo-China. Following the visit of Jean Letourneau, the French Minister in charge of relations with Indo-China, in March 1953, the Menzies Government reassessed its position on assistance to the associated states, offering over £A1.5 million in capital and technical assistance.[61] John Rowland, Chargé d'Affaires in Saigon, suggested that Australia was in a prime position to take advantage of increasing tension between US and French authorities by showing a real 'interest in the future of the three countries'. Local discontent towards the French and the US presence also heightened the potential political mileage which might be obtained from a speedy supply of assistance. For these reasons, Rowland felt that Australia's Colombo Plan contributions, 'relatively small though they may be, have a political importance that they possess nowhere else'.[62]

In the years after the Second World War, the economic, political, and psychological vacuum left by decolonisation concerned policy-makers across the Commonwealth. Australian politicians and bureaucrats hoped that Colombo Plan aid would help to transfer not only the practical tools for material progress, but also the moral, cultural and spiritual virtues necessary to transform Asia into an economically self-sustaining, non-communist region. The Colombo Plan rationale — that economic progress would act as an ideological bulwark against communism — was nurtured by intertwined ideas. Fear about Australia's future in the Asian region combined with a seductively simple understanding of economic advancement to produce the Colombo Plan's *raison d'être*. Yet the rigidity of realist, Cold War ideology precluded other interpretations. The desire to develop Asia along non-communist lines through the application of Western ideas and technology, and the tendency to see aid as an oblique instrument of economic and cultural control, reinforced Australian preconceptions about the region: Asia was poor, weak, malleable — always at risk of quick conversion by communists or capitalists.

What was already apparent was that the Colombo Plan was going to have a greater impact on Australian perceptions of the region than on the economic advancement of member states. Casey's attention to public relations and personal diplomacy would be a defining mark of his tenure as foreign minister. It marked a critical shift away from using aid to catapult the ailing economies of Asia (although he continued to speak publicly of the catalytic potential of Australia's contributions) and it would soon take the Colombo Plan into areas not considered at the program's inception. The distinction between prosecuting a war against communist insurgency and building Australia's economic, cultural and diplomatic links through foreign aid was to become increasingly blurred.

A 'new deal' for Japan

Early in 1950, Colonel William Hodgson, head of the Australian mission in Tokyo, wrote to Percy Spender to explain the political and commercial benefits that would accrue should Asia spend its foreign aid on capital goods from industrialised nations such as Japan. He claimed that not only would this foster a more dynamic regional economy, the creation of Japan as a South–East Asian trading hub would then help the United States gradually relinquish its role as regional financier. Japan's 'progress towards self-sufficiency would be assisted and the need for American aid funds reduced, while the Asian countries concerned would be provided with the means to obtain, mostly from Japan, supplies needed in developmental and rehabilitation projects'.[63] Hodgson was not proposing that Japan join the embryonic Colombo Plan. Nor did he identify a clear role for Australia, possibly because the mere suggestion of Japanese commercial expansion would arouse anxiety. But he did say that Australia would have to chart a careful diplomatic course because preventing Japan from 'playing an essential part in world recovery, would not only be damaging from an international point of view but also would arouse the hostility of both America and Japan'.[64]

By 1950, the Truman administration had determined that the regional integration of a highly-developed Japanese economy remained essential to ensure progress and stability across Asia. American objectives for Japan shifted from reform to reconstruction, with the long-term goal of preventing Soviet control of industrial and military activity in the region.[65] Secretary of State, Dean Acheson, told the British in December 1949: if 'Japan [were to be] added to the Communist Bloc, the Soviets would acquire skilled manpower and industrial potential capable of significantly altering the balance of world power'.[66] The key to this policy of containment lay in the economic links between Japan and the Asian hinterland. The National Security Council decided that Japan would only be able to maintain present living standards if it could 'secure a greater proportion of its needed food and raw material (principally cotton) imports from the Asiatic area, in which its natural markets lie' and expand intra-regional trade.[67]

Japan was willing to oblige. Fearful of further alienating the region, Japan's Prime Minister, Shigeru Yoshida, resolved to pursue a policy of 'economic diplomacy', structured around strengthening export and trade links with South–East Asia, the provision of technical and capital assistance, and membership of international associations such as ECAFE and the Colombo Plan.[68]

Not until the Colombo Plan had achieved some stability did Australia begin to contemplate Japan's admission. Australia had offered tentative support for Japan's gradual return to the international economic community via membership of the UN, the International Monetary Fund (IMF), and the International Bank of Reconstruction and Development (IBRD), but inviting a former enemy into the congenial Colombo Plan fraternity was likely to be more problematic. In March 1952, senior officials at the DEA swapped ideas on the issue. Joining the program, they suggested, would be a means of 'binding Japan to the democratic camp', and offer some protection against communist states. As Casey explained publicly, the major threat to Australia's regional security came from communist expansion, not Japanese aggression. 'The immediate problem we have to consider is the security of Japan, even more than security against Japan'.[69] Japan's resurgence as an economic leader also reflected the nationalist aspirations of many other nations in the area; Asian governments might even demand compensation should Australia deny them easy access to the aid Japan was so eager to give.[70] Importantly, some in the Department of External Affairs (DEA) felt that conceding Japan's entry into the fold represented an ideal opportunity to impress the Americans, for any effort Australia took which made the integration of the Japanese economy easier would 'have US blessing'.[71]

The legacy of the Pacific War deeply affected Japan's relations with the region. For Australia, there were sensitive economic and political matters, including Japanese rearmament, pearl fishing in Australian waters, compensation for former prisoners of war, the trial of Japanese war criminals, Japanese war dead in Australian territory, and Japan's potential inclusion in SEATO and the General Agreement on Tariffs and Trade (GATT).[72] (GATT was a series of multilateral trade agreements aimed at the abolition of quotas and the reduction of tariff duties). But boosting Japan's economic power in the name of regional stability and progress was difficult for many to understand. To the generation with close and sharp memories of Kokoda, Changi and Sandakan, it seemed an absurd irony. Both Britain and Australia were wary of the potential danger of Colombo Plan finance facilitating the commercial and political exploitation of smaller South–East Asian nations. Sir Gerald Templer, from the British High Commission in Malaya, told the Foreign Office that there was a 'clear danger of this being [a] cover for economic penetration, particularly in [the] field of fisheries and mining [with] which we were familiar before the war. We hope, therefore, that [the] matter [of Japanese admission] will neither be raised nor pressed'.[73] DEA officials worried that if Australian aid found its way to Japan, 'however devious the route', the public hostility towards Japan might spill over and damage the standing of the Colombo Plan program itself. Whatever the concern, the issue seemed 'likely to remain "hot" for some time'.[74]

Yet it was always going to be difficult for Australia or Britain to use fear of political domination as a public reason to deny Japan access to the Colombo Plan. For to suggest that Japan could use their member status to dominate smaller South–East Asian economies might imply that current donor countries could do the same. So instead of the real reason, the DEA cited Japan's balance of payment problems and its inability to provide adequate assistance to recipient nations as the principal reason for recommending that Australia not admit Japan. The DEA assumed, however, 'that the real opposition lies in [the] doubts of Australian people'. The immediate and convenient solution for Australia, New Zealand, and the United Kingdom was to do nothing, but this did not rule out the possibility of a change of heart. Rather the DEA thought the move '"premature" rather than inconceivable'.[75]

American officials worried about Australia's capacity to tolerate a more intimate association with Japan. The State Department noted that because Australia had a positive influence on other Western powers, 'every effort should be made to prepare the ground through diplomatic channels before [attempting] new measures which might be misunderstood'.[76] The Americans, however, were impatient and appeared intent on denying the British Commonwealth the luxury of slowly coming to terms with the issue of Japan's full return to the international community.

All the while endeavouring to 'avoid the appearance of aggressive sponsorship', the US embassy in Tokyo asked British officials about the possibility of Japan's attending the 1952 meeting of the Consultative Committee in Karachi as an observer.[77] On hearing of the discussions, Alan Watt, Secretary of the DEA, immediately informed the United Kingdom that Australia was not keen about any motion to admit Japan to Consultative Committee proceedings.[78] A cable from Canberra explained that although the DEA was aware that Japanese admission would most likely have a positive economic impact for Colombo Plan countries, 'formal participation of Japan would naturally have important political implications and [the] Australian Government is unlikely to agree in the near future'.[79] When the United Kingdom reported to the United States that Australia and most of the other committee members were 'implacably opposed' to the suggestion, the Americans dropped the issue in deference to such widespread and deeply felt opposition.[80]

Eighteen months later, the question of Japanese membership stalled once more, this time, a result of Japanese fishing activity in the Arafura Sea. The Japanese Peace Treaty stipulated that the Japanese government negotiate with Australia to ensure the conservation of oyster beds located in Australian waters. In August 1953, while negotiations were in progress, Japanese pearlers recommenced fishing, reputedly taking over 1,000 tons of shell (compared to the Australian harvest of 170 tons).[81] Moreover, some of this activity was taking place off the coast of Darwin. With memories of the attacks on Darwin and Sydney still alive, the presence of Japanese so close to home unsettled many Australians. Negotiations between Japan and Australia broke off. Haruhiko Nishi, the Japanese Ambassador in Canberra, met with Watt in late 1953 and told him that Japan could not conform to Australia's demand that it restrict pearl-fishing activities in Australian waters. Nishi then immediately questioned Watt on Japan's potential admission to the Colombo Plan. Watt's reply was curt, 'indicating that this was hardly a propitious time to raise this second question'.[82] The Australian government formally asked Japan to recognise the validity of Australian restrictions on activity on the Indonesian continental shelf — before it would consider their application to join the Consultative Committee. This distraction annoyed US officials, who asked their representatives why the Australian Government would 'interject apparently extraneous issues into what US considers a desirable objective'.[83] Assistant Secretary, James Plimsoll, explained to Arthur Emmons, First Secretary of the US embassy in Canberra, that Australia would not bargain with Japan over territorial matters: 'The question of the Colombo Plan and of pearling were linked only in one way: that the fishing dispute had not made the atmosphere a suitable one for raising the question of further concessions to Japan'.[84] Plimsoll also took the opportunity to remind Emmons of the devastation brought upon Darwin during the Second World War and the considerable level of hostility still felt towards the Japanese.

Anxious predictions about Japan's political and economic future continued to dominated parliamentary debates and stymied any chance of Australian support for their membership in the Consultative Committee. Australian representatives in Washington remained unconvinced by American assurances. A State Department official had explained that it would be 'easier to influence Japan against undue commercial exploitation in the area if she were associated with the rest of us in the plan'. The cable concluded, however, that 'American thinking on the economic side is rather woolly'.[85] Where Australia did agree with American assessments was over the capacity of the Colombo Plan to dissipate anti-Japanese feeling in South and South–East Asia, stimulate intra-regional trade, and encourage other Asian countries to export primary commodities to Japan.[86]

In the early 1950s, Japan was Australia's second largest buyer of wool. However, Australia was increasingly vulnerable to the vicissitudes of the Japanese economy, the stabilising of which was of paramount importance if the market for Australian exports was to be maintained. This was crucial if Australia was to maintain its export potential. Another problem was to redress the gross trade imbalance between Australia and Japan. In 1952/53, Japan purchased around £A84 million worth of goods (mainly wool), whereas Australia purchased just £A5 million worth of Japanese goods. The imbalance was set to increase into the decade.[87] With the war in Korea nearing an end, Japan was so short of sterling that 'adequate allocations cannot be made even for the purchase of Australian wool. Sterling aid to Japan therefore now seems more necessary than Japanese aid to the sterling area'.[88]

The very idea of aid finding its way to a former enemy caused some concern. When the Japanese press began enthusiastically reporting that the Australian government was seriously considering widening the scope of the Colombo Plan to include them, an Australian representative in Rangoon refused to believe such audacious claims. 'I feel sure that this is a cunning ruse originating from some interested Japanese quarters', the embassy reported to Canberra:

> *It would amount to sheer madness. A country need not for all time entertain ill feelings against her former ruthless enemy, but it would be sheer folly to go out of her way and give substantial help in rebuilding industries … History will be meaningless if a country does not learn by the happenings in the past and model her actions by past events and experiences.*[89]

Apparently, the author had mistakenly assumed that Japan would be a recipient of aid, not a donor. The embassy's obvious surprise also suggests the degree to which Casey and the DEA kept the detail of their thoughts private.

Casey, however, sensed the potential for a new era of regional engagement. The Japanese search for prestige was a relatively transparent strategy — one that handed Casey a powerful diplomatic tool. As he explained to Tange, 'Japan's wish to get into the Colombo Plan may be a rather heaven-sent opportunity on which we might base our "new deal" towards Japan'.[90] He recorded in his diary that he would endeavour to 'make as much of this' search for acceptance as he could.[91] The integration of Japan via the goodwill of the Colombo Plan emerged as a politically palatable alternative to direct financial assistance. By helping Japan's earning potential in Asia, the government hoped that the balance of payments deficit would ease and allow a more stable trading partnership with Australia. The prospects were good for Australian exports.[92] Over the decade, the demand for wool in Japan increased rapidly, with consumption per head rising from 0.2 kg in 1950 to 1.1 kg in 1960, at which time Japan replaced the United States as Australia's largest wool market. The major obstacle to a more equitable balance of trade was Japan's negative image and the reluctance of Australian consumers to buy Japanese goods. To remedy this and to prepare the ground for economic concessions, Menzies took to the air waves to explain Australia's complex economic predicament. A transfer of the prestige associated with the Colombo Plan to the Japanese was another important factor the government thought would help the sale of Japanese imports in Australia.

Cabinet's decision to admit Japan to the Colombo Plan coincided with the general adoption of a more liberal attitude toward Japan. Although Cabinet approached the liberalisation of Australian relations with Japan 'reluctantly', the meeting did identify sound commercial and political advantages — apart from keeping Japan away from the embrace of China. Assisting Japanese economic integration with South–East Asia would increase Japanese earnings and enable her to buy more Australian wool. The committee was even prepared to accept the loss of Australian exports (such as tractors and diesel locomotives) when Japanese industry became more efficient. Any disadvantages were 'far outweighed by the necessity of ensuring that Japan was a strong bidder for [Australian] wool' and the 'psychological effect' of 'influencing them towards association with Western Powers'.[93] And any disadvantages likely to arise from Japanese penetration of Asian commercial markets were subordinated to strategic objectives. On 27 August 1954, Cabinet agreed to support Japanese membership in the Colombo Plan, on condition that it received support from a majority of member nations, including the United Kingdom and the United States.

Unaware of the Cabinet decision, the US State Department continued to place pressure on Australia, implying that if Australia made concessions to Japan they could expect reciprocal concession, not only in Japanese tariffs, but in US tariffs as well. The timing of this request suggests that the 'concessions' the United States expected from Australia included Japan's full admission to the Colombo Plan. The DEA proceeded cautiously, aware of the strange nature of the proposal: 'The unusual character of the American proposal is appreciated but we are not at this stage in a position to indicate whether or not the Government can take it up'.[94] The cable instructed Washington staff to seek US views on a possible reduction in the duty on wool as the basis of future negotiations.

Although the offer turned out to be an empty distraction, sometime in late August 1954, the DEA, presumably with Casey's approval, resolved to take a much more active role at the Consultative Committee meeting to be held in Ottawa in October. On 27 August, the DEA sent a telegram to relevant posts announcing the decision to support Japan's admission as a donor to the Colombo Plan. Much to the surprise of New Zealand, Canada, and the United Kingdom, the DEA even offered to sponsor Japan's application.[95] Unaware of the US promise to Canberra, New Zealand's Minister for External Affairs, Clifton Webb, greeted Australia's sudden change of heart with suspicion. Remaining steadfastly opposed to the admission of Japan, officials in Wellington regarded the amount of pressure brought to bear by the Americans as excessive.[96] On 8 September 1954, Webb conveyed his misgivings about Australia's diplomatic manoeuvring to his Washington ambassador: 'The Australians, who originally opposed

Japanese admission more strongly than we did, have now turned about-face and want to make a "dramatic gesture" by sponsoring Japan themselves, in the hope that this will secure some goodwill. Is this not "rather woolly"?[97] Nevertheless, the major Western allies and Asian Colombo Plan nations had agreed on their stance toward Japan. Facing further isolation, New Zealand capitulated and agreed to vote in favour of admission.[98]

What had led to Australia's change of heart? Was it the promise of more attractive trade arrangements? Was it the desire to impress the United States and the Japanese? Or was it an attempt to garner greater support for the Colombo Plan and Australia's regional reputation? Superficially, it looked as though Australia had only succumbed to US pressure when offered a means to offset any losses incurred through the displacement of local produce by cheap Japanese goods. However, it is unlikely that the US offer of further GATT concessions was more than a minor factor in the decision to take a more active role. At most, the promise of GATT concessions from the State Department simply stiffened the resolve of Australian officials. By August 1954, Australia had already determined that it was as much in Australia's interest as it was in the United States' to admit Japan. Sponsoring Japan, as opposed to merely allowing her admission, was a relatively painless way to maximise the seemingly magnanimous nature of Australia's decision. Sponsorship also restored the goodwill lost as a result of the protracted negotiations.

The Japanese embassy in Canberra suspected American involvement and asked the DEA directly whether Australia was acting at the behest of the United States. Counsellor Masayoshi Kakitsubo came dangerously close to the mark when he said that the United States was trying diligently to have Japan admitted to GATT and had pressured Australia to have Japan as a Colombo Plan donor. Naturally, his suggestion was 'firmly rejected', the DEA informing him that the initiative had been undertaken independently — in the interest of Japanese relations with Australia and the Colombo Plan region.[99] Curiously enough, after Australia's decision to sponsor Japan, Under-secretary of State General Walter Bedell Smith expressed 'his gratification at Australia's decision and agreed that nothing should be read in any way which would suggest that [its] decision had not been completely on [its] own initiative'.[100]

Casey withheld the decision from parliament. Fearful of a premature announcement and hoping to achieve maximum publicity at the official meeting in Ottawa, Casey claimed only to have heard a 'tentative proposal' that another country was being invited to join the program.[101] The DEA had asked some journalists who had learned of Australia's plans not to announce anything before the Consultative Committee agenda had been set. On 22 September 1954, Menzies, replying to a Question on Notice, gently announced the decision to support Japan's admission to the Colombo Plan. There was no debate, just as the government desired.[102]

Canberra also went to considerable effort to ensure that the formal admission procedure held during the Ottawa meeting went as smoothly as possible.[103] The DEA guided Japan through the application procedure, thus ensuring that India did not take credit (as she was appearing to do) for officially proposing Japanese membership. Now actively encouraging Japan's economic resurgence, the DEA's Assistant Secretary to the United Nations Division, Patrick Shaw, encouraged Japan to apply for full membership of the Consultative Committee (as opposed the more limited membership of Technical

Council) because it 'gave Japan access to the economic planning of a number of countries in which Japan presumably was interested from a commercial point of view'.[104] In the event, Japan received full membership, but confined its initial contributions to just $US40,000 in technical aid.[105]

Two days after Japan's admission, Nishi meet with Tange and Shaw in order to thank the Australian government formally. The First Secretary of the Japanese embassy, Y. Yamamoto, visited the DEA later that evening offering more appreciation for achieving a 'milestone in Japanese–Australian relations'. In keeping with the transparent and deferential nature of Japanese diplomacy of the time, Yamamoto then announced that he looked forward to the next milestone — 'the abolition of discrimination in import licensing against Japanese goods'.[106] Indeed, that milestone, embodied in the 1957 Australia–Japan Agreement on Commerce and Trade, was still a few years away.

Cabinet had based its decision to admit Japan to the Colombo Plan on interrelated economic, political, and strategic issues. As a raw material supplier and importer of industrial products, Australia was part of the South–East Asian resource hinterland that Western strategists considered fundamentally important for regional stability and prosperity. Against this background, the Truman Administration's support for a $US250 million loan through the IBRD in August 1950 was a tangible expression of the US desire to see Australia develop as a key feeder nation supporting Japanese capitalist expansion.[107] However, the Colombo Plan served as an important political and diplomatic tool that allowed the Menzies Government to manoeuvre itself into a stronger position. Once more, the congenial alliance suggested by universal support for Japanese inclusion in the Colombo Plan belied the complex interplay between anti-communist containment and the Anglo–American approach to economic regionalism.

For those concerned to extend the Colombo Plan's reputation as a unifying symbol of resolve against the communist bloc, Japan's admission came just in time. For the following year, the Soviet Union launched its own foreign aid program for the developing nations of Asia, a program which placed renewed pressure on the Colombo Plan.

A red Colombo Plan for Asia

The Western world received scant warning about Soviet intentions to create an aid program for Asia. During the early 1950s, Australian representatives abroad detected few signs of a communist alternative to Western development initiatives, merely an increasing number of pronouncements about the necessity of the underdeveloped world to embrace the socialist model. Then, in 1955, the Soviet Union burst onto the foreign aid arena. At a cost of over $US200 million, the Soviets announced a commitment to build the Bhilai steel plant in India, intended as a global demonstration of communist planning, technological capacity, and concern for oppressed people. With much fanfare, the Soviet Union took over the ambitious Aswan high dam project in 1956 when the United States withdrew in retaliation for Egypt's recognition of China and its weapons deal with Czechoslovakia. The blustering and ebullient leader of the Soviet Union, Nikita Khrushchev, would not officially challenge capitalist leaders to a peaceful competition in the underdeveloped world until 1957, but the Soviet 'economic offensive', as the White House called it, had already begun.[108]

Australia's role in the ensuing battle would be an auxiliary one, but it was equally alarming. 'ASIA GETS A RED COLOMBO PLAN' ran the headline in the

Melbourne *Herald* for a story by English foreign affairs analyst Barbara Ward. She cautioned Western powers not to be complacent about their own aid programs because Russia was making a start on a Colombo Plan of its own. Russian training programs seemed to be 'going forward more ambitiously' and might soon outnumber those offered by Australia and her allies. She spurred the West to act, for 'upon the horizons of Asia may be the portent of vast political upheavals still to come'.[109] Ward's observations proved prescient. With the launch of Sputnik — a striking symbol of modern scientific progress — and a burgeoning industrial capacity, the Soviets demonstrated an apparent technological and economic superiority over the West. The communist model of economic planning, not to mention the generous conditions of Russian foreign aid, appeared increasingly attractive to Asians looking for a means to embrace the modern age.

Western aid provided to Asia under the Colombo Plan and multilateral aid programs dwarfed Soviet finance. But a number of important features distinguished the communist program and jolted the confidence of Western policy-makers. Focusing on major 'prestige' projects in fewer countries, the Soviet Union deliberately provided low-interest loans instead of outright gifts; the latter option was considered condescending and demeaning. Significantly, they also accepted repayments in local currencies or in exports, a feature especially attractive to countries with balance-of-payment problems. According to Western perceptions, the Soviet Union was unfettered by democratic procedure and could bring its highly centralised industries more quickly to bear on Asia's economic needs. Many also believed that the supposed absence of a profit motive in the communist economy might allow the Soviets to eliminate competitors and to dominate Asian markets with consummate ease. The combination of these features, warned the US Director of International Cooperation Administration, J.R. Smith, meant that the communists were 'much better equipped than we are to wage economic warfare'.[110]

The propaganda deployed by the Soviets was no different from the methods and language adopted by the Western sponsors of the Colombo Plan. Communist aid emphasised impact projects that would not only assist the region's economic advancement, but also generate maximum publicity. Writing in Moscow's *Journal of International Affairs*, Viktor Rymalov celebrated the Soviet Union's 'unselfish' supply of 'material and cultural assistance to backward and oppressed peoples'. And he criticised the Colombo Plan's emphasis on agricultural production as a trick to restrict Asia's role to that of a plantation economy, capable of suppling much needed primary commodities. The Soviet program, on the other hand, funded both industrial and agricultural expansion.[111] Of course, the reality was that, as with the United States, post-war reconstruction left the Soviets with an oversupply of capital goods and a need for new markets in exchange for Asia's raw materials.

Always critical to Western geo-strategic assessments of Asia, the avowedly neutralist Indian government seemed particularly open to the blandishments of both socialists and capitalists. Seemingly paralysed by the audacity of the Soviet program, Australia's High Commissioner in New Delhi, Peter Heydon, believed that the Indian government felt politically obliged to balance its receipt of Western aid with Russian assistance. While he thought it unlikely that India would be 'swept off her feet [or] … allow herself to be inextricably entangled in any Russian economic web', he worried about the added allure of the 'exceptionally quick' delivery of high quality goods, the competitive prices, and the acceptance of local currency. Heydon's recommendations were a mixture of resignation and resolve. 'It is difficult to point any way for Australia', he said:

> *We are given some credit for the Colombo Plan, but late deliveries result in some loss. We cannot attempt to match volume with the USSR or the USA, but we could perhaps improve our performance. Speedier delivery of equipment if possible would help, but selection of an individual project for assistance, as an Australian project, would be immeasurably better if limitations on Colombo Plan aid could be relaxed.*[112]

The arrival of Soviet aid forced Australia to engage with countries hitherto ignored. In Burma, wrote Lewis Border, Australia's Ambassador in Rangoon, 'we have little trade and we have little in common in other directions' and without the Colombo Plan Burma would be cut off from the Western world. It was therefore necessary for Australia to balance communist aid and not leave Burma vulnerable to an 'influx of technicians, experts, cultural groups, etc. from the communist countries and to a campaign of penetration and subversion'. He believed the buses already donated by Australia served as a 'positive reminder that the government does not have to turn to the communist countries for its aid'. Equally, communist aid helped expose the flaws and fallacies that had grown up around the provision of aid as a political and cultural antidote. Francis Stuart, Australian Minister to Cambodia between 1957 and 1959, oversaw the implementation of many Colombo Plan projects, including a municipal vehicle and machinery workshop in Phnom Penh.[113] However, the machines and vehicles fixed by Australian technicians had in fact been donated by the communists! So much for the idea that foreign assistance would transmit democratic values and endear Asians to Western designs for regional development, simply by virtue of its geographic origin.

Nevertheless, American military and non-military aid (including the supply of surplus agricultural produce) increased conspicuously from 1955 on, despite public claims that the United States would not attempt to counter Soviet aid.[114] Of course, the Soviet economic offensive was not the only reason the United States re-examined its aid programs, but most members of Congress considered the region too important, and too unstable, to stand back and let the Soviets move in unopposed. One member of Congress metaphorically thumped the lectern: 'The Soviet strategy has been changing again, and so must ours ... We cannot be guilty of "too little too late", for the fate of humanity is at stake'.[115] In this climate, the Americans were not about to abandon the Colombo Plan, its Commonwealth taint now a distinct advantage. Although senior US bureaucrats maintained their reservations about the loose nature of the Consultative Committee and the fact that 'little if any pressure is exerted upon [recipient countries] regarding the management of their economic affairs', the 'family link' between Commonwealth nations was to be savoured. Extolling the Colombo Plan's virtues, J.H. Smith Jr. told the Under Secretary for Economic Affairs:

> *Among the interesting features of the Colombo Plan are that it excludes the Soviet bloc countries, antedates the Sino–Soviet economic offensive, and is regarded by the Asians as their own organisation. The Russians cannot attack it as they attacked SEATO [South East Asia Treaty Organisation] and the Asians are not likely to leave it.*

An American attempt to rework the Consultative Committee into a more coercive, multilateral agency — led by Harold Stassen, Director of the Mutual Security Agency — collapsed when it failed to garner Congressional or widespread Asian support. The failure turned out to be a blessing. Although the Americans continued to explore ways they could strengthen the regional integration of Colombo Plan nations without challenging the bilateral framework, it was in fact better, Smith said, for Asian countries to work through an 'admirable institution such as the Colombo Plan' rather than to adhere to a rigid multilateral agency closely identified with the United States. The highly regarded program prompted Smith to suggest that his country should do more to associate its aid programs with the Colombo Plan name.[116]

Beyond these limitations, the Colombo Plan administrative framework proved a resilient and flexible structure for negotiating foreign-assistance programs. The Consultative Committee framework was a product of the economic nationalism that pervaded post-colonial Asia. This structure, and the strict adherence to bilateralism, also went some way to preserving the economic and political autonomy of Asian nations. That bilateral negotiations partly contradicted the regionalism the Colombo Plan designers hoped to foster mattered less than the achievement of bringing disparate governments together to discuss common problems. In 1960, international affairs expert Creighton Burns identified the diversity and complexity falling under the Consultative Committee rubric:

> *It links countries already bound by military alliances to either Britain or the United States with those which have maintained an uncommitted stand in foreign policy. It is politically eclectic,*

*combining traditional Western liberal democracies
and their Asian models with military dictatorships
and left-wing experiments in collective leadership.
Of the current ideologies, Communism alone is
unrepresented. The economies of the Colombo
Plan countries shade the spectrum from semi-
feudal through qualified free enterprise to those
with a high degree of central control.*[117]

Paradoxically, the politically benign nature of the
Colombo Plan Consultative Committee ensured its survival
in a fractious international climate. Positive, if superficial,
dialogue between Asia and the West was maintained
precisely because it avoided overtly political language and
strategy. Indeed, this non-political forum did not stop
Western governments from privately — and sometimes
secretly — attempting to incorporate political and military
strategy within aid programs. The triumph of bilateralism
and the willingness of the Soviet Union to embark on a
foreign economic program ensured the legitimacy of
political neutralism. The fact that recipient governments
could also draw from a Soviet source gave them bargaining
power and protected their political autonomy. Economist
John P. Lewis succinctly explained the situation concerning
India. The Indian people, he wrote, 'do not want to be
thrown into the same statistical bin with two or three dozen
other countries':

> *they fear the inappropriate egalitarianism that
> international politics injects into the parceling out
> of funds under multilateral operations. The Indian
> Government ... wants to keep its foreign aid
> bargaining dispersed ... Not only may the present
> arrangement occasionally allow India to play off
> one benefactor against another; it maximises the*

*autonomy of Indian developmental planning. And
the latter is something that a government of the
independence and stature of the Indian is no
readier to surrender to the World Bank or the
United Nations than it is to the United States or
the Soviet Union.*[118]

The continuation of the Colombo Plan's original
bilateral architecture helped maintain the nation–state
bilateral dialogue and that, in turn, helped to sustain the
combative, bipolar nature of global relations. In the
absence of an overarching regional organisation dedicated
to economic development, the 'bidding war' became an
entrenched component of Cold War politics. For the next
forty years, the two power blocs vied for influence and
recognition in Asia.[119] It is, of course, debatable whether
a multilateral, regionally-integrated program (supported by
a substantive increase in US funds) would have had a
greater impact on the economic development of Asian
countries. The inexorable force of international commodity
markets and tariff manipulations was infinitely more
damaging to Asia's economic progress. More important for
the Australian government was the prospect that a
multilateral agency would absorb Australian contributions
and leave no trace of their origins. Thus, by maintaining
the Colombo Plan's bilateral framework, Australia's role as
contributor to and creator of a major Asian aid forum was
preserved, if not enhanced. It also ensured that Australian
efforts to generate maximum dividends from its nascent
links to the region would continue unabated.

Footnotes

1 'Australia and S.E. Asia', *Eastern World*, vol. 7, September 1953, p. 22
2 *CPD (HoR)*, vol. 206, 21 March 1950, p. 978
3 *CPD (HoR)*, vol. 211, 28 November 1950, p. 3166
4 Note, R. Harry to A. Tange, 16 April 1952, A1838, 3004/11 part 1, NAA
5 *CPD (HoR)*, vol. 206, 21 March 1950, p. 973
6 A. Tange, 'Political objectives of the Colombo Plan – working paper', 19 March 1952, A1838, 3004/11 part 1, NAA
7 Cable, W.T. Doig to Spender, 9 March 1951, A1838, 250/10/1/1/1 part 1, NAA
8 Tange, 'Political objectives of the Colombo Plan – working paper'
9 R.G. Casey diaries, 10 March 1954, vol. 16, box 27, MS 6150, NLA; Memo, J.V. Moroney, Secretary, Department of Primary Industry, 20 January 1960, A463, 1960/3126, NAA
10 Tange, 'Political objectives of the Colombo Plan – working paper'; 'The Colombo Plan: an appraisal', 1952, A4311, 145/1, NAA
11 Despatch, J.C.G. Kevin to Casey, 30 May 1953, A4231, 1953/Djakarta, NAA
12 'The Colombo Plan: an appraisal'
13 Memo, J.B. Rowland, Charge d'Affaires, Saigon to Tange, 4 December 1954, A4529, 65/1/1/1954, NAA
14 'US objectives and programs for national security: annexes to NSC 68/3', 8 December 1950, *FRUS*, 1950, vol. 1, p. 447
15 'Strategic importance of Ceylon: Royal Ceylon Navy, record of conversation with Commodore Rajan Kadirgamar', 4 & 10 February 1957, A1838, TS697/5 part 1, NAA
16 F. Shedden to Burton, 'The strategic importance of Ceylon', 17 May 1947, A5954, 1554/7, NAA
17 'A descriptive summary of current Australian participation in economic development projects as at 30 November, 1956', 11 January 1957, A11604, 704/1 part 1, NAA; 'The Colombo Plan: an appraisal'
18 Australian News and Information Bureau, *Australia in Facts and Figures*, various issues, 1950–1970
19 P. Charrier, 'ASEAN's inheritance: the regionalization of South–East Asia, 1941–1961', *The Pacific Review*, vol. 14, no. 3, 2001, p. 326
20 'The Colombo Plan: an appraisal'
21 The full titles of these operations are: United Nations Relief and Rehabilitation Administration, International Refugee Organization, United Nations Korean Reconstruction Agency, United Nations Children's Emergency Fund, United Nations Relief and Works Agency for Palestine Refugees, United Nations Expanded Program for Technical Assistance, International Bank for Reconstruction and Development.
22 G. Greenwood & N. Harper, eds., *Australia in world affairs 1961–1965*, Melbourne, F.W. Cheshire, 1968, pp. 228–29

23 The Colombo Plan for Economic Development in South and South–East Asia, *Fifth annual report of the Consultative Committee*, Wellington, New Zealand, December, 1956

24 Colombo Plan Council, *Technical co-operation under the Colombo Plan — report by the Colombo Plan Council for Technical Co-operation in South and South–East Asia, 1 July 1964 to 30 June 1965*, Ceylon, Colombo Plan Bureau, Government Press, 1965; Colombo Plan Bureau, *Report of the Consultative Committee of Economic Development in South and South–East Asia: fourteenth annual report of the Consultative Committee, Karachi, November 1966*, London, HMSO, 1967

25 *Yearbook of the Commonwealth of Australia*, 1960, Canberra, Commonwealth Bureau of Census and Statistics, p. 827

26 R. Harrod, *Towards a dynamic economics*, London, Macmillan, 1948; P. Rodan-Rodenstein, 'Problems of industrialisation in Eastern and South–Eastern Europe', *Economic Journal*, vol. 52, pp. 202–11; W. Lewis, *The principles of economic planning* (1949), London, Unwin University Books, 1970; R. Nurkse, *Problems of capital formation in underdeveloped countries*, Oxford, Basil Blackwell, 1953; W.W. Rostow, *The stages of economic growth: a non-communist manifesto*, Cambridge, Cambridge University Press, 1960

27 W. Lewis, 'Industrialization of the British West Indies', *Caribbean Economic Review*, vol. 2, 1950, p. 36

28 *New Zealand parliamentary debates*, vol. 289, 12 July 1950, p. 340

29 Rostow, *Stages of economic growth*, pp. 4–16

30 D. Porter, *United States economic foreign aid: a case study of the United States Agency for International Development*, New York, Garland Publishing, 1990

31 H. Laugier, 'The first step in the international approach to the problems of underdeveloped areas', *The Milbank Quarterly*, vol. 26, no. 3, 1948, p. 256

32 C.W. James, 'The Colombo Plan passes halfway', *Australian Outlook*, vol. 9, no. 1, March 1955, p. 42

33 Commonwealth Bureau of News and Information, *Australia in Facts and Figures*, no. 42, May 1954, p. 18; Note, P. Shaw to Casey, 'Colombo Plan aid to Indonesia', 4 June 1954, A10299, C15, NAA; *Canberra Times*, 29 April 1953. Originally, Australia considered sending 600 buses, but subsequently revised the number to 100.

34 'US Objectives and Programs for National Security: Annexes to NSC 68/3', 8 December 1950, *FRUS, 1950*, vol. 1, p. 448

35 G. Whitwell, 'The social planning of the F & E economists', *Australian Economic History Review*, no. 26, 1985, pp. 1–19

36 H.C. Coombs, *Trial balance*, Melbourne, Macmillan, 1981, pp. 60, 89

37 P. Hasluck, 'A policy for New Guinea', *South Pacific*, vol. 5, no. 1, 1951, pp. 224–28; P. Hasluck, 'The economic development of Papua and New Guinea', *Australian Outlook*, April 1962, pp. 5–25

38 T.B. Paltridge, 'Report on some aspects of Colombo Plan aid in Ceylon', 23 October 1957, A1838, 160/10/2/4, NAA

39 Commonwealth Consultative Committee, *The Colombo Plan for Cooperative Economic Development in South and South–East Asia: a report by the Commonwealth Consultative Committee*, London, 1951, p. 9

40 Commonwealth Consultative Committee, *The Colombo Plan for Cooperative Economic Development in South and South–East Asia: a report by the Commonwealth Consultative Committee*, London, 1950, pp. 46, 55, 63.

41 V. Vithal Babu, *Colombo Plan and India*, New Delhi, Atma Ram & Sons, 1950, pp. 14–15

42 Commonwealth Consultative Committee, *The Colombo Plan for Cooperative Economic Development in South and South–East Asia: a report by the Commonwealth Consultative Committee*, London, 1950, p. 63; CPD (HoR), vol. 211, 28 November 1950, p. 3166–68; P. Spender, 'Partnership with Asia', *Current Notes on International Affairs*, vol. 22, January 1951 (reproduction of his *Foreign Affairs* article), p. 12; *Sydney Morning Herald*, 14 May 1953

43 'The Colombo Plan: an appraisal'

44 C. Burns, 'Progress report on the Colombo Plan', *Australia's Neighbours*, January 1954, p. 4; Consultative Committee, *Second Annual Report of the Consultative Committee, New Delhi, October 1953*, London, HMSO, pp. 125–30

45 Council for Technical Co-operation in South and South–East Asia, *The Colombo Plan*, Colombo, Colombo Plan Bureau, 1954, p. 6

46 R. Harry, *The diplomat who laughed*, Melbourne, Hutchinson, 1983, pp. 48–49. For more on Spender's career in Washington, see D. Lowe, 'Mr Spender goes to Washington: an ambassador's vision of Australian–American relations, 1951–58', *Journal of Imperial and Commonwealth History*, vol. 24, no. 2, May 1996, pp. 278–95

47 W. Crocker, *Travelling back: the memoirs of Sir Walter Crocker*, Melbourne, Macmillan, 1981, pp. 187–90

48 P.M. Williams, ed., *The diary of Hugh Gaitskell 1945–1956*, London, Cape, 1983

49 Walter Crocker, interview with author, 28 August 2001, Adelaide

50 A. Watt, *Australian diplomat: memoirs*, Sydney, Angus and Robertson, 1972, pp. 31–35; W. Crocker, *Australian ambassador: international relations first-hand*, Melbourne, Melbourne University Press, 1971, pp. 65–66; P. Hasluck, *The chance of politics*, Melbourne, Text Publishing, 1997, p. 87; W.J. Hudson, *Casey*, Melbourne, Oxford University Press, 1986, pp. 25–27, 241

51 R. Casey, 'The conduct of Australian foreign policy', *Current Notes in International Affairs*, vol. 23, no. 9, September 1952, pp. 461, 478

52 Cabinet submission 21, 'Australian contributions to the Colombo Plan', 28 May 1951, A4905, vol. 2, NAA; R.G. Casey diaries, 4 October 1954, MS 6150, vol. 17, box 28, NLA. See also R.G. Casey diaries, 8 October 1954, MS 6150, vol. 17, box 28, NLA

53 Note, Casey to Plimsoll, 14 August 1953, A10299, C15, NAA

54 'Publicity for the Colombo Plan', no date, *circa* November 1951, FO 953/1202, PRO, UK; I.P. Bancroft, 'Colombo Plan: the Stent paper', no date, *circa* May 1952, DO 35/2724, PRO, UK

55 'US objectives and programs for national security: annexes to NSC 68/3'
56 Great Britain Economic Information Unit, *New hope for Asia*, Commonwealth Office of Education for the Department of External Affairs, Canberra, 1951, p. 6
57 Despatch, Gilchrist to Casey, 21 July 1952, A4231, 1952/Djakarta, NAA
58 Despatch, J.C.G. Kevin, Djakarta, to Casey, 30 May 1953, A4231, 1953/Djakarta, NAA
59 Note, Casey to Menzies, 18 August 1954, A462, 610/8/1, NAA
60 Cable, Australian Embassy, Djakarta to DEA, 21 April 1953, A1838, 3034/7/7 part 1, NAA
61 'Joint communiqué of the Minister for External Affairs, the Rt Hon. R.G. Casey and the French Minister in Charge of Relations with the Associated States, Mr. Jean Letourneau, 11 March 1953', *Current Notes in International Affairs*, vol. 24, no. 3, March 1954, pp. 165–66
62 Memo, J.B. Rowland to A. Tange, 4 December 1954, A4529, 65/1/1/1954, NAA; Note, Patrick Shaw to Casey, 'Colombo Plan: Indo-China', 21 July 1954, A1838, 2020/6/5 part 1, NAA
63 W.R. Hodgson, 'Japan's possible contribution to the economic rehabilitation of South and South–East Asia', 27 April 1950, A1838, 479/2 part 3, NAA; Memo, Hodgson to DEA, 27 April 1950, A1838, 479/2 part 3, NAA
64 Despatch 14/1950, Hodgson to Spender, 10 February 1950, A1838, 479/2 part 3, NAA
65 J.L. Gaddis, 'The strategy of containment', T.H. Etzold & J.L. Gaddis (eds.), *Containment: documents on American policy and strategy, 1945–1950*, New York, Columbia University Press, 1978, pp. 25–38
66 'Informal memorandum by the Secretary of State (Acheson) to the British Ambassador (Sir Oliver Franks)', 24 December 1949, *FRUS*, 1949, vol. 7, p. 927
67 United States Department of Defense, *United States–Vietnam relations, 1945–1967*, vol. 7, Washington, US Government Printing Office, 1971, pp. 226–64
68 S. Sudo, *The Fukuda doctrine and ASEAN: new dimensions in Japanese foreign policy*, Singapore, Institute of South–East Asian Studies, 1992, pp. 37–48
69 *CPD (HoR)*, vol. 216, 6 February 1952, p. 20
70 Note, 'Japan and the Colombo Plan', 10 March 1952, A1838, 3103/9/3/3, NAA; Note, 'Colombo Plan — Japanese participation', undated, A1838, 3103/9/3/3, NAA
71 Note, 'Japan and the Colombo Plan'
72 Casey, 'Cabinet submission 30', 28 July 1954, A4940, volume 1, NAA
73 Telegram, Gen. Sir G. Templer, Malaya to Foreign Office, 13 March 1952, FO 371/101248, PRO, UK
74 Note, 'Japan and the Colombo Plan'
75 Note, 'Colombo Plan – Japanese participation'
76 'Politics and problems in relations between the United States and Australia', 21 April 1950, *FRUS*, 1950, vol. 6, p. 192

77 Memo, Gay to Allison, 3 December 1952, RG 59, 890.00/12-352, USNA; Telegram, CRO to UK High Commissioner, Karachi, 'Colombo Plan and Japan', 15 March 1952, FO 371/101248, PRO, UK; Cable, Australian High Commission, Karachi, to DEA, 21 March 1952, A1838, 3103/9/3/3, NAA

78 Cable, Watt to DEA, Canberra, 8 March 1952, A1838, 3103/9/3/3, NAA

79 Cable, DEA to Australian High Commission, Karachi, 'Japan and the Colombo Plan', 14 March 1952, A1838, 2080/13, NAA

80 Telegram, UK High Commission to CRO, London, 'Japan and the Colombo Plan', 17 March 1952, FO 371/101248, PRO, UK

81 D.P. O'Connell, 'Sedentary fisheries and the Australian continental shelf', *American Journal of International Law*, vol. 49, no. 2, April 1955, pp. 187–88

82 J. Plimsoll, 'Interview with Mr Emmons', 15 October 1953, A1838, 2080/13, NAA

83 Telegram, Department of State, Washington to US embassy, Canberra, 13 October 1953, RG 59, 890.00/10-1353, USNA

84 J. Plimsoll, 'Interview with Mr Emmons', 15 October 1953, A1838, 2080/13, NAA

85 Cable, Australian embassy, Washington, to DEA, 12 August 1954, A1838, 156/5, NAA

86 'Report of the Asian Economic Working Group concerning the inauguration of large-scale, long-range program of economic assistance', 30 August 1954, *FRUS*, 1952–54, vol. 12, part 1, p. 818

87 A. Rix, *Coming to terms: the politics of Australia's trade with Japan 1945–57*, Sydney, Allen & Unwin, 1986, pp. 163–69

88 'Annex B: background paper on Japanese participation', *circa* late 1953, A1838, 2080/13, NAA

89 Note, Rangoon to DEA, 2 August 1954, A1838, 2080/13, NAA

90 Note, Casey to Tange, 16 August 1954, A1838, 2080/13, NAA

91 Casey diaries, 17 August 1954, vol. 17, box 28, MS 6150, NLA

92 E.A. Boehm, *Twentieth century economic development in Australia*, Melbourne, Longman Cheshire, 1979, pp. 91–93

93 Cabinet minute, 17 August 1954, A4906, vol. 1, NAA

94 Cable, DEA to Australian embassy, Washington, 20 August 1954, DEA, CRS A6366/1 item WAS54/1, NAA

95 Cable, DEA to various, 27 August 1954, A1838, 3103/9/3/3, NAA

96 Cable, Australian High Commission, Wellington, to DEA, 1 September 1954, A1838, 3103/9/3/3, NAA

97 Telegram, NZ minister for External affairs to NZ Ambassador, Washington, 8 September 1954, Foreign Office 371/111908, PRO, UK

98 Cable, DEA to Australian High Commission, Ottawa, 'Japan and the Colombo Plan', 12 September 1954, A1838, 3103/9/3/3, NAA

99 P. Shaw, 'Record of conversation with Mr. M. Kakitsubo, Counsellor, Japanese embassy', 28 August 1954, A1838, 2080/13, NAA; Cable, DEA to Australian High Commission, Ottawa, 'Japan's association with the Colombo Plan', 2 September 1954, A1838, 3103/9/3/3, NAA

100 Cable, Australian embassy, Washington to Casey, 2 September 1954, A1838, 3103/9/3/3, NAA

101 *CPD (HoR)*, vol. 4, 25 August 1954, p. 588

102 *CPD (HoR)*, vol. 4, 22 September 1954, p. 1525

103 Cable, Australian embassy, Washington, to DEA, 3 September 1954, A1838, 3103/9/3/3, NAA

104 P. Shaw, 'Record of conversation with His Excellency Mr. H. Nishi, Japanese Ambassador', 16 September 1954, A1838, 3103/9/3/3, NAA

105 P. Shaw, 'Record of conversation with His Excellency Mr. H. Nishi, Japanese Ambassador', 20 September 1954, A1838, 3103/9/3/3, NAA

106 P. Shaw, 'Record of conversation with His Excellency, Mr. Nishi, Japanese Ambassador', 7 October 1954, A1838, 2080/13, NAA

107 'Economic development in Australia', *FRUS*, 1950, vol. 6, pp. 205–06; 'Problems in relations between the United States and Australia', *FRUS*, 1950, vol. 6, pp. 193–94

108 Despatch, B.C. Hill to Casey, 'Soviet and communist tactics, December 1953', 1 January 1954, A5462, 117/1/1, NAA; Despatch, B.C. Hill to Casey, 'Soviet and communist tactics, February 1954', 3 March 1954, A5462, item 117/1/1, NAA

109 *Herald* (Melbourne), 27 July 1955; Note, Oldham to Casey, 28 July 1955, A4311, 14/20, NAA

110 Goldman, *Soviet foreign aid*, New York, Praeger, 1967, pp. 204–05; 'Letter from the Director of the International Cooperation Administration (Smith) to the Chairman of the Council on Foreign Economic Policy (Randall)', 7 February 1958, *FRUS*, 1958–60, vol. 4, p. 7

111 Goldman, *Soviet foreign aid*, p. 115; V. Rymalov, 'Soviet assistance to underdeveloped countries', *International Affairs* (Moscow), September 1959, pp. 23–31

112 Heydon, 'Visit of Soviet leaders to India: November–December 1955', 4 January 1956, A4231, 1956/New Delhi, NAA; Heydon, Australian High Commission, New Delhi, 'Despatch no. 23', 5 December 1956, A4231, 1956/New Delhi, NAA

113 Memo, Border to Tange, DEA, 20 November 1964, A1838, 2020/1/24/1, NAA; For the details of this and other projects provided to Cambodia under the Colombo Plan, see L.P. Goonetilleke, *A compendium of some major Colombo Plan assisted projects in South & South–East Asia*, Colombo, Colombo Plan Bureau, 1972, pp. 35–37; Francis Stuart, interview with author, 5 April 2001

114 'Brief to PM: United States' policy in Asia', June 1956, A1838, 250/10/7 part 2, NAA; C. Wolf, *Foreign aid: theory and practice in South-East Asia*, Princeton, Princeton University Press, 1960, pp. 221–22; J.D. Montgomery, *The politics of foreign aid*, New York, Praeger, 1962, pp. 32–35

115 Quoted in B.I. Kaufman, *Trade and aid: Eisenhower's foreign economic policy, 1953–1961*, Baltimore, John Hopkins University Press, 1982, p. 70

116 'Memorandum by the Director of the Office of Financial and Development Policy (Corbett) to the Assistant Secretary of State for Economic Affairs (Waugh)', 24 August 1954, FRUS, 1952–54, vol. 12, part 1, pp. 781–82; J.H. Smith to C.D. Dillon, 'The Colombo Plan', 22 August 1958, RG 59, 890.00/8-2258, USNA; 'Classified report of United States delegation to the Colombo Plan Consultative Committee meetings, Wellington, November 5 – December 8, 1956', 11 April 1957, RG 59, 890.00/4-1157, USNA

117 C. Burns, 'The Colombo Plan', *The year book of world affairs*, vol. 14, 1960, pp. 179–80

118 J.P. Lewis, *Quiet crisis in India: economic development and American policy*, Washington, D.C., The Brookings Institute, 1962, pp. 263–64

119 S. Hoffman, 'The role of international organisation: limits and possibilities', *International Organisation*, vol. 10, no. 3, 1956, p. 369; Organisation for Economic Cooperation and Development, *The flow of financial resources to countries in the course of economic development*, 1960, [no place, no publisher]

5. A GOOD SHOE-HORN FOR OUR INTERESTS

Richard Casey struggled throughout his career to generate interest in Asia and in Australia's foreign aid program. In 1954 he lamented in his diary that Australians were 'living in a fool's paradise of ignorance about the East'. 'Most people', he continued, 'are hostile to the UN — hostile to the Colombo Plan — and unsympathetic with Asia'.[1] Strict export restrictions and the Treasury department's reluctance to look beyond domestic economic concerns were constant thorns in Casey's side. But the essence of the problem, as he explained to diplomat Walter Crocker, was that his colleagues simply saw 'no immediate material advantage' in giving away millions of pounds. Lacking Percy Spender's punch, Casey's verbose Cabinet orations compounded the problems.[2] His biographer notes succinctly that he was 'not tough enough, cunning enough or politician enough to carry Cabinets with him'. Moreover, he felt that Treasury and the Cabinet ignored his attempts to pursue Colombo Plan objectives in a financially restrained and responsible way. In fact, he believed it worked to his disadvantage. 'Being honest and accommodating doesn't seem to pay', a forlorn and frustrated Casey noted in his diary.[3] But he learned quickly that grafting Cold War priorities onto his submissions generated greater momentum and interest for Australian aid initiatives. In August 1954, Casey outlined his vision to Menzies:

> The Colombo Plan is a good shoe-horn for our interests. What we most want to see in South East Asia is the development of stable, democratic and friendly governments. In other words — a group of reliable buffer states between ourselves and the Communist drive to the South — although we must never call them that. I believe our main endeavour should be to give further positive aid towards attaining this objective with every weapon in our armoury — ranging from diplomatic relations, through increasing cultural contact and economic support, to less respectable activities.[4]

Over the decade, as the Menzies Government employed the Colombo Plan to fight in the Cold War, Casey tested the political and moral limits of Australia's aid program.

By the mid-1950s, Australia's Cold War objectives in South–East Asia were to support friendly and stable anti-communist governments, improve economic development, exchange security intelligence with friendly nations, build strategic alliances with the United States, and improve cultural and diplomatic relations with Asia. In the longer term, the Government initiated a more nebulous campaign to convince Asia's political elites, and the population at large, that communism was not in their interests.[5] Exploratory discussions about Cold War activities took place in December 1954 when an inter-departmental committee met to consider the development of a coordinated Western approach to Cold War planning.[6] The committee concluded that a tightly-defined Cold War plan was essential and that it was important for a single department to be made responsible for Australia's effort.[7] On 7 January 1955, Cabinet approved Casey's submission that he, and his department, should assume full responsibility for coordinating Australia's Cold War planning.[8]

The Colombo Plan appeared to be an easy and relatively inexpensive way to solidify political and military support in an unstable regional context, in conjunction with the Western alliance. While responding to a defence appreciation, which concluded that overt military conflict in South and South–East Asia was unlikely, Casey told Cabinet that non-military measures were likely to assume greater prominence and yield more success than conventional military strategies. He warned that the political situation to the north remained no less grave in the light of the reassessment. Emphasising the point, Casey argued that Australia's direct interest in the outcome of the Cold War was 'greater than that of any other non-Asian power'. To meet the new situation, Australia needed to exchange information with other Western powers, provide technical assistance to local security forces, produce propaganda and information to counter communist activity, promote democratic and pro-Western values, and eliminate communist influence in schools, trade unions, youth organisations, and other political, cultural, and religious organisations. Foreign aid emerged as one of the few measures which could be applied to such a diffuse and difficult task. The challenge to incorporate the Colombo Plan into a sophisticated propaganda strategy clearly excited Casey, who demanded that 'we must be prepared to pursue policies in the Cold War with no less energy than is required for the preparedness of our armed forces'.[9]

The nature of the work probably took Casey back to his time as a deception planner during the Second World War. Days after Cabinet had approved his control of Cold War planning, Casey wrote to Arthur Tange, Secretary of the Department of External Affairs (DEA), about the need to enhance Australia's Cold War effort. 'The whole of this business of anti-subversive work is almost a virgin field', he enthused. 'It has fascinating possibilities for the exercise of imagination. We must organise discussion groups of selected individuals to meet periodically — men likely to strike fire from uninhibited discussion with each other'. While Casey restated the central importance of foreign aid to Cold War strategy, he cautioned Tange that the 'ordinary accepted aims' of the Colombo Plan might have to be 'stretched' to accommodate the new campaign.[10]

Casey was eager to supplement the growing pool of talent working for the DEA, in order to facilitate these 'uninhibited discussions'. In January 1955, he mentioned to Tange the possibility of seconding John Hood to Canberra to lead a section devoted to Cold War activities. Hood had developed a reputation as a diligent and reflective political analyst during the war while working as an adviser to Colonel W.R. Hodgson (Secretary of the DEA between 1935 and 1945), and then as External Affairs Officer in London. Hood's pen, according to Casey, was 'his sharpest and most effective tool',[11] making him highly suitable as a 'senior back room thinking boy'.[12] Casey's praise was more than an idle comment, because three days later Tange recalled Hood from Bonn for six months' work in Canberra. On his way to Australia, he discussed Cold War planning with the British Foreign Office, before meeting Casey in Bangkok for the Manila Treaty Conference.[13]

The establishment of Australia's Cold War campaign was, of course, secretive and sensitive. However, the Australian press soon became aware of Hood's appointment as director of the 'psychological warfare campaign'.[14] While visiting London, Tange, realising what was at stake, sent a sharp directive to Acting Secretary James Plimsoll and the Minister:

> *I strongly believe, while it may be inevitable and even desirable that some of our proposals be publicly discussed, we shall make ourselves suspect all over Asia if these activities are described as 'Cold War' exercises ... In any case we will be embarrassed by persistent enquires from other Governments if there is too much public talk of Hood's functions in the Department and I want public explanations kept to an absolute minimum.[15]*

Australia's growing propaganda and security interests in South–East Asia were bringing the DEA and Casey into much closer relations with defence and intelligence strategists. Casey's diaries and correspondence reveal his consuming interest in developing a propaganda machine. The warm and intimate tone of Casey's letters to Alfred Brookes, the first director of the Australian Secret Intelligence Service (ASIS), was a departure from his characteristic formality. The large number of letters they exchanged suggests that they had a series of discussions and meetings about subversive techniques to counter the infiltration of the police, armed forces, government departments, and the priesthood. In one letter to Brookes, Casey remarked that, given the 'insidious methods' deployed by the communists, he felt obligated to do his utmost to expose publicly these underhanded tactics. Casey then asked Brookes for his opinion on the idea of creating a 'corps of whisperers' working in South–East Asia.[16] This intriguing mention of a team of spies was followed up a year later with a cryptic diary entry. Casey wrote that the propaganda campaign was all about 'helping the goodies and unhelping the baddies [and] helping the local governments on the security side and inspiring people to say the right things'.[17] Was this a reference to the 'corps of whisperers' Casey hoped to have roving the halls of Asia's political institutions?

The apparent scientific and technological superiority of the Soviet Union — which culminated in the launch of Sputnik on 4 October 1957 and the beginning of the missile age — hardened Australia's commitment to covertly fighting the Cold War with foreign aid. Competition for political and economic control would now extend rapidly into the realms of science, technology, economic and social development, and propaganda. And perhaps, thought Western political leaders, the increasingly restive and assertive leaders of Asia would be convinced that the future lay with the Soviet model of economic planning. Away from the traditional front line of Cold War confrontation in Europe, Australian posts across Asia carefully reported the development of relations with the communist bloc. The High Commission in Ceylon, for example, reported to Canberra as early as September 1956 on an agreement signed between Russia and the Ceylonese that included plans for diplomatic representation, trade cooperation, and a tour by educationalists and a troupe of 'ballerinas [who were to] visit a large number of schools, attend cultural shows, and hold conferences with teachers' unions'.[18] Later, the ubiquitous 'Skoda' trademark was registered in Ceylon to cover vehicles, machinery, and metallurgical products.[19] The Australian High Commission remained optimistic that Ceylon's lack of traditional markets in the communist bloc would prevent it from becoming dependent on them for vital commodities; it subsequently reported in 1958 that there had been little impact on either Australian or British trade relations.[20]

Likewise, the British Foreign Office grew wary of the new situation emerging in South Asia. Although the official political assessments were notably calm, British officials recommended that aid donors place greater emphasis on propaganda and give the Colombo Plan Information Unit a more prominent role. The Russians aimed at 'extending their prestige and influence in South–East Asia through various offers of economic assistance', one Foreign Office official wrote. Their aid initiatives might have been small, but 'comparisons apart, it is still a significant amount, and there is no doubt that the Russian economy is wealthy enough to provide it … [and] we may be certain that Soviet propaganda … will make the most of it'.[21] The 'promise of Russian aid' spurred Casey to boost the profile of Australia's Colombo Plan programs. In addition to the likes of Brookes, Hood, and Galvin, Casey liaised regularly with Senator (and future Prime Minister) John Gorton and Brigadier Dudley-Clark, head deception planner for the United Kingdom in the Middle East during the Second World War. At Casey's request, Dudley-Clark submitted a detailed report on propaganda strategies Australia might consider implementing.[22] Among the extensive proposals, use of the Colombo Plan as part of a 'bolder approach to the whole matter of advertising Australia to other countries' featured prominently.[23] The report also included a section on 'influencing the Australian mind' in relation to South–East Asia. Casey immediately wrote to Tange recommending that the DEA restructure the Colombo Plan. 'We should drag our feet on the economic aid side and speed up the technical assistance side', he wrote. 'The latter is the side that has inherently vastly more publicity potential, which we must exploit'.[24]

One person Casey hoped would push the intellectual boundaries of the DEA's propaganda strategy was the multi-talented John Galvin. A journalist by training, Galvin joined the British Special Operations Executive in Hong Kong during the Second World War. Casey knew him to be a difficult character, but was convinced of his 'genius'.[25] After making his fortune by purchasing Malayan tin mines immediately after the Japanese surrender, Galvin moved to San Francisco where he occasionally associated with the Australian Consul-General, Stewart Jamieson.[26] Casey wrote to Laurence R. McIntyre, Senior External Affairs Representative in London, about the elusive Galvin:

> With the Cold War hotting up in South East Asia, Galvin might well be of use to us. He's an imaginative fellow — and not obsessed with too many scruples — and I'd expect that he knows a good many people of S.E. Asia. If I were 'by chance' to run across him again, it might well be that we could, between us, evolve some means of his being useful to us, possibly in unorthodox ways.[27]

In fact, the CIA became interested in using Galvin as part of a covert weapons shipping operation to Indonesia, but decided against him because of his unpredictable and flamboyant nature. It is not clear whether Galvin ever became a member of Casey's Cold War team, although it seems unlikely. He was last reported to have fled America for Ireland in the late-1950s, closely pursued by the US Inland Revenue Service.[28]

Other members of the Commonwealth Public Service shared Casey's interest in fighting the Cold War in Asia through propaganda and development projects. He diligently and enthusiastically recruited these individuals during his time as minister. The result was a diverse collection of people who came together to generate ideas about how to engage with Asia, both in a defensive sense with propaganda, and in a more progressive way through cultural and educational links. This counters the myth that Casey was a lone advocate of engagement with the region. Certainly, Casey did have trouble persuading his Cabinet colleagues of the importance of his work, but he had the support of a dedicated department which, under Tange, pursued a dynamic and forthright development of South–East Asian foreign policy. Although the DEA was responsible for the overall coordination of Australian Cold War planning, ideas and strategies were drawn from a range of people and departments. Key members of the Cold War activities committee — which later became the Overseas Planning Committee (OPC) — included Tange, John Hood, A. Griffith, James Plimsoll, Charles Kevin, Malcolm Booker, and William Landale. The members from outside the DEA were Allen Stanley Brown (Secretary of the Prime Minister's Department), R.J. Randall (Treasury), Brookes and R. Ellis[29] (ASIS), Arthur Noel Finlay (ABC), Kevin Murphy (ANIB) and A.P. Fleming (Defence). Other DEA staff who contributed much to the development of ideas generated at these committee meetings included John Quinn, David McNicol, John E. Oldham, John Davis, and the future director of ASIS, Ralph Harry.

The OPC devised a basic set of principles to guide Australia's information activities in South–East Asia. The critical aspects of the policy can be summarised in three general points. First, Australia was to be depicted as being in the early stages of development and thus sharing many Asian developmental problems. Second, Australia was not a great power and should not be feared; 'on the contrary the existence of a stable neighbour such as Australia should be a source of reassurance'. Third, propaganda was expected to emphasise the ways in which Australia's economic stability benefited the entire region — 'cooperation was advantageous to all'.[30]

In order to achieve these goals, Australia's Cold War planners argued that propaganda activity needed to address specific problems faced by Asians, in a manner that was not overly theoretical or didactic. They hoped to counter communism by focusing on people's daily concerns and promoting the material benefits of democratic institutions, rather than by relying merely on negative scaremongering. Paradoxically, the OPC was wary of promoting democracy too forcefully, as this might offend undemocratic — but nevertheless anti-communist — governments, upon which Australia depended to resist the red menace. Policy-makers determined that Australia should support a stable, but undemocratic government in the absence of a viable alternative, lest a dangerous political vacuum be created. Australian influence would be best achieved by emphasising the virtues of Australia's advanced social, industrial, and administrative infrastructure and by educating Asians about how they could achieve this level of development. The final, but by no means least significant, goal was to convince Asians that Australia's immigration policy did not imply any animosity towards Asians.[31]

The committee was keenly aware that the United States and the United Kingdom were spending considerable sums on propaganda. Australia's much smaller financial capacity heightened the DEA's sense that a carefully targeted program would have to be initiated to avoid merely being lost in the flood of Western propaganda already testing the 'digestive capacity of the area'.[32] With some success, Casey and his department appointed diplomatic personnel who ensured that stories about Australia (many involving Colombo Plan projects) were distributed to local media.[33] In September 1956, a distressed British Embassy staffer in Rangoon, P.H. Gore Booth, wrote to the Foreign Office about the lack of publicity for British Colombo Plan projects. He lamented that he never heard about British endeavours but saw that the Australian and New Zealand programs received 'constant publicity' in local Burmese and English papers. Gore Booth even claimed that ministers and politicians invariably spoke as if 'Australia and New Zealand were alone running the Colombo Plan'. He ended his letter with a plea: 'I really do hope that you will be able to find some solution. But bluntly, the Australian and New Zealand effort, particularly in regard to photographs, makes us look like a lot of bungling amateurs'.[34] Evidently, diplomatic staff had heeded Casey's drive to extract every ounce of publicity from Colombo Plan projects, at least in Burma. That such publicity was making an impression at the highest level would have pleased Casey greatly.

From the DEA's point of view, the more people who came into direct contact with Australian aid projects the better. Indeed, the DEA cited this as one of the major reasons for supplying 100 diesel buses to Indonesia: 'they would be an especially tangible form of aid which would bring the Colombo Plan to the attention of the mass of the inhabitants of Djakarta'.[35] To remove all confusion about the origin of the buses, a hand-sized plate with a map of Australia was fixed at eye-level near the front entrance.

Visibly branding Australian projects became an important feature of the Colombo Plan. Just as donated equipment came well-labelled, by the mid-1960s students, too, were encouraged to display their Colombo Plan credentials with a special badge, lapel pin, or broach made of an 'antique silver' alloy, which the designers promised would never tarnish in tropical conditions.[36]

The effectiveness of Australian-sponsored aid projects affected their value as propaganda. Conversely, the overwhelming emphasis on shallow publicity had a direct bearing on the long-term benefits generated by the Colombo Plan. Western aid donors quickly learnt how fickle aid recipients could be and just how tenuous attempts to instigate a deep ideological shift with foreign assistance could be. In 1954, the British reported from Afghanistan (which joined the Consultative Committee in 1963) that Soviet propaganda conducted by the technical experts sent to carry out the development project meant that 'the Afghan population as a whole tends to become pro-Soviet in direct response and proportion to the material benefits which it receives'. However, the Afghan government's staunch non-alignment policy ensured that Western attempts to match or compete with Soviet programs would see the acceptance of a Soviet overture in order to maintain an appropriate balance. This frustrating commitment to neutralism meant that the government of Afghanistan will 'never be won over to the spirit of Western cooperative effort or allow that spirit to effect [sic] their political attitude. They can, in short, be politically bought but not politically converted'.[37]

The DEA's ideas about propaganda exposed their assumptions about Asian people and their political institutions. A common theme in the department's thinking was that Asian political structures seemed to possess a natural tendency towards authoritarianism and corruption. Moreover, it was believed that ordinary citizens passively accepted these flaws as an intrinsic part of the political and cultural landscape. As one OPC paper suggested: 'A certain amount of despotism seems unavoidable in some Asian countries and is often taken as a matter of course by the population. Where we have to work with and through despotic government, there is nothing much we can do about it anyway'.[39] Some members of the department, such as Counsellor John Oldham, head of Information Branch, posited theories about the changes occurring in Asia, despite having almost no experience of Asians. Asians, he claimed, were more susceptible to propaganda because they endured poverty, feudalism, and anti-colonialist rhetoric and, generally, suffered from a 'lack of experience of genuine freedom and responsible government'.[39] But Oldham was hopeful, sensing a movement in Asian philosophy away from fatalism towards a belief in development and progress through social and political change.

Clearly, increasing aid to Asia did not necessarily correspond to a more detailed understanding of decolonisation and the complex interplay between nationalism, communism, and post-colonial power struggles. In fact, political rhetoric about the transformative power of foreign aid tended to reinforce the simplistic, yet powerful, idea that poverty acted as a seedbed for communism, and that liberal democracy was inseparable from economic individualism. While such theories were deeply seductive, a more moderate and complex interpretation was available to the government. Four years after his 'Goodwill Tour' of Asia in 1948, Melbourne academic Macmahon Ball published *Nationalism and Communism in East Asia*, one of the first attempts to comprehend the political, social, and economic aftermath of decolonisation in Asia from a Western perspective. While he thought it important for Western democracies to win the support of non-communist Asia, he argued that the current strategy was destined to fail. He warned against heavy-handed military solutions, stressed the dangers of assuming that 'Western ways have universal appeal', and criticised Western policy-makers' view of the talismanic role of science and technology. By explaining that there was 'no simple correlation between poverty and Communism', Macmahon Ball undermined the foundations of the Western aid policy. He feared that if economic aid merely increased national income with no regard for its equitable distribution, productivity increases were likely to exacerbate social disintegration rather than reduce it — except, of course, in the case of technical and scientific training.[40]

The OPC agreed. They reasoned that the Colombo Plan and other 'do-good schemes' may have been able to improve living standards generally, but they had a tendency to 'make the rich richer', thereby exacerbating social and political tensions.[41] Such interpretations, however, did not lead to a reassessment of the effectiveness of the aid program itself and the welfare programs in place in Asian countries. Instead, they lent support to arguments for covert strategies to deal with communist activity, strategies that would supposedly take effect more quickly than the long-term development projects, the impact of which was less tangible.

Shortly after the inception of the Colombo Plan, Australian diplomatic posts throughout Asia received requests to train local personnel in police and security methods. Spender had made it clear to Cabinet in 1951 that, 'short of armed force', improving the efficiency of police administration in the region was the only means of securing stable democratic governments. The Thai police department was the first to request assistance, in October 1951, followed by Burma, Pakistan and Ceylon.[42] In September 1953, Pakistani officials approached the Australian High Commission in Karachi about the possibility of police officers undertaking further training in Australia. DEA staff explained to Casey that, provided instruction was restricted to criminal investigation methods and did not extend to ASIO or special branch training, the requests could be funded under the technical assistance program because the civil police organisation was a component of the public administration infrastructure.[43] Plimsoll, as Acting Secretary, wrote to Alan Watt, former Secretary of the DEA and now the Australian Commissioner in Singapore, about the possibility of police and military training for Burmese officers. Among other matters, Plimsoll briefed him on talks with the UK and US delegations and emphasised that officers should not portray police and military training 'as Cold War activities'. However, his qualifying remarks are significant:

> the broad objective of the Colombo Plan is to combat communism, [and] we have been careful in the past to keep our contributions quite apart from politics. With regard to military training, it seems essential that the Burmese should not be given the impression that we regard this as an anti-communist move as they might then consider it an infringement of their neutrality and even reconsider their use of Australian facilities.[44]

In 1955, Casey breached the distinction between public administration training and covert counter-propaganda training, further politicising the Colombo Plan. He met with Charles Spry, Director General of ASIO, and asked him to train a small group of English-speaking Thai police in anti-subversive techniques — training that would ostensibly be financed under the Colombo Plan budget.[45] By October 1955, training was well underway and state police departments expressed a willingness to participate in a much larger program. The DEA then asked Manila Treaty countries whether they needed further assistance in this field.[46] Spry immediately indicated that ASIO, pending available funding, would organise two courses a year for Asian intelligence officers in counter-subversion techniques.[47] A complete record of the number who undertook these courses does not exist, but there is direct evidence of security training of Asian officials taking place in Australia.[48] One notable trainee was Tran Van Khiem, ex–press secretary to the President of Vietnam, who completed four months of training in the period 1955–56 with ASIO and the Victorian and NSW police on a Colombo Plan scholarship. He was trained in security methods that he hoped would provide him with the skills to 'cope with the terrorist war in Saigon'.[49]

Some members of the DEA and ASIO expressed doubts about the practicality of security training and were inclined to refer such requests to UK Special Branch divisions, which had begun advanced courses in counter-espionage in Malaya and Singapore during the mid-1950s. Spry also raised concerns about the 'language problem' and the embarrassing ignominy of providing training to potentially hostile countries. The DEA dismissed such reservations because they had the potential to undermine the entire basis of Colombo Plan training. As Max Loveday, acting head of the Defence Liaison Branch, suggested: 'If we follow Spry's reasoning we should consider cancelling other Colombo Plan offers — because I don't think the security training courses [are] much different from, say, an engineering course if we are considering the dangers of training potential enemies'.[50] The number of Colombo Plan police trainees rose substantially after 1956, to over 100 by 1965.[51] The figures, however, do not distinguish between the types of courses undertaken. Of course, given the politically sensitive nature of the training, it is debatable whether these courses would appear in official statistical sources.

As the likelihood of a direct military assault in the region receded, the need to address subversive disruption emerged as a higher priority for the Menzies administration. Talk of a protracted 'psychological war' became commonplace, both inside and outside government circles.[52] Police training was deemed an appropriate way to combat attempts to overthrow government institutions, but such training had little impact on the attitudes and opinions of local citizens, academics and community leaders. Despite Loveday's assurances, police training was risky, likely to prove counter-productive and diplomatically embarrassing should a government change (or be overthrown) and the allegiance of the police force shift to support a political structure unfriendly — even hostile — to Australia and the West. The DEA spent considerable time developing means by which it could bypass the government and appeal directly to the people. Radio was the medium which captured the Department's imagination.

Australia's overseas broadcasting service, Radio Australia, began operating in 1939, its mission to explain Australian and British policies to people in Asia and the Pacific. John Oldham and others in the DEA proposed that Australian propaganda disseminated to the region move beyond negative, anti-communist rhetoric.[53] He believed that the most effective means of increasing awareness of the 'Australian point of view' was an objective and factual presentation of current affairs. The United States Far

Eastern Bureau told Oldham that, in the face of a pervasive anti-American sentiment, Australia was more likely to succeed in promoting a pro-Western viewpoint to Asians. Radio Australia had already proved successful, particularly in Indonesia, and its content and transmission range warranted expansion. The OPC also expected that a sophisticated broadcasting infrastructure, both in Australia and throughout Asia, would yield strategic benefits should war actually break out.[54] Late in 1954, Oldham suggested that an ambiguously worded May 1950 Cabinet directive, which conferred discretionary control of Radio Australia broadcasts on the editor, be amended to bring information services under direct DEA control. He believed this would 'increase the technical efficiency of Radio Australia and … make the programme material more effective in countering Communist propaganda and subversion in Asia'. Funding would also be required to bolster ailing infrastructure that was still using equipment assembled in 1945. The network, consisting of one 50-kilowatt transmitter and two 100-kilowatt transmitters in Shepparton and a 10-kilowatt in Lyndhurst (both in Victoria), was especially vulnerable to jamming by powerful communist radio waves. The Department of Defence was particularly concerned because there was no reserve power to cope with breakdowns, as the system was operating at maximum capacity. Australia would need to build a relay station in New Guinea in order to maintain the clarity and reach of the broadcasts.[55]

Earlier, in May 1950, Spender had written to the Chairman of the Australian Broadcasting Commission, Richard Boyer, informing him that it was crucial that 'Radio Australia be looked at as an instrument of foreign policy'.[56] Throughout the decade, the DEA demonstrated its determination to exercise a stronger influence over the content of Radio Australia broadcasts. In 1955, Casey escalated the campaign to take control. Predictably, his argument to Cabinet emphasised the importance of radio 'from a political warfare point of view', in addition to its ability to establish and maintain a political and cultural dialogue with the region.[57] In a letter to Tange, he outlined his strategy:

> *we will need to clear our own minds as to where we want to go and the extent to which Radio Australia broadcasts are to be extended, and the extent to which we would propose to increase their political content — and how this political content is to be compiled and canalised into the Radio Australia machine. Maybe we will have to seek direct control in respect of material to constitute the political content of Radio Australia broadcasts. In other words, we may have to bring it about that External Affairs and not Radio Australia determines what goes into these broadcasts on the non-entertainment side.*[58]

Radio Australia's struggle for autonomy and editorial independence is not the focus of this chapter. Suffice to say that the organisation did not yield easily to the persistent attempts by the DEA to influence content and presentation. However, from August 1955, Radio Australia based its news commentaries on material provided by the DEA, which ensured that relations between the two organisations continued to be antagonistic.[59]

The decision to use radio as the principal instrument to provide information to Asia brought the Colombo Plan to the forefront of attempts to forge political and cultural links between Australia and Asia. While attending a meeting with the United States Information Agency (responsible for Voice of America's international broadcasts), Percy Spender suggested that the fundamental objectives of Voice of America broadcasts were the same as Radio Australia's, and he envisaged a much closer relationship between the two agencies. Casey proudly told officials of Australia's effort to distribute short-wave and medium-wave radios to village leaders and teachers throughout Asia.[60] Speed was the key. In early March 1955, the DEA enlisted E.S. Heffer, a radio engineer for Amalgamated Wireless Australasia, to conduct a six-week technical survey of the capacity of Indo-China and Thailand to use and maintain portable radio receivers. The department envisaged that around 1,000 sets would be distributed across the area, with South Vietnam as the highest priority.[61] At the request of the South Vietnamese Minister for Defence, Australia used Colombo Plan funds to supply military units with petrol-driven generators for use in wireless transmission.[62] The example of Vietnam reflected a wider trend towards promoting the use of radio in Asia. By the mid-1960s around 6.5 per cent of Australia's Colombo Plan allocations for capital aid was being spent on radio equipment, having risen from just 2 per cent in the 1950s.[63]

The Australian Embassy in Djakarta expressed concern about the effect the expansion of Radio Australia might have on the Colombo Plan. They warned that, without seeking the active participation of the recipient country in the development of radio programs, 'the Indonesians may come to dislike it [thus] affecting the attitude towards the Colombo Plan generally'. Second Secretary Wilfred Vawdrey doubted if any demand for instructional radio existed among the populace. Indonesians, he wrote, seem 'to have little interest in anything but musical programmes and perhaps the news'. As for English lessons, they were already available through

Radio Indonesia and the BBC, and 'the family circle is probably not going to take kindly to talk on tractor maintenance in place of "listener's choice"'.[64] Vawdrey also added that, in any case, a successful teaching program needed trained staff with specialist knowledge about the cultural particulars of each region: 'Surely this would prove a costly undertaking', he surmised. Had the need to get something off the ground not been so pressing, such concerns may well have received a sympathetic response. But, with reports flowing back to Canberra warning of the pervasive impact of the communists' propaganda and the effect of the 'Communist radio technique', Australia had to join the fray with whatever resources it could muster.[65] By September 1955, Indonesian broadcasts had been increased from one to two hours daily, Thai broadcasts from one hour a week to one hour per day, and the hour of Mandarin was due to become two hours daily. Response was positive with almost 3,000 letters, presumably complimentary, received from Indonesian listeners between March and September 1955. In November, over 800 were received. Desperate for any indication of the impact of radio broadcasts, the DEA, on analysing these letters, concluded that the programs were reaching a 'fairly intelligent audience'.[66] Travellers to Asia were also aware of Radio Australia's credibility and integrity, characteristics not afforded as readily to Voice of America. Other letters indicated that listeners considered Radio Australia more friendly and cheerful than the BBC.[67]

For Casey, the English language was more than a means of communication. It connoted modernity, progress, and civilisation: concepts which he considered essential to establishing and maintaining a pro-Western relationship with Asia. As Casey told Brookes, English was a fundamental political and psychological tool, 'a weapon in our hands'. Other forms of media occupied Casey's thoughts during the OPC meetings. Writing to Brookes, months after Oldham had first suggested the idea of employing Colombo Plan monies to bolster South–East Asian newspapers with anti-communist predilections, Casey posed the question: 'Might it not kill at least two birds with one stone if we were to offer to take some free-Asian journalists for attachment and training with selected newspapers in Australia?' The two birds that Casey referred to were the twin desires, to make Australians more aware of their Asian neighbours and to expose Asians to the virtues of Australia's free press. The results were another publicity triumph for Casey. After a team of Indian editors toured Australia in 1957, Peter Heydon, Australia's High Commissioner in New Delhi, rejoiced when he reported to Canberra that on their return to India they wrote enthusiastically about 'the hard-working character of Australians generally and our egalitarianism'.[68]

One of the English-language 'weapons' Casey had in mind was *Hemisphere*, a monthly journal published from March 1957.[69] Designed specifically to influence the growing Asian student body, the publicly-stated objective of the magazine was to provide a positive and engaging example of the 'tolerant, thoughtful and sceptical spirit of democracy and liberalism' to be found in Australia. However, *Hemisphere* was 'not designed for publicity in the ordinary sense' despite its obvious suitability for such a purpose.[70] John Hood described the magazine as a 'natural and effective cover for contact and penetration among Asian students', fulfilling its 'covert objective of enabling contact to be made with these students in order to influence them for anti-communist ends'. A suppressed copy of the same committee report disclosed that in addition to its overt purpose of publicising Australian life and conditions and promoting friendly relations with

South–East Asia, 'the magazine will serve as cover to M.O.9. [codeword for ASIS] in making special contact with Asian students in Australia and also as a link in anti-communist penetration in countries of South and South–East Asia'.[71]

With the magazine produced jointly by the DEA and the Commonwealth Office of Education (COE), the use of Colombo Plan funds to finance it forced the government to take particular care 'not to raise any suspicions of propaganda motives'.[72] The emergence of other magazines on Asian–Australian affairs also impelled *Hemisphere's* editors to produce a high-quality and visually appealing journal, lest the government be left with a publication which looked 'second rate by comparison'.[73] With regard to language, the DEA asked the COE to consider revising the 'preview' issue to remove words potentially offensive to Asians, such as 'Chinamen', 'sinister little Japanese', and 'rickshaw coolies'. Ironically, by adhering to such high standards, Australian representatives in Asia reported that *Hemisphere's* expensive and glossy appearance, which made the magazine so popular, caused some Asians to query its apparent editorial independence. They advised that the inclusion of more controversial material might allay some of these misgivings.[74] Nevertheless, circulation rose quickly from around 3,000 in 1959 to around 15,000 in 1967, half of which went to Asia.[75] Government officials even approached Trans-Australian Airlines (TAA) and Ansett Australian National Airlines (AANA) about the possibility of placing *Hemisphere* on domestic flights as the in-flight magazine. The airlines declined, 'not because *Hemisphere* was propaganda … just that the policy of the airline was to avoid anything which might be regarded as "political"'.[76]

During the mid- to late-1950s, there was a general feeling among DEA officers — no doubt influenced by

Casey — that Australia was too passive in its approach to cultural relations. In 1953, the High Commissioner to Pakistan, Raymond Watt, wrote to Casey about the 'urgent need to make Australians more Asia-minded' and suggested that the Colombo Plan needed to transcend its focus on economic and technical progress 'when on the cultural level so much extra could be done, at so little cost, to promote better relations'. Inevitably short of finance, Casey encouraged non-government and non-political groups, such as the Australian–Asian Association, to remedy the cultural malaise.[77]

Building cultural links with Asia saw Casey attempt to establish a subsidy program for selected works of Australian literature to be sold in Asia. The scheme was intended to compete with a similar program initiated by the Soviet and Chinese governments.[78] The books also formed an important part of Casey's plan to educate Asian readers and 'remove misconceptions about Australia and Australian policies'.[79] Casey approached the managers of Angus & Robertson and Penguin Books, who both agreed to create a series of Australian texts, selected by the DEA, to be sold well below the normal price of books available in Asian countries. A staggering 10,000 copies of each of the following titles were planned to be distributed to Colombo Plan countries: Ernest Titterton's *Atomic energy*, Vladimir Petrov's *Empire of fear*, Francis Ratcliffe's *Flying fox and Drifting sand: the adventures of a biologist in Australia*, and Douglas Mawson's *Home of the blizzard*.[80] Despite widespread enthusiasm for the idea and the allocation of £A8,000, the DEA abandoned the Cheap Books subsidy program after more than ten years of discussion because no one could agree on which titles should be included.[81] However, throughout the decade, the Australian government sent substantial numbers of books as gifts under the Colombo Plan to universities and libraries across Asia.

Casey had a strong sense of the images of Australian life he wanted to promote to Asian audiences. Indeed, in his quietly egotistical way, Casey, according to his private secretary Harold Marshall, was particularly pleased with the content and title of his own book, *Friends and neighbours: Australia and the world*, destined for Asia under a US subsidy program.[82] But, in general, he placed considerable importance on distinguishing Australia from the United States, at a time when he felt it was difficult to express a solely Australian viewpoint in world affairs. It was vital, Casey thought, to establish a regional identity that was independent and non-threatening, an identity that would not attract the ire of an increasingly assertive Asia:

> *The kinds of themes I have in mind would include the absence of racial prejudice in Australia, the idea of Australia as a waterless land unsuitable for mass settlement, Australia's past and continuing pioneering efforts — the absence of that decadence attributed to capitalist societies in communist propaganda, our progressive social reforms and the egalitarian nature of Australian society, our request [sic] for human and spiritual rights without the extreme materialism of either Communism or American individualism, the primitive nature of our aborigines and of the New Guinea peoples, and even the beneficial aspects of colonial regimes.*[83]

It is interesting that Casey positioned Australian society between the Cold War power blocs and the values they appeared to represent. Australia's strength lay in the fact that it was not a major colonial power, but the successful product of a colonial regime serving as a model to the region. There is something else of note in Casey's musings about creating meaningful links with Asians. In a 1956 submission to Cabinet, Casey argued that Australia was different from other Western countries, not just in terms of its location and former dominion status, but in having something to offer Asia, materially and culturally. He wrote that a concerted effort was needed to convince Asians that Australia was not 'an outpost of an alien culture, antipathetic towards coloured races'. A change from reactor to actor is evident — it was Australia's responsibility to initiate a more positive and meaningful relationship.[84] It was not surprising that the re-orientation suggested by Casey's words was slight. While this was a long way from an endorsement of racial and cultural pluralism, such a comment suggests a re-conceptualising, if an equivocal one, of Australia's regional identity and was perhaps indicative of the beginnings of a deeper cultural shift.

Casey's faith in the broader cultural impact of the Colombo Plan extended to the domestic arena. Always searching for avenues to muster support for the program and maintain dialogue between Asians and Australians, Casey mooted the idea of inviting members of the public to subscribe to the plan on a 'pound for pound' basis with the government. He believed this had the potential to capitalise on the 'considerable public consciousness of the value of the Colombo Plan … and give people an opportunity to express themselves in a practical way'. Casey also proposed that particular Australian cities adopt a town or city in one of the Colombo Plan nations and send money or gifts.[85] The DEA did not take up the idea.

Typically, educational aid proved to be the most enduring way of binding many regional countries to Australia. In 1957 the DEA expanded the South–East Asian Scholarship Scheme to include Pacific and North

Asian countries outside the Colombo Plan area. Like the Special Commonwealth African Assistance Plan (SCAAP), which offered small numbers of scholarships to African students, the tiny number of students funded under the Australian Overseas Scholarship Scheme were intended to connect Australia to as many non-Colombo Plan countries as possible. In the case of Korea — which did not join the Colombo Plan until 1962 — Australia was particularly interested to broaden her international contacts, compensate for Britain's 'lack of interest' and vary the 'very full American diet with which Koreans are served'.[86] With characteristic impetuosity, Casey later toyed with the idea of extending the program to Iraq.

Although not financed under the Colombo Plan, the 'Asian Visits Fund' was devised by the DEA with similar objectives in mind. No doubt inspired by the American 'International Visitor Program' created under the 1948 Smith–Mundt Act as part of a plan to promote the United States and foster mutual understanding, the modest Asian Visits Fund aimed to build cultural relations between Australia and Asia. Once again, a covert rationale appeared mandatory, with the scheme 'not established purely as a goodwill measure or for cultural exchange, but as a means of achieving definite objectives in the context of the Cold War'. According to Cabinet records, Australia could lure teachers, journalists, government members, trade unionists, or broadcasters from the region with an invitation to explore 'some practical project in which the invitee is interested. It would then be sought in the course of the visit to indoctrinate him generally in relation to [the] Australian way of life'. Conversely, tours by Australians would help introduce Asians to influential and charismatic Australians, in much the same way as the expert program. An annual allocated sum of £A25,000 would fund the travels of around

40 people. Cambodia's Prince Sihanouk — who happened to possess a detailed knowledge of Australian tennis history —requested that the ambassador organise a reputable tennis coach to visit and train young Cambodian players. Good manners were vital, the DEA determined. The department deemed Jack Hopman (brother of Harry Hopman) an appropriately 'conscientious and good-living man' and he later took the four-month job under the auspices of the Asian Visits Fund. By 1964, 377 Asians, Africans and Pacific Islanders had travelled to Australia under the program and 119 Australians had visited South and South–East Asia.[87]

Cultural exchanges, such as through sport, also had definite, if somewhat ill-defined, strategic benefits. Alex Borthwick, First Secretary to the Australia High Commission in Singapore, proposed the funding of sportsmen to travel and coach in Asia. He suggested that Australia pay men such as track-and-field athlete John Landy, swimmer Harry Nightingdale, and tennis champion Frank Sedgeman to coach young athletes in Asia. (In fact, Sedgeman had already played in Ceylon during the 1952 Colombo Exhibition staged to celebrate the beginning of the Colombo Plan). Suggesting the Colombo Plan as a source of funding, Borthwick wrote that he thought the idea 'not entirely bizarre' and perhaps a valuable 'exercise in the Cold War'.[88] Although he was not in the circle of men Casey had inspired to 'strike fire' from uninhibited discussion of Australia's Cold War effort, Borthwick's ideas would have been a welcome addition to the department's thinking. Sport had greater mass appeal than the performing arts or visiting politicians and it had little of the stigma of aid 'hand outs'. From the mid-1950s, the DEA instructed Asian posts to distribute Australian sporting magazines and newsletters and directed Radio Australia to give greater attention to sporting events. Later, Colombo Plan finance was used towards the supply of sporting equipment, the construction of sporting fields and arenas, and physical education scholarships. Of course, Australian officials were responding to communist endeavours to cultivate relations with Asia. The Soviet Union established sporting contacts and funded the construction of sporting venues, thus reaping a 'harvest of publicity', according to the DEA.[89] Colin Moodie, High Commissioner in Rangoon, suggested that Australia stood to gain a great deal by organising athletes to visit the region:

> *Particularly in the fields of tennis, golf, swimming, soccer and athletics, there is a considerable field for making a mark on numbers of Burmans who will be able to judge for themselves the bearing of the visitors and their freedom to move and speak as they wished compared with visitors they may receive from the Communist group of countries.*[90]

There is a sub-text to Moodie's words. Contact with Asia through sport was more than a chance to build rapport with ordinary Asians; the mere presence of Australian visitors was a subtle advertisement for Western values. Like many others, Moodie thought that the athletes, through their bearing and attitude, would exude the virtues of freedom and democracy. However, the benefit was double-edged, for not only did it involve Australians travelling and making contact in Asia, the DEA saw it as a 'means of promoting awareness and … understanding of Asian countries among Australians generally'.[91]

Casey, counter-propaganda and Osmar White's Colombo Plan tour

By the mid- to late-1950s, the Colombo Plan became a useful tool for addressing a variety of defensive, political, and cultural issues affecting Australia's place in the region. Casey's influence over the direction and scope of the program remained strong, but he had failed to build any appreciable enthusiasm for the program in Cabinet. Although he was respected, his weak performance in Cabinet was symptomatic of a growing alienation from political life. To some extent, this was self-imposed. Arthur Tange recalled that Casey reinforced his isolation from his department and his political colleagues by refusing to base himself in Canberra, instead returning 'home' to Melbourne each weekend.[92] Now in his late-60s, he flagged under the strain of the demanding portfolio. Even before the Suez affair and a humiliating defeat in his bid for the position of deputy leader of the Liberal Party, those close to Casey noticed that he looked 'worn and strained', having also developed a nervous, twitching eye.[93] The Colombo Plan became something of a crutch, a means of gaining personal exposure while simultaneously promoting Asian affairs to other bureaucrats and members of Cabinet. Crocker, who knew Casey on a professional and personal basis, observed that as Casey became 'befogged' by the complexity of foreign relations 'the more desperately he [clung] to the Colombo Plan', turning it into a 'huge advertising racket for himself'.[94] Casey's attachment to the plan meant he saw any criticism of it as a personal attack, despite his protestations. In July 1956, he complained to Tange about the 'considerable campaign against the Colombo Plan and against me personally — that the Sydney *Truth* and *Mirror* are conducting. Scarcely a week goes by without a virulent savage article. I don't believe it is important — but it goes on'.[95]

Publicity for the Colombo Plan occasionally stimulated the community's latent hostility towards foreign aid. With Australia so visibly supporting Asians, it is not surprising that Casey also received his share of racist hate-mail demanding the end of the Colombo Plan and more.[96] However, despite the generally positive and even-handed treatment in the media, few Australians were aware of the impact Australian funds were actually having on economic and social progress in Asia. Development was, after all, the bedrock of the simplified public rationale for the operation of the aid scheme. Under pressure to bolster his own position in Cabinet, Casey embarked on his most sustained attempt to convince his political colleagues and the public that the Colombo Plan was worthy of financial and moral support.

In 1958, Casey and the DEA became increasingly interested in discovering how effective Australian aid projects were in fulfilling the objectives of the Colombo Plan. A public debate about the use of Australian donations under the plan helped force the government's hand. In April 1958, R.E.G. Cunningham, a former employee of the UN Food and Agricultural Organization, spoke to a Parliamentary Joint Committee on Foreign Affairs and then to the press. He criticised Colombo Plan projects in Pakistan, claiming that he had seen Australian tractors rusting in fields and that 100 sheep sent as part of a breeding program had all died. The criticisms forced Casey to try to minimise the damage. He rebutted the claims, stating that there was a 'degree of experimentation' in such programs and losses were to be expected. But he denied strongly the suggestion that aid money was wasted or misappropriated. Australia worked in 'close consultation with the recipient nations to ensure that equipment was of the right type'.

Furthermore, Casey emphasised that Colombo Plan experts, diplomats, and other officials reported regularly on the effectiveness of Australian aid programs. Casey did receive reports about the effectiveness of Colombo Plan aid, but on a more sporadic and piecemeal basis than he acknowledged publicly. Two months before this flare-up, David Hay, Assistant Secretary of the DEA, had written to Casey lamenting the excessively general nature of the assessment of Australian Colombo Plan projects. Any accurate assessment, he said, could 'only be produced by an experienced "inspector general" able to spend a year or so travelling extensively in the area'.[97] Hay's idea lay dormant in Casey's mind until after the Cunningham incident.

But Casey chose counter-propaganda over sponsoring an objective assessment of Australian aid projects. In July 1958, he began searching for a 'top line' journalist who would undertake a lengthy tour of the Colombo Plan region and report to the Australian people. The DEA deliberately looked outside government ranks for an independent spirit — a man who could write 'lively, intelligent articles', and more significantly, a man 'who could not be regarded by his fellows as writing material to order'. The man whom Casey eventually commissioned was *Herald and Weekly Times* reporter Osmar White. White had had a distinguished career as a wartime correspondent in the Pacific and Europe. In 1945 he published *Green armour*, an evocative and influential account of the war in New Guinea and the Americans' battle for the Solomon Islands. His intimate knowledge of the region and his clear support of the Allied cause made Casey's decision straightforward. In December 1958, White and Australian News and Information Bureau (ANIB) photographer James Fitzpatrick (not to be confused with the American film producer-writer-director of the same name) left for Pakistan. Their brief was to gather stories, photographs, and film on the impact and influence of Australia's Colombo Plan contributions. When they returned in June 1959, they had visited 14 countries: Pakistan, India, Nepal, Ceylon, Burma, Thailand, Cambodia, Vietnam, Malaya, Sarawak, North Borneo, Singapore, the Philippines, and Indonesia.[98]

In addition to writing a series of news feature articles, the two men were to produce a documentary film and an illustrated information booklet. Although the DEA had relied on the sporadic reports from Colombo Plan experts and diplomatic dispatches for information on the effect of foreign aid, the White tour was more an opportunity to promote the virtue of Australian aid to Asia than a systematic or comprehensive attempt to assess the impact of Australian economic and technical assistance. Casey had struggled throughout the 1950s to generate Cabinet interest in the aid scheme. The decision to send these two men was part of Casey's strategy to garner popular interest and support for the Colombo Plan. The DEA also hoped to enhance awareness and appreciation of Australian aid among recipient nations.[99]

Before the DEA officially commissioned White for the job, Casey summoned him to Canberra to discuss the objectives of the exercise and, it would seem, to question him about his political beliefs. Later, White wrote to Colin Moodie, Assistant Secretary of the DEA, restating his understanding of his primary responsibility to 'produce feature articles designed to inform the public, how, in human terms the plan is operating, and what value it has' and to write an information booklet. Moodie cautioned White about assigning the booklet secondary importance 'in view of its very considerable long-term importance ... [and its] value to us for publicity purposes for some years to come'.[100] That Moodie was at pains to correct White's seemingly casual comment suggests that he sensed White had a different understanding of the tour's purpose. White saw his role as providing a broad, critical, and impartial assessment of the program, whereas the DEA saw the production of good publicity as White's principal function.

Casey was particularly concerned to avoid the appearance of government involvement and agreed that White should send his material 'direct to the Features Service for distribution, without the Department exercising any editorial authority'. The DEA publicity machine swung into action and White was provided with a list of former Colombo Plan scholars and fellows who 'for some interesting personal reason, such as their personal charm, their zest for the programme in Australia, their appreciation of life in Australia, etc., placed them a cut above their CP compatriots'. Although the DEA went to some lengths to ensure White's experience would be positive and fruitful for the Australian government, at this stage, government officials relinquished control over the outcome of White's tour. White left Australia believing Casey had giving him 'carte blanche'.[101]

Neither White (even with his four years as a war correspondent in Europe and the Pacific) nor Fitzpatrick was prepared for their experience in South and South–East Asia. They arrived in Pakistan in the midst of a gastro-enteritis epidemic, and the first two weeks felt like a year. Within a month, the pressure of their fast-paced tour and the strain of adapting to the differing work protocols of Asia began to take their toll. As White complained to his wife, Mollie:

> The administrative inefficiency of these people has to be observed — or suffered — to be believed. We both spend endless hours drinking cups of tea, making diplomatic speeches, accepting promises and the only thing that causes some action is a complete screaming blow-up. Against the grain,

*I now behave like a burra sahib almost from
the beginning, and snap, bark, shout and roar at
the drop of a hat. It works, but it's hard on the
blood pressure.*

Almost immediately, White became concerned
because his articles were not being published and Fitzpatrick's
photographs were slow to be developed. 'I refuse to worry
about this', he continued. 'If the dopes muck up the
newspaper side of the assignment, it's their own bloody fault.
I have enough trouble with the Paks [Pakistanis] as it is,
without taking on our own public service into the
bargain'.[102] White later told Moodie that he suspected that
Asian officials were only showing him the most successful of
Australian Colombo Plan projects and that 'unfavourable
facts were being deliberately concealed'. When shown the
200 tractors donated by Australia, White's instincts were
aroused: 'My newspaperman's radar indicates most strongly
the presence of a rat!' Anticipating a disastrous tour and a
series of negative articles, he reminded Moodie of the
assurances provided by the DEA for a free editorial hand.[103]

White, a strong believer in the objectives of the
Colombo Plan, was disheartened to find widespread waste
and neglect in Australian-funded projects and equipment.
After five weeks in Pakistan, White and Fitzpatrick arrived
in New Delhi and informed Indian High Commissioner
Walter Crocker of their moral dilemma. Crocker recorded
in his diary that the two men

*had found so much corruption and inefficiency and
waste in the use of Australian Colombo Plan aid
that they could not write their articles, which
Casey said could be completely free, without
dealing with that side. And if they did the reaction
in Australia might well be to put an end to the*

Colombo Plan aid and even to put Casey out of office. Should they go on with their mission?

Crocker felt also the pressure of his allegiance to Casey. He felt unable to talk freely about his own misgivings about the Colombo Plan, 'always safeguarding' Casey during his discussion with White and Fitzpatrick. Cautiously, Crocker suggested that White telegram Casey himself. He did so, telling Casey that his first duty as a journalist was to report the situation as he saw it and that he had accepted the job only on the condition that he had full editorial control. Yet, White remained torn between his belief in the developmental and anti-communist objectives of the Colombo Plan and his journalistic desire to 'make headlines'. He told Casey it was the 'knottiest professional problem' he had encountered since the war. Continuing with the tour, White explained his predicament to Robert Furlonger, Acting High Commissioner in Karachi:

> *it had become apparent that the cumulative effect of publication might make all CP [Colombo Plan] projects unpopular with the Australian public — an effect which, apart from the terms of my present brief, I would deeply regret. So I simply passed the ball to the Minister and will await his reaction before deciding what I must write and how.*[104]

Casey, sensing the implications of an ambitious and comprehensive assessment by White, requested that he not lose sight of the 'original objectives' of the tour. He asked White to confine his attention to the particular rather than the general: 'I believe there are many stories with individual human interest and appeal which we can look to you to exploit. I would particularly like to see publication of a number of articles about Australian-trained Asians holding responsible positions or carrying out colourful jobs back in their own countries'. In this case, White faced no moral dilemma, but a real problem: in Pakistan he simply could not find a success story. As he explained to Casey, 'I am searching diligently for individual human stories but so far have found that trainees mostly have been swallowed up in routine public service jobs often unrelated to skills which their Australian training sought to develop'. Again Casey sympathised, but asked him not to circulate his articles prematurely until he had visited more countries, by which time he might have 'a different view of Colombo Plan achievements and shortcomings'. Casey was in the invidious position of imploring White not to reveal his findings, lest they 'make it impossible for him to maintain parliamentary support for the plan'. Clearly, White had stumbled across a myriad of problems associated with aid-giving procedures, but he may have been overzealous in searching for examples of waste and neglect. While passing through India, White complained bitterly to an official about the 'shocking waste' of Australian Colombo Plan material in Nepal, when in fact the Australian goods destined for that country had not even arrived in India.[105]

The exchange between Casey and White continued a month later, when White's tour took him to South Vietnam. The issue of waste and mismanagement had not receded. Casey claimed that the Australian government had avoided large-scale infrastructure projects and attempted to supply more experts to oversee and monitor aid projects. Yet Casey's attitude towards the waste was revealing. He warned White not to be perturbed by it, because 'in underdeveloped countries we must inevitably expect more waste and even less efficiency'. Moreover, a loss of effectiveness might be necessary in order to emphasise the non-political nature of the aid. Casey explained his theory to White:

> *Asian countries [are] extremely sensitive — often*
> *peculiarly so — to any implication they are*
> *incapable of running their own affairs on their*
> *terms … I believe that the success of the Colombo*
> *Plan and the goodwill Australia has won through it*
> *is largely due to our basic practice of dealing with*
> *Asian governments on a basis of full equality. To*
> *achieve this we have had sometimes to accept a loss*
> *in efficiency.*

'We are', he explained, 'relative new boys in the foreign aid business'. Even the more conspicuous and more rigorously supervised American projects suffered from allegations of waste and inefficiency. Moreover, critics berated the United States for interference in other countries' international affairs. All things considered, Casey assured White, 'we have not done so badly in getting a return for money spent in the past, especially when you take into account the intangible factors that I need not stress to you'. Once more, we see Casey focusing on the 'intangible factors', the goodwill and prestige, which he hoped would materialise in the minds of those associated with Australian Colombo Plan projects. White would eventually come to share at least a little of Casey's faith. But for the moment, he continued to struggle with his instincts as a journalist. Days after receiving the cable from Casey, White wrote to Kevin Murphy of the ANIB:

> *As a newspaper man all my instincts are to scream*
> *my head off and be damned to the consequences …*
> *The Colombo Plan and other aid is about the only*
> *effective weapon our mob has against the Comms*
> *[Communists] in the Mysterious East, and to tell*
> *the tough truth to the long suffering taxpayer will go*
> *a long way towards blunting the weapon.*[106]

Talk of censorship found its way to Cecil Edwards, editor of the *Herald and Weekly Times*, who suspected the DEA was vetting White's material. Although White would later deny that he was censored, Edwards asked that White supply him with a list of what he had written in order to determine if 'stories had gone astray'.[107]

The professional exposure White was receiving in Australia was some compensation for the intense work. He told Mollie: 'I'm writing for the whole bloody Australian press, now twenty-four articles in all plus five TV scripts and about 40,000 words of confidential reports. This stuff is being used at an intensity which the News and Information Bureau claims is an all-time record for placements'. But, after nearly four months in the field, White's partner, Fitzpatrick, had 'just about packed up under the continued pressure. He's completely slap happy, and has started bullying Burmans and trying to make every shot perfect'. White warned Fitzpatrick that if he continued in this manner he would be recalled. The arduous physical and emotional conditions, combined with Casey's insistence on his holding his fire, undoubtedly tested White's mettle. Venting his frustrations to Mollie, White responded to the challenges by stiffening his resolve to explain the effect of the Colombo Plan exactly as he saw it: 'we've been making the most fearful boners in pure ignorance and the Tiger [Casey] is ruthlessly copping the lot. As you say, my job is to see — and by gum I'm seeing, and he's getting told'. Nonetheless, White's view of the overall effectiveness of the Colombo Plan improved as the tour progressed. In March, he claimed optimistically in a cable to Edwards that the Colombo Plan

> seems to be an effective instrument of foreign policy, and in all countries I've seen so far — with the possible exception of India — it had generated a

surprising amount of goodwill. Furthermore, the CP organization has, on the psychological level, handled aid-giving infinitely better than the American ICA [International Cooperation Agency] which, although it has spent vast sums on badly needed projects, is resented and distrusted by Asians — far more so than is warranted by its demerits.

White, however, exercised more tact than his sharp letters might suggest. In late June he met with Casey and Moodie. Once more Casey pleaded that 'public criticism of the Colombo Plan would militate against our national interest'.[108] White reiterated the major themes of his extensive report, clearly describing the waste and inept management (from both Asian and Australian officers) he had seen while on tour. Yet he also said he wanted to see the plan continue on a more effective and efficient basis. His subsequent articles, such as 'Colombo Plan has been partly successful' and 'Colombo Plan "waste" unavoidable', were, he thought, constructive compromises intended to bolster the program rather than scuttle it in favour of a more censorious headline.[109]

In 1960, the DEA published White's booklet, *The seed of freedom: Australia and the Colombo Plan*, the title having been adapted from President Dwight D. Eisenhower's evocative speech about the 'seeds of conflict' to the 1958 meeting of the Consultative Committee in Seattle. Government printers produced a staggering 50,000 copies for the first edition in Australia, with an additional 20,000 sent to Colombo Plan nations throughout Asia.[110] In July 1961, a further 30,000 copies were printed.[111] It might not have been a bestseller, but it was a significant free publication distributed by diplomatic posts. The culmination of the Australian government's attempt to extract the maximum amount of publicity material from the work submitted by White and Fitzpatrick was a 30-minute documentary entitled *The Builders*, produced by the Australian Commonwealth Film Unit and released in late 1959.[112] The film was an important example of the DEA's attempt to manufacture an image of Asia under the Colombo Plan that would resonate with Australian and Asian audiences. The DEA oversaw the production of *The Builders* but granted White considerable discretion over the script and basic storyline. Although the Australian Commonwealth Film Unit had already produced films on Colombo Plan students, such as *Our Neighbour Australia*, *The Builders* came to be something of a flagship public relations document on Australia's relations with Asia.[113] Its significance, for the government at least, was enhanced by the fact that it was a product of a broad set of guidelines governing the content and style of official audio-visual representations of Australia and Asia.

In the mid-1950s senior bureaucrats determined that the objectives of this media policy were to improve Australian relations with other nations, explain national policies, assist in counteracting 'Russia's ... politico-economic drive', help to expand trade and commercial relations, and provide Australian representatives abroad with readily accessible information describing Australia's position on international issues. Specifically, the DEA said films should be of excellent quality (to ensure maximum commercial distribution), avoid the 'squalid aspects of Australian life', and avoid patronising language and slang expressions. Nor were they to encourage Asians to adopt Australian customs. The government hoped that such films would convey the themes of the 'strength and virility' of Australia, the lack of racial discrimination, the importance of private enterprise, the harshness of the Australian environment and its lack of arable land, the need for cooperative efforts in the Asian region, the 'dignity of labour', and the message that 'Asian countries could also develop to [Australia's] stage'. Where possible, 'the pomp and circumstance of official occasions should be included, since Asians liked this'. The DEA distributed *The Builders* to Asian posts for dubbing into local languages and screening in commercial movie houses and mobile cinemas provided under the Colombo Plan. In Asia, it received a limited, but generally positive, reception. In Australia, commercial television stations and the ABC broadcast the documentary between 1960 and 1961.[114]

Immediately after the film's release, concern among some Australian diplomats began to trickle back to the DEA. Lionel Wigmore, Australian High Commissioner in Delhi, complained to Murphy of the ANIB that the documentary made little reference to India and paid particular attention to Colombo Plan projects in Pakistan. 'Indians are quick to notice any such disparity', he warned. He then asked if it was possible to provide an alternative version with a greater emphasis on India.[115] But pandering to Asian sensitivities had its limits. The ANIB's John Murray quipped:

> *Imagine the situation if, at some Colombo Plan Conference, an enthusiastic Indian delegate recommended that the Conference should see the very fine film Australia had made about the Colombo Plan … and the meeting agreed to have a screening. If the Conference was being held in Kuala Lumpur, the film would be provided by our Malayan friends — the version that was made to please the Malayans! (Crowd noise — exeunt all!)*

Avoidance proved the better course. Murray suggested that Wigmore return the print to Australia lest 'some curious person might whiz it away for screening to the very people you do not want to see it'. While *The Builders* had served its purpose in Asia, he was confident that it would be 'useful for a long time yet in Australian schools'.[116] His comment was apt because the documentary and the story of how it was created said far more about Australia and its attempts to grapple with its place in the region than it did about the collection of nations they called Asia.

———————

The long-term developmental programs created under the auspices of the Colombo Plan were only going to yield benefits for Australia's security in subtle, ill-defined and inconclusive ways: perhaps more subtle than Casey and the Cold War Planning Committee may have wished. However, the fundamental rationale of the influential 1952 report into the United Kingdom Overseas Information Service still held sway in Australia into the 1960s. Its principal conclusion was that seemingly inconsequential programs and decisions were likely to have consequences far beyond their size: 'the effect of propaganda on the course of events is never likely to be more than marginal. But in certain circumstances it may be decisive in tipping the balance between diplomatic success and failure'.[117] The battle for the mind of Asia was a close contest. A small effort could tip the balance, by influencing a parliamentary committee, or helping to deliver a single vote that might sway a decision in Australia's favour. Dudley-Clark made this very point to Casey in 1956 when he said success in the Cold War could only come 'out of a long and patient effort in a hundred minor gains ... it must inevitably be a war of attrition'.[118] The impact would be almost impossible to quantify and governments could make only the most subjective and tentative assessments about the effect of these programs. In official circles, the Cold War was conceived of as a mental battle as much as a strictly political and economic one — a Manichean contest that simply had to be won. Casey saw the battle for hearts and minds as a most serious one, where an Australian propaganda campaign, orchestrated under the rubric of the Colombo Plan, could play a pivotal role.

Towards the end of the 1950s, the Australian government convinced itself that the Colombo Plan, in association with other aid programs, had retarded the effectiveness of communist insurgents. The 1959 ANZUS communiqué 'noted the growing awareness on the part of Asian countries of the threat posed to life and liberty by Communist imperialism'. Ministers believed that economic and social progress would continue to render 'Communist political subversion and sabotage in the area increasingly difficult'. But there remained an ever increasing 'need for other free countries to devote a large share of their resources through … channels such as the Colombo Plan, for technical and economic development assistance to countries of the area'.[119] The fading boundary between non-military and military-aid — although it was always a problematic distinction — continued into the 1960s. With Australia on the brink of armed commitment to Vietnam, the role of the Colombo Plan as a support program for more tangible military goals became even more pronounced. In May 1960, the Acting Minister for External Affairs, Garfield Barwick, authorised a shipment of battery-operated transistor radios to South–East Asian countries, including South Vietnam, Laos, and Thailand. Unlike the shipment of transmitters made in the mid-1950s, the government publicised this gift. A great problem for the governments of South–East Asia, Barwick said publicly, was 'how best to dispel ignorance and to counter false rumours and propaganda'. Australia's donation would 'assist in the dissemination of information and teaching to school children and villages in remote areas'.[120] Early in 1964, Australia provided 15 railway carriages to the South Vietnamese government under the Colombo Plan, ostensibly because they would play a role in economic and commercial development. But as Hasluck explained to Cabinet, from a 'strategic point of view' the gift was important for 'the carriage of troops, equipment and military supplies' between Saigon and the northern provinces.[121]

The DEA began to develop a more critical appreciation of the problems facing the execution of Australian foreign policy, yet the department's attitude and approach to propaganda in South–East Asia remained essentially unchanged from the early-1950s. Considering the pervasive fear of communist aggression and the primacy of the Menzies Government's defence imperatives, it seemed almost inevitable that the government would use the Colombo Plan to implement paramilitary and counter-subversion operations. In 1961, the Information Branch of the DEA produced an analysis of Australia's propaganda activities in South–East Asia. Among other things, the report reflected on the politicisation of Australian foreign policy. Specifically, it contended that 'the Cold War now extends into nearly every nook and cranny of information activity ... The Cold War has limited our capacity for self-expression and this is a handicap which has to be accepted in information activity as in other fields'.[122] The response is understandable, given the international and domestic contexts in which these decisions were made. However, it narrowed Australia's perception of what was possible in its engagement with Asia. Casey worked assiduously to develop a workable propaganda strategy, drawing on expertise from across the public service and abroad. The results of the planning committee he created are difficult to quantify, but more importantly, we can see where the dictates of the Cold War, combined with a rudimentary understanding of Asia and its people, circumscribed the department's imagination and language. This process dominated the department's concept of engagement throughout the decade and would continue to do so for another. That the Cold War ethic was considered a *fait accompli* also encapsulates the reactionary nature of the department's strategy. Naturally, the Colombo Plan and its associated programs, as key features of Australia's involvement in the region, were inexorably caught up in this environment.

The Colombo Plan embodied the growing tension between a coercive intervention, oriented toward short-term objectives, and a constructive, less prescriptive form of engagement. On one hand, it reaffirmed Australian nationalist sentiment, summed up by the widely voiced idea that the Colombo Plan offered a chance 'to show them [Asians] that, in our way of life, there is something worthwhile'.[123] Yet it also cast stronger light on Australian isolationism and forced policy-makers to re-examine other policies. From deep inside the bureaucracy, a tentative shift in regional awareness began to take a more influential form. When contemplating the political objectives of the Colombo Plan, Arthur Tange reflected that it was the white Australia policy and a 'history of isolation' that had led to a 'wealth of misunderstanding' between Asia and Australia. And although he thought irreconcilable differences on complex international issues were likely to remain, the Colombo Plan had allowed Asians and Australians to 'mix together in a way which [had] not been otherwise practicable'.[124] In its most defensive guise, the Colombo Plan aimed to relieve the anxieties associated with living next to Asia, to stimulate resistance to communist subversion, and to reinforce the boundaries between Australia and the region.

Yet the cultural interaction promised by the Colombo Plan was set to challenge and transgress the very barriers the government thought the program would maintain.

Footnotes

1   T.B. Millar, ed., *Australian foreign minister: the diaries of R.G. Casey 1951–60*, London, Collins, 1972, p. 82; R.G. Casey diaries, 28 July 1954, vol. 16, box 27, MS 6150, NLA

2   Letter, Casey to Crocker, New Delhi, 25 March 1953, A10299, C13, NAA; G. Woodard, 'Ministers and mandarins: the relationship between Ministers and Secretaries of External Affairs 1935–1970', *Australian Journal of International Affairs*, vol. 54, no. 1, 2000, p. 87

3   W.J. Hudson, *Casey*, Melbourne, Oxford University Press, 1986, p. 288; Casey diaries, 28 July 1954, vol. 16, box 27, MS 6150, NLA

4   Memo, Casey to Menzies, 18 August 1954, A462/5, 610/8/1, NAA

5   'Cold War – outline notes – working paper', 23 September 1955, A7452, A359, NAA

6   A.P. Fleming, 'Conference on Cold War planning, Department of External Affairs, 20 December 1954, A7936, B/4/2 part 1, NAA; Cable, DEA to Washington, 13 January 1955, A1838, 156/1/1, NAA

7   Fleming, 'Conference on Cold War planning'

8   Cabinet Minute, no. 262, 7 January 1955, A4940, C1147, NAA

9   Casey, Cabinet Submission 241, 'Australian activities in the Cold War', A4940, C1147, NAA

10 Casey to Tange, 10 January 1955, A10299, A21, NAA

11 Casey to Tange, 10 January 1955

12 Draft letter, Casey to Pearson, *circa* January 1955, A1838, TS383/1/1/1 part 1, NAA

13 Cable, Tange to Hood, 13 January 1955, A10299, A21, NAA

14 *Herald* (Melbourne), 26 February 1955

15 Cable, Tange to Plimsoll and Casey, 26 February 1955, A1838, TS383/1/1/1 part 1, NAA

16 Letter, Casey to Brookes, 17 January 1955, A10299, A21, NAA

17 R.G. Casey diaries, 10 February 1956, vol. 20, box 28, MS 6150, NLA

18 Memo, J.M. Starey to Tange, 'Relations with communist countries', 21 December 1957, A1838, 160/11/3, NAA; Memo, Starey to Tange, 'Relations with communist countries', 18 January 1958, A1838, 160/11/3, NAA

19 'Communist economic penetration in Ceylon: report for quarter ending 31 December 1958', A1838, 160/11/3, NAA

20 'Communist economic penetration in Ceylon: report for quarter ending 30 June 1958', A1838, 160/11/3, NAA

21 Minute, J.O. Rennie, 'Combating communist propaganda', 19 December 1955, FO 953-1636, PRO, UK

22 R.G. Casey diaries, 8, 13, 21 December 1955, vol. 19, box 28, MS 6150, NLA

23 See Dudley-Clark's report, A7133/5, 22, NAA

24 Letter, Casey to Tange, 3 January 1956, A7133, 22, NAA

25 B. Toohey & W. Pinwill, *Oyster: The story of the Australian Secret Intelligence Service*, Melbourne, William Heinemann Australia, 1989, pp. 73–74

26 Letter, Casey to Jamieson, 10 January 1955, A1838, TS 383/1/1/1 part 1, NAA

27 Letter, Casey to L.R. McIntyre, 10 January 1955, A1838, TS 383/1/1/1 part 1, NAA

28 J. Smith, *Portrait of a cold warrior*, New York, Putnam, 1976, pp. 234–38

29 R. Ellis should not be confused with Charles Howard 'Dick' Ellis, also of ASIS, who was suspected of being a German and then a Soviet double agent during the Petrov Affair. See, R. Manne, *The Petrov affair: politics and espionage*, Sydney, Pergamon, 1987, pp. 228–29

30 'Cold War – outline notes – working paper', 23 September 1955, A7452, A359, NAA

31 'Cold War – outline notes – working paper'

32 'Cold War – outline notes – working paper'

33 'Meeting of the Cold War Planning Committee', 6 April 1955, A1838, 383/1/1/1 part 2, NAA

34 Letter, P.H. Gore Booth, Rangoon to P.F. Grey, London, 13 September 1956, FO 953/1638, PRO, UK

35 Memo, Shaw to Casey, 23 July 1954, A1838, 2020/6/5 part 1, NAA

36 *Ceylon Daily Mirror*, 30 October 1963

37 Letter, D. Lascelles, Kabul to W.J.M. Paterson, South East Asia Department, Foreign Office, 12 October 1954, FO 371/111908, PRO, UK

38 'Cold War – outline notes – working paper'

39 Memo, Oldham to Tange, 20 December 1954, A10299, A21, NAA

40 W. Macmahon Ball, *Nationalism and communism in East Asia*, Melbourne, Melbourne University Press, 1952, pp. 190–205

41 'Cold War – outline notes – working paper'

42 John Hood, 'Police training for Asian nationals in Australia', undated (*circa* June 1954), A1838, 3004/11 part 2, NAA

43 Memo, 'Colombo Plan – training for Pakistan police officers', A10299, C13, NAA; Letter, Plimsoll to Beavis, High Commissioner in Pakistan, 15 September 1953, A10299, C13, NAA

44 Memo, Plimsoll to Watt, 18 February 1955, A1838, TS 383/1/1/1 part 1, NAA

45 Memo, Casey to Plimsoll, 19 January 1955, A10299, A21, NAA

46 'Overseas Planning Committee: summary record of meeting, 10 October 1955', A7936, B/4/2 part 1, NAA. Police Training also took place in South Australia. See, for example, Letter, H.C. Avent, Secretary, Public Service Board of South Australia to Secretary, South Australian Police, Office of the Commissioner, 20 August & 13 December 1956, GRG 37/1/1951/68, SRSA

47 'Overseas Planning Committee: summary record of meeting, 10 October 1955'
48 Cable, DEA to Australian Legation, Phnom Penh, 27 August 1956, A1838, 688/9/4, NAA
49 Cable, Australia Legation, Saigon to DEA, 13 August 1955, A1838, 688/9/2, NAA; Letter, Landale to Attorney-General's Department, 21 December 1955, A1838, 688/9/2, NAA
50 Memo, Loveday to Booker, 24 August 1956, A1838, 688/9/4, NAA
51 Australian News and Information Bureau, *Australia in facts and figures*, various issues, 1955–1965
52 See, for example, 'Overseas Planning Committee: summary record of meeting at Department of External Affairs, Friday, September 23, 1955', A7452, A359, NAA; *Herald* (Melbourne), 26 February 1955
53 Fleming, 'Conference on Cold War planning'
54 'Overseas Planning Committee: summary record of meeting at Department of External Affairs, Friday, September 23, 1955', A7452, A359, NAA
55 Memo, Oldham to Tange, 20 December 1954, A10299, A21, NAA; James Wood, *History of international broadcasting*, London, Peter Peregrinus, 1992, pp. 162–67; 'Meeting of the Cold War Planning Committee', transcript, 6 April 1955, A1838, 383/1/1/1 part 2, NAA; 'Special Planning Committee (South and South East Asia) review of activities', 2 September 1955, A1838, 383/1/1/1 part 2, NAA
56 Letter, Spender to Boyer, 9 May 1950, Boyer papers, MS 3181/2/15, NLA
57 Casey, Cabinet submission 241, 'Australian activities in the Cold War', A4940, C1147, NAA
58 Casey to Tange, 10 January 1955, A10299, A21, NAA
59 E. Hodge, *Radio wars: truth, propaganda and the struggle for Radio Australia*, Melbourne, Cambridge University Press, 1995. See also K. Inglis, *This is the ABC: the Australian Broadcasting Commission 1932–1983*, Melbourne, Melbourne University Press, 1983, pp. 156–58, and C. Jones, *Something in the air: a history of radio in Australia*, Kenthurst, Kangaroo Press, 1995, pp. 53, 83
60 Hodge, *Radio wars*, p. 67
61 Letter, Shaw to Heffer, 5 April 1955, A1838, 383/1/1/1 part 2, NAA
62 R.G. Casey diaries, 14 February 1955, MS 6150, NLA
63 Australian News and Information Bureau, *Australia in facts and figures*, no. 48, December 1955, pp. 37–38; Australian News and Information Bureau, *Australia in facts and figures*, no. 84, December 1964, pp. 67–69
64 Memo, Vawdrey to Tange, 12 May 1955, A11604, 704/1, NAA
65 Memo, Australian Delegation, Seoul to Tange, 24 September 1954, A1838, 3004/12/5 part 1, NAA
66 'Overseas Planning Committee: summary record of meeting at Department of External Affairs, Friday, September 23, 1955'
67 Inglis, *This is the ABC*, p. 157; 'Meeting of the Cold War Planning Committee'
68 R.G. Casey, *The future of the Commonwealth*, London, Fredrick Muller Limited, 1963, pp. 132–34; Memo, Casey to Brookes, 8 August 1955, A10299, A18, NAA; Memo, Oldham to Quinn, 2 February 1955, A10299,

A21, NAA; Memo, Casey to Brookes, 8 August 1955, A10299, A18, NAA; Memo, 'Visit to Australia by Indian editors', 18 June 1957, A1838, 3004/11/33 part 2, NAA

69 C. Waters, 'A failure of imagination: R.G. Casey and Australian plans for counter-subversion in Asia, 1954–56', *Australian Journal of Politics and History*, vol. 45, no. 3, 1999, pp. 347–61

70 Circular memorandum, L.J. Arnott to various, 29 October 1957, A1838, 563/6/2 part 2, NAA

71 'Special Planning Committee (South and South East Asia) review of activities: top secret: repeal', 2 September 1955, A7452, A359, NAA

72 'Overseas Planning Committee, 27 May 1955', 7452, A359, NAA; J.W.C. Cumes, 'Meeting of the advisory committee on *Hemisphere*: 3 October 1958', 10 October 1958, A1838, 563/6/2 part 3, NAA

73 O.L. Davis, for Secretary, DEA, to J. Weeden, Director, Commonwealth Office of Education, 10 October 1958, A1838, 563/6/2 part 1, NAA

74 See file A1361, 50/2/4 part 1a, NAA

75 See file A1838, 563/6/2 part 7, NAA

76 Note, D.W. Hood, 15 February 1961, A1361, 50/9/1 part 3, NAA

77 *Herald* (Melbourne), 27 April 1956; *Sydney Morning Herald*, 29 June 1956

78 R.G. Casey diaries, 8 October 1955, vol. 19, box 28, MS 6150, NLA

79 Letter, Casey to Holt, 14 August 1959, A1838, 563/6/5, NAA

80 Letter, Casey to Holt, 14 August 1959, A1838, 563/6/5, NAA

81 Letter, A.M. Morris the Secretary, Prime Minister's Department, 30 November 1960, A1209, 1960/1048, NAA

82 H. Marshall, *Ignorance to enlightenment: fifty years in Asia: Australians in Asia series, no. 18*, Brisbane, Griffith University, Centre for Australian–Asia Relations, 1997, pp. 5–8; Memo, Casey to Heydon, 12 May 1959, A1838, 563/6/5, NAA

83 Letter, Casey to Holt, 14 August 1959, A1838, 563/6/5, NAA

84 Casey, 'Goodwill contacts with Asian countries': draft Cabinet submission, undated, *circa* 1956, A1838, 3004/11/33, NAA; 'Australian overseas publicity', January 1955, A1838, TS677/7, NAA

85 Note, Casey to Tange, 11 November 1954, A10302, 1956/170, NAA

86 D. Dexter to A. Tange, 23 August 1957, A1838, 2047/1, NAA; H. Marshall to Loomes, 12 August 1957, A4529, 65/1/2/1955 part 1, NAA

87 Minute, 'Asian visits fund', August 1956, A1838, 3004/11/33, NAA; Minute, 'Asian visits fund', 29 May 1956, A1838, 3004/11/33, NAA; Casey, 'Goodwill contacts with Asian countries'; Cabinet minute, 'Submission 222', 16 June 1964, A4940, C3265, NAA; on visitors to Cambodia, see file A1209, 1960/925, NAA

88 Letter, Borthwick, Singapore to Tange, 19 May 1956, A1838, 3004/11/33, NAA

89 'Sport as a means of contact with Asian countries', 17 May 1956, A1838, 3004/11 part 4, NAA

90 Memo, Moodie, Rangoon to DEA, 12 February 1955, A1838, TS383/1/1/1 part 1, NAA

91   'Sport as a means of contact with Asian Countries'
92   A. Tange, *Monologue: recording of a personal narrative made in February and August 1989 intended as a supplement to the 1989 interview with J.D.B. Miller*, TRC 2447, Oral History Collection, NLA
93   Crocker diaries, 10 May 1956, MS G20735, p. 535, NLA
94   Crocker diaries, 17 October 1955, MS G20735, pp. 754–55, NLA; Walter Crocker, interview with author, 28 August 2001, Adelaide
95   Letter, Casey to Tange, 9 July 1956, A10302, 1956/170, NAA; Editorial, 'Menace lurking in Colombo Plan', *Daily Mirror*, 21 August 1953
96   See, for example, Letter, Anonymous to Casey, 13 June 1956, A10302, 1956/170, NAA
97   Telegram, Donald Born, United States Embassy, Canberra to Department of State, Washington, 20 May 1958, RG 59, 890.00/5-2058, USNA; Memo, D.O. Hay to Casey, 21 February 1958, A10302, 1958/170, NAA
98   Casey diaries, 11 July 1958, MS 6150, vol. 23, box 29, NLA; Memo, Moodie to Dexter, 7 May 1958, A1838, 2048/2 part 7, NAA
99   Letter, Moodie to Secretary, Treasury Department, 27 August 1959, A6895, N58/164, NAA; Letter, Moodie to Gorton, 30 March 1960, A1838, 2020/1/2 part 3, NAA
100 P. Torney-Parlicki, *Somewhere in Asia: war, journalism, and Australia's neighbours 1941–75*, Sydney, University of New South Wales Press, 2000, p. 117; Sally White (daughter of Osmar), pers. comm., 2 September 2001; Letter, White to Moodie, 16 September 1958, OWP; Letter, Moodie to White, 23 September 1958, OWP
101 Letter, White to Jack Waters, Managing Director of the *Herald and Weekly Times*, 28 September 1958, OWP; Letter, Arthur Smith, DEA Welfare and Liaison Officer to White, 28 November 1958, OWP; Letter, White to Mollie White (MW), 3 January 1959, OWP
102 Letter, White, Karachi to MW, 18 December 1959, OWP; Letter, White to MW, 3 January 1959, OWP
103 Cable, White to Moodie, 14 January 1959, OWP
104 Crocker Diaries, 19 & 27 January 1959, MS G20737, p. 1752, NLA; Cable, White to Casey, 23 January 1959, OWP; 'Foreign Affairs Committee: notes on discussion with Mr. Osmar White', 2 July 1959, OWP; Cable, White to Furlonger, 21 Jan 1959, OWP
105 Cable, Casey to White, 28 January 1959, OWP; Casey diaries, 30 January 1959, MS 6150, vol. 24, box 30, NLA; Cable, White to Casey, 29 January 1959, OWP; Cable, Casey to White, 11 February 1959, OWP; Cable, White to Edwards, 30 March 1959, OWP; Crocker diaries, 11 July 1959, MS G20737, NLA
106 Australian News and Information Bureau, *Australia in facts and figures*, various issues, 1950–1970; Cable, Casey to White, Saigon, 25 February 1959, OWP; Cable, White, Rangoon to Murphy, 27 February 1959, OWP

107 Cable, Edwards to White, 16 March 1959, OWP; Cable, White to Edwards, 30 March 1959, OWP

108 Letter, Murphy, ANIB to White, Rangoon, 10 March 1959, A6895, N58/134 part 2, NAA; Letter, White, Rangoon to MW, 27 March 1959, OWP; Cable, White to Edwards, 30 March 1959, OWP; Casey diaries, 23 June 1959, vol. 24, box 30, MS6150, NLA

109 *Herald* (Melbourne), 15 September 1959; *Herald* (Melbourne), 16 September 1959. For other articles by White, see: *Sun* (Sydney), 3 February 1959; *Herald* (Melbourne), 4 February 1959; *Daily Telegraph*, 2 March 1959; *Herald* (Melbourne), 26 February 1959; *Sydney Morning Herald*, 5 March 1959; *Daily Telegraph*, 9 March 1959; *Canberra Times*, 9 February 1959

110 O. White, *The seed of freedom: Australia and the Colombo Plan*, Canberra, Department of External Affairs, News and Information Bureau, 1960; Letter, Moodie to White, 13 January 1960, A6895, N58/134 part 2, NAA

111 Letter, Brady, DEA to Hills, Government Printing Office, 23 July 1961, A6895, N58/164, NAA

112 Australian Commonwealth Film Unit (ACFU), *The Builders*, Canberra: Department of the Interior, 1959, Screen Sound (SS), Canberra

113 Department of the Interior, *Report for Colombo*, 1952, Canberra, SS; Movietone News, *Australian Experts Teach Asians Food Science*, 1954, SS

114 'Record of discussion on films policy', 10 February, 1956, A1838, 156/1/1, NAA; 'Australian overseas publicity', January 1955, A1838, TS677/7, NAA; *New Light of Burma*, May 14, 1960; *The Reporter* (Burma), 14 May 1960; Letter, Murphy to Moodie, 18 March 1960, A6895, N58/165 part 2, NAA; Letter, Murphy to Moodie, 15 February 1960, A6895, N58/165 part 2, NAA; Letter, John Edwards, Tasmanian Television Limited, to Murphy, 3 July 1961, A6895, N58/165 part 2, NAA

115 Lionel Wigmore, New Delhi to Kevin Murphy, 12 May 1960, A6895, N58/165 part 2, NAA

116 John Murray to Lionel Wigmore, 14 September 1960, A6895, N58/165 part 2, NAA

117 'Australian overseas publicity', January 1955, A1838, TS677/7, NAA

118 Letter, Dudley-Clark to Casey, 5 January 1956, A7133, 22, NAA

119 *Current notes on international affairs*, vol. 30, no. 10, October 1959, p. 578

120 *Current notes on international affairs*, vol. 31, no. 5, May 1960, p. 231

121 Cabinet submission 454, P. Hasluck, 2 October 1964, A5827, vol. 14, NAA; Cable, L.A. Crozier to Tange, Canberra, 14 May 1962, B300, 9268/4, NAA, South Australia

122 'Australian information policy in South East Asia', 16 August 1961, A1838, TS696/1/2 part 3, NAA

123 *CPD (HoR)*, vol. 207, 9 May 1950, p. 2256

124 A. Tange, 'Political objectives of the Colombo Plan – working paper', 19 March 1952, A1838, 3004/11 part 1, NAA

6. FACE TO FACE WITH ASIA

In 1953, a group of recently-arrived Indonesian Colombo Plan scholars waited for a tram to take them into central Sydney. Among them was Sumadi, later to become a senior official in the Indonesian Department of Information: 'Everybody looked at us, everybody stared. We all joked among ourselves, "No matter how much we dress up we still [felt like we were at] Taronga Zoo ... they consider us the orang-utan." Everybody always stare ... and we felt there must be something wrong with us. Then we realised that maybe because at that time not many Australians have ever come face to face with Asian students'.[1] The arrival of Colombo Plan students was one of the most striking and conspicuous manifestations of Australia's foreign policy and the most tangible aspect of Australia's program of international aid. Privately-funded scholars from Asia outnumbered sponsored students by five to one, but such was the publicity afforded to the Colombo Plan that when Australians saw any Asian student they invariably assumed they were sponsored under the program, thus artificially magnifying the scheme's impact. While the Department of External Affairs (DEA) spent more on large-scale infrastructure projects, the scholarship scheme had an immediate effect on the lives of many Australians and a lasting impact on Australia's social and political landscape.

The influx of private and government-sponsored students from Asia in the 1950s coincided with the arrival of over 1,000,000 immigrants, mainly from Britain and Europe. While mass migration made Australia more culturally diverse, that diversity did not include Asia. In 1954, just 0.4 per cent of the population was born in South or South–East Asia, only marginally higher than in 1933. By 1961, the figure had increased only slightly, with fewer than 60,000 Asians living in Australia, representing 0.6 per cent of the population. Between 1951 and 1965, Australia hosted nearly 5,500 students and trainees, 16 per cent of the 33,000 places offered by all donor nations contributing to the Colombo Plan. Australia's Colombo Plan scholars came from 15 nations across Asia; three-quarters came from Malaya, Indonesia, India, Pakistan, and Ceylon, while smaller numbers came from Burma, Brunei, Cambodia, Korea, and Afghanistan.[2] The expansion of the Colombo Plan program corresponded with a dramatic shift in the destinations of private Asian students. By 1965 around 5 per cent of the student body were international scholars — with most coming from South–East Asia. Somewhat shocked by the shift way from Britain and America, the DEA thought that 'something of a revolution' was taking place.[3] The rising importance of the Colombo Plan student program corresponded with a declining faith in the ability of large-scale infrastructure projects to deliver benefits for Australia. Within five years of the inception of the Colombo Plan, the DEA became increasingly worried by negative reports about Australian-funded capital projects. In part, government officials blamed recipient nations for their lack of planning and management, but Australian procedures were also at fault. The DEA's experienced Assistant Secretary, John Keith Waller, told Casey that Australian administration had been 'ill-considered … cumbersome and slow'.[4] By contrast, the scholarship program was something of an unexpected success. Australia's High Commissioner to India, Walter Crocker, who usually cautioned his Canberra superiors against expecting gratitude or benefit from foreign aid, was uncharacteristically positive when it came to the scholarship program. In 1953 he reported to Alan Watt, Secretary of the DEA, that 'the best publicity we have received so far has been from students who have been studying in Australia. In fact I am inclined to feel that the only political value which Australia has got out of its Colombo Plan efforts has been from the students'.[5] The early success of the program was even more surprising because the government had neglected to anticipate the basic needs of overseas students or the problems they might encounter. The cavalier embrace of Asian students was the same in Britain. The goal, reasoned the Foreign Office, was simply to get as many Asian students into the country as possible; it mattered 'much less what they do when they arrive … as long as they do not waste their time'.[6] Nevertheless, Asian delegates attending the Colombo Plan Consultative Committee meetings expressed high regard for Australian training, overwhelming Australian representatives with nominations. Cabinet needed little encouragement to trim some of the Colombo Plan's more profligate capital enterprises. In order to minimise waste, reduce demand on scarce primary materials, and capitalise on the goodwill stimulated by the training scheme, Cabinet insisted on diverting funds from the capital aid program. Over the next ten years, the proportion of aid devoted to education, training and the supply of equipment increased steadily, from 22 per cent in 1954/55 to 46 per cent in 1963/64. By 1970, the government split the Colombo Plan budget equally between capital aid projects and technical assistance.[7]

Australia's scholarship scheme focused on giving Asians skills they could pass on to others once they returned home. Students studied a broad range of subjects, including agricultural production, animal husbandry, fruit culture, textiles, wool technology, food preparation, mining, road construction, civil aviation, railway administration and technology, education, industrial welfare, social services, nursing, public administration, sewerage construction, and water conservation. Courses in science, engineering, health, and education were by far the most popular, with more than 70 per cent of trainees (1,400) taking degrees in these field by the late-1950s. By the mid-1960s, the number of students acquiring these skills had increased to more than 4,000, but as a proportion of the total number of scholars, it had dropped to 60 per cent. This change did not represent a fundamental shift in attitude or policy; rather it was a consequence of the increasingly diverse number of courses made available, largely in response to requests from recipient nations. Notable growth took place in the numbers of students studying agriculture, industrial production, mining and mineral research, police and legal training, wireless operation and maintenance, journalism, film production and broadcasting. Under pressure to expand the reach of Australian training, the DEA launched a Colombo Plan correspondence scheme in 1955. By June 1961, nearly 1,000 students had completed a correspondence course and more than 1,800 students were then receiving training under the program.[8]

The basic political and cultural imperatives served by the Colombo Plan scholarship program remained largely unchanged during the 1950s and 1960s. In January 1962, Arthur Tange, Secretary of the DEA, submitted a statement on the demand for tertiary courses from foreign countries to Leslie Martin, Chairman of the Australian Universities Commission. He predicted that Australia was likely to continue to grow as a preferred destination for overseas students in the Asia–Pacific region and explained that the Colombo Plan education program 'incidentally' fulfilled political and cultural objectives. First, it was a practical demonstration of Australia's intention to assist 'countries geographically near us from which Australia has been cut off culturally until the last 15 years'.[9] Secondly, students who had lived and studied under the program were generating goodwill and prestige for Australia. As one official put it, returning students had 'something of a snowball effect' as they took up positions of influence.[10] At the heart of Australian management of the Colombo Plan student program, however, was a concern to minimise the negative impact of the white Australia policy. 'Questions of race and colour play a large part in determining the attitudes of the Asian and African States to many significant international problems', the DEA explained to the Committee on the Future of Tertiary Education in Australia in 1962:

> In these circumstances Australian aid programmes like the Colombo Plan ... which gain wide and favourable attention are a valuable testimony to

the absence of racial prejudice in our foreign policies. The presence of Asian and African students in Australia and their experience of the tolerance and friendliness of the Australian people are an effective counter to the charges of racial discrimination which are sometimes levelled against us.[11]

The number of Colombo Plan scholarships on offer rose from 434 in 1959 to 656 in 1965. Despite the steady rise, demand for scholarships always outpaced supply. As numbers of international students increased, naturally so did the pressure on universities to accept them. The principal of Melbourne High School, George Langley, crystallised a fundamental government concern when he told Menzies about the 'international aspect' of the failure of some Asian scholars to find places at Melbourne University's medical course owing to restrictions on the number of places available to foreigners. Langley suggested that, considering the prominent role 'played by Australia in the launching and implementation of the Colombo Plan', it was logical for the Commonwealth to fund the expansion of medical education. 'Panic' among overseas students, he warned, 'might lead to ill considered letters home and poor publicity'.[12]

During the first few years of the program, the DEA struggled to integrate the rising numbers of Colombo Plan — and private overseas — students into the academic and social community — sometimes with tragic consequences. Between 1950 and 1951, three Asian students studying at the University of Western Australia committed suicide and another suffered a mental breakdown, all ostensibly suffering from social isolation. The neglect of the growing student body had the potential to jeopardise the guiding

maxim of the student program — namely, the idea that
the students' exposure to Australian culture should be a
positive experience. Casey raised his concerns with Menzies
as early as July 1951: 'My department has for some time
been concerned that accommodation difficulties, problems
of orientation and a good deal of ordinary loneliness may
not only lead to occasional instances of personal tragedy,
but also leave the way open to Communist influences'.[13]
Douglas Wilkie, journalist and ex–war correspondent,
wrote publicly of the risk to Australia's foreign policy
objectives of failing to provide adequate housing. It was, he
said, 'anomalous to bring Asian students here and then force
them to live in drab boarding-houses or in isolated
communities because we could not "afford" an International
House'.[14] Ian Clunies-Ross, chairman of CSIRO, exploited
Casey's preoccupation with shielding students from
communism, when he asked that Colombo Plan funds be
applied to the construction of a hostel for international
students. He also suggested that by closely integrating
Asians and Australians, the government would escape any
allegation that it supported racial segregation. The opening
of International House in Melbourne in 1957 (built with
the help of £A50,000 of Colombo Plan finance) certainly
suggested a new-found consciousness of Asia, yet it also
reflected the anxiety and defensiveness that underpinned
that awareness. Non-government groups moved much
faster to fill the growing demand. Keen to awaken the
churches' obligations to international education, Anglican
Archbishop Howard Mowll moved to create a hostel for
overseas students immediately after the establishment of
the Colombo Plan. Through his work, the International
Friendship Centre officially opened in the Sydney suburb of
Drummoyne in 1952, initially housing 19 men, including
two Colombo Plan students.[15]

The abstract benefits generated by the Colombo Plan did not allay fears that students were a threat to Australia's social and political fabric. During the early years government officials and the media tended to typecast Asian students as potential spies or vulnerable innocents, open to communist blandishments. In federal parliament, one member believed that Colombo Plan scholars might come into contact with 'undesirable elements in our community ... we may be sending back rabid Communists to the South East Asian countries ... I am not ashamed to say that we should also attempt to bring some moral influence to bear on these students'. Lawrence Arnott, who headed the DEA's Economic and Technical Assistance Branch between 1952 and 1956, warned Casey in 1951 that if the government did not protect students from subversive forces, they risked 'nullifying [their] efforts under the Technical Assistance Programme'. The *Daily Mirror* wondered if Colombo Plan students were travelling the countryside taking pictures of airports, army camps, and defence installations, and asked readers to remember the 'bowing Japanese students and businessmen' who had come to Australia before the war. That the Petrov inquiry in 1954 named a Colombo Plan student as a left-wing activist fuelled such perceptions. The DEA even denied a request for financial assistance from the student-oriented East–West Committee to stage an exhibition of Asian culture because ASIO investigators suspected that communists would use the occasion to distribute propaganda.[16]

The government's concerns, while understandable, were largely unfounded. In response to a request from the Malayan government, that the Malayan Students' Association and Colombo Plan trainees were falling under the influence of Australian communists, ASIO reported that although the association was left-wing and nationalist, there was little evidence to suggest a significant communist presence.[17] The anxiety expressed by conservative media about the vulnerability of Asian students was similarly misplaced. For example, the Melbourne *Sun* ran the alarmist headline 'REDS WORKING ON ASIAN STUDENTS HERE' for a story about the failure of communist groups to attract Colombo Plan students.[18] The popular Singapore-based newspaper, *Malay Mail*, reported a more common scenario: after six years studying at the University of Melbourne, 'Anthony' Ng Beh Tong said that his fellow Malayan students were completely absorbed with their studies and 'had no time for politics'. Furthermore, he said, they feared that if they dabbled with leftist politics they might not be let back into Malaya.[19]

Private industry was nervous about trainees taking back trade secrets that might be used against Australia. Secretary of the Department of Labour and National Service, Henry Bland, explained in a review of training procedures that 'fear that the knowledge gained will be used in enterprises in Asian countries which, in many cases, are direct competitors with Australian manufacturers, has led to some hesitancy in certain sections of private industry to provide training when requested'.[20] The impact of such anxiety, however, proved to be limited, with only a few Colombo Plan students being denied placements in industries where Australia competed heavily with Asia, such as leather goods, tanning and meat-processing.

Information on the academic performance of Colombo Plan students is scarce, although there is enough evidence to suggest that they performed reasonably well. Of the 309 individuals who sat for Bachelor's degrees in 1956, 206 (66.7 per cent) passed. The most successful national group was Malayan, with a 93 per cent pass rate, followed by Ceylon (86 per cent) and Singapore (74 per cent). Pass rates for post-graduate degrees were higher. As the DEA expected, students who had a greater command of English and were familiar with British-styled education systems fared better. Over the decade the implementation of an increasingly rigorous selection process and compulsory English classes helped to improve academic performance. By 1963, the overall pass rate for Colombo Plan students had risen from 71 to 79 per cent, with the pass rate for those completing the first year of a Bachelor's degree increasing to 77 per cent — higher than the equivalent statistics for Australian students.[21]

The experiences of students in Australia were private and deeply personal, and evade easy generalisation. The case of a group of Colombo Plan students studying in NSW provides an interesting example of problems faced by visitor and host alike. Twelve Burmese students studying mining technology at the NSW University of Technology experienced the ignominy of getting the worst academic results of the 1956 intake, with all of them failing their exams. Although the DEA blamed the students for their general 'attitude to the course', a closer examination of the reports reveals a more complex picture. Language difficulties appeared to be the most significant and persistent barrier to success for the Burmese students. Physics teacher, E.F. Palmer, noted that the natural shyness and 'embarrassing amount of courtesy' displayed by the students was in marked contrast to the 'brusque manners' of the Australian miners who provide practical demonstrations in the mines. Teachers and students frequently misunderstood each other, and the generally passive and withdrawn nature of the Burmese students compounded these difficulties. C. Harrison, the coal-mining instructor, noted that in some cases when 'students received little encouragement' they hid in dark recesses of the mine, avoiding miners altogether. The students — suffering from sustained exposure to Australian cuisine — escaped to the rear of the hostel on weekends to cook traditional meals on campfires by the riverbank.[22]

In addition to the cultural shock, many students faced the difficulty of living on a substantially reduced income, compared to what they might have been accustomed. Students most likely to have the education and language skills to benefit from courses in Australia were likely to come from families which, if not wealthy, at least had been free of basic wants and had a little to spare. Such students were acutely conscious of their need to scrape by and of their poverty in relation to some Australians, and appealed to their parents for funds. Reports of the inadequacy of the living allowance flowed back to the DEA. Patrick Shaw, Assistant Secretary of the Economic and Technical Assistance Branch, wrote to Casey in 1956: 'Dissatisfaction with these rates under present conditions is general and we have received copies of reports to their own Governments from trainees who have returned home, stressing the inadequacy of the living allowance we are paying'.[23] In practice, management of Colombo Plan students was reactive, and turned on considerations about the damage a disgruntled student might do on returning home. But not everyone was aware of, or sympathetic to, their plight. 'Wet-nursed' students, claimed the *Daily News*, were met on arrival, given accommodation, books, travel subsidies, and a living allowance![24] Perhaps expecting scholarship recipients to be more demure and grateful, some government officials interpreted assertiveness as greed. A Commonwealth Office of Education (COE) officer from Western Australia complained to the national director, William ('Jock') Weeden, that 'some sponsored students appear to take everything for granted, and seem to think that the Branch Office representative has nothing to do but suit their convenience in every detail'. The officer wondered whether, in its approach to the scholarship program, the department had been too eager to please. Stipends were increased, but with the allowance not intended to support a family, the DEA suggested to its Asian posts that they 'discreetly endeavour' to discourage married men and women from applying.[25]

Student experience became increasingly important, particularly when it came to fulfilling the foreign policy objective of instilling in students an appreciation of Australian mores. During the early 1950s, the administration and integration of Colombo Plan students had been a sporadic, ad hoc affair. In order to create a more flexible, 'less haphazard procedure', the DEA delegated various administrative functions to other government instrumentalities and shifted responsibilities to private community organisations.[26] Guided by the COE, the Coordinating Committee for the Welfare of Overseas Students brought together the functions of middle-class community organisations across Australia. Fortunately for the DEA and the Menzies Government, a significant base of support became active. These groups included Rotary Clubs, Apex Associations, the Asian Student Council, the YWCA, the Malayan Students' Association, the Australian–Indonesian Association, the Country Women's Association, the Thai Students' Association, and many others. Together these groups shouldered much of the burden of integrating overseas students into the wider community.

Colombo Plan scholarship holders still occupied a privileged place among the student fraternity, primarily because of the publicity attached to their presence. As Bevan Rutt, head of the University of Adelaide branch of the COE, observed, Colombo Plan scholars were so well provided for that they invariably received more invitations for holidays and other forms of hospitality than they could accept.[27] Private students, on the other hand, received less attention and were often left to their own devices. The potential neglect of the private student body prompted some university administrators to offer guidance to Australians on how to best interact with and support overseas students. The Reverend Frank Borland, Warden of the Union at the University of Adelaide and President of the Australian–Asian Association in South Australia between 1957 and 1958, sent letters to 'potential hosts' of Asian students and short booklets to those already providing accommodation, offering instructions on how to prepare their homes and how to converse with Asians. 'Their happiness and well being is greatly influenced by the hospitality they receive', he advised. 'But please do not over-mother them or smother them with attention. They like to be independent, and are able to make their own plans and decisions'.[28] Others pointed out that Asians were not that different from Australians. In 1954 C. Sanders told the audience at the Pan-Indian Ocean Science Association and British Psychological Society conference that Asian scholars enjoyed interacting with Australians, were keen to improve their language skills, and preferred to live with private families or in smaller hostels. Sanders also reminded the audience that Australians also 'suffered emotional upset' if isolated from familial support and that such feelings were not, as some were inclined to believe, peculiar to the Asian temperament.[29]

Contact with Australians, especially for those who boarded with local families, was marked by the shyness of students, and their sometimes overly polite nature. Nervous yet congenial encounters were the rule; overt racism or discrimination, the exception. In homes and hostels across the country a more intimate bond formed between Asians and Australians. Few could have guessed the impact Asian students would have on host families and the community in general. With accommodation shortages a perennial problem, the response from ostensibly middle-class families was striking. The changing sentiment towards Asian students took Meredith Worth, DEA Liaison Officer at the University of Melbourne, by surprise. Placing the first wave of Colombo Plan students in acceptable lodgings had been difficult because the 'right type of landlady' was hard to find and few were even aware of the existence of Colombo Plan students, let alone interested in helping them. Worth informed Casey:

> The position now is very different, mainly due, I think to the excellent impression which Colombo Plan students have made here and to their willing co-operation with all efforts to publicise the Colombo Plan and the importance of closer relations between Australia and South East Asia. I now receive many unsolicited offers of good accommodation and the recent appeal in the 'Sun' and over 3DB for hospitality … has resulted in over fifty offers of hospitality in Melbourne as far afield as East Gippsland.[30]

Hosts often felt compelled to express publicly their support for Asian students and their discomfort with the immigration policy. Mrs M.G. Swinburne of Surrey Hills in Melbourne provided board and lodging to three Colombo Plan students and in 1954 sent in these observations to the editor of the *Age*:

> Our contact with these young men proves to us that they are normal, natural boys from good homes. They have distinct personality, are generally of excellent character, good intelligence,

> *fine sensibilities and very likeable ... We find that*
> *to know these students better is to regret very*
> *much that we are debarred by our own*
> *immigration law from having them as our real*
> *next-door neighbour.*[31]

Swinburne's reference to the 'distinct personality' of her boarders is particularly significant. She simultaneously acknowledges and challenges a version of the nineteenth century 'Asian hordes' metaphor which had been transplanted into a Cold War context, where Asians were seen as being homogenous and vulnerable to communist influence. Swinburne's letter prompted Irtaza Zaidi to write to the newspaper:

> *It is through personal contacts that we know and*
> *understand each other fully well and not merely by*
> *reading in schools and colleges ... I do not want to*
> *indulge in controversy on whether Australia should*
> *allow Asians to settle here or not — a point raised*
> *by Mrs Swinburne — but I think Australia should*
> *at least encourage more and more Asians to come*
> *and visit Australia on social and cultural missions.*
> *At the same time Australians should be*
> *encouraged to visit different countries of Asia.*[32]

In these two letters the acceptance of Asia is genuine — if circumspect. These personal encounters were perhaps the most important factor in altering Australian perceptions of Asians and their ability to live harmoniously with Anglo–Australians. Their academic success may have given rise to new stereotypes of Asian diligence and dedication, yet it debunked the myth of Asian intellectual inferiority or backwardness. Collectively, Colombo Plan students (and private Asian scholars) were a non-threatening, but powerful, challenge to conventional

stereotypes of non-Europeans and epitomised their ability
to adapt and assimilate to Australian conditions. Indeed,
their socio-economic background facilitated their ready
integration. Colombo Plan students were typically male,
from middle-class families, educated, and able to speak
adequate English. Importantly, scholarship holders could
not take permanent employment (although vacation jobs
were acceptable) and were required to return home on
completion of their studies. As visitors, they could not be
condemned as an economic or social threat; nor did they
appear to threaten Australia's racial integrity.

Capitalising on the growing support for Asian
students, Worth proposed that the Good Neighbour
Council, created by the Chifley Government in 1949 to
assimilate migrants, establish a sub-committee dedicated to
Colombo Plan recipients. Committee members would greet
students on arrival, assist in finding appropriate
accommodation, organise social events, help with personal
problems, and arrange publicity. In 1953, Casey created the
'Meet Your Neighbours Campaign', whereby Colombo Plan
students attended arranged dinner parties with Australian
families. 'While they have returned to their home countries
armed with much information and professional and
industrial experience', Casey said, 'few have known the
average Australian working man in his own home
surroundings. Yet this is hardly a less vital part of their
education'.[33] Casey expected that these 'casual' meetings
would counter perceptions that Western citizens led selfish
and indolent lives, surrounded by limitless wealth.

Contented and articulate Asian scholars were perfect
grist for the government's slick publicity mill. In 1956, the
Australian News and Information Bureau published *My life
in Australia*, the story of Filipino dramatic arts student
Minda Feliciano. Later broadcast through Radio Australia

and local Manila radio, Feliciano recalled that by talking about 'our common interests, our way of life, and our aspirations I found that not only have I told others a great deal about my land, but now I have been indoctrinated in the way of life of this land of which I knew so little'.[34] In another government publication about a group of Ceylonese photography students, laudatory justifications of the white Australia policy prevailed. Victor Sumathipala wrote: 'I was aware of the so-called White Australia policy — a term which, I soon learned, has no official existence in Australia'. He went on to say: 'What very few Asians can appreciate until they visit Australia, is that Australia's immigration laws are aimed not at the exclusion of individuals, but at the preservation of national unity among a people faced with great problems in developing their country'.[35] Awkward and manufactured as they were, such statements reveal the government's continuing preoccupation with social stability and the idea that Asians would, after a period, uncritically adopt Australian values. Yet using Asians as ciphers for propaganda had its drawbacks and the surge of publicity surrounding the Colombo Plan sometimes offended the very students the government hoped to befriend. This sentiment emerged in a letter to the government-financed *Hemisphere* magazine in March 1959, when a student wrote angrily to the editor: 'I am sick of being constantly asked if I am a Colombo Plan student — a fact which goes to show how poorly the Press in general has informed the Australian public. Probably your magazine can put more stress on the private students and use the words "Colombo Plan" with less relish'.[36]

Given that the government policy-makers hoped the Colombo Plan student program would minimise negative opinion about Australian immigration and foreign policy, it is no surprise that recipients were officially forbidden to engage in political activity. But while serious public criticism was unlikely to come from conscientious scholarship holders absorbed with their studies, government attempts at censorship were only partly successful. On 9 August 1965 the Perth *Daily News* interviewed Asian students at the University of Western Australia about the Labor Party's decision to drop 'white Australia' from its policy platform. Although they had some reservations about the political motivations behind the change, the students welcomed the removal of a phrase they found personally offensive and damaging to Australia's international reputation. The article carefully let readers know that their objections to immigration restrictions did not imply that they wanted to remain in Australia. 'We like Australia, and we have had a pleasant time here', said one student, 'but our countries are home to us'.[37] One month later, the seemingly unremarkable story was front-page news because senior External Affairs officers visited the two Colombo Plan students quoted in the story. Abdullah Toha and Jimin Bin Idris were both admonished for breaching their undertakings to avoid pubic statement on Australia's foreign and domestic policy. The *Daily News* claimed the government interrogated the students and threatened them with deportation. While on campus, the DEA officers also took the opportunity to remind the organisers of an upcoming conference of the Overseas Students' Association in Adelaide that Colombo Plan students could not be involved in a proposed discussion of immigration policy. The organisers later dropped the forum from the conference agenda. On hearing about these events, Jimin's anthropology lecturer, D'Arcy Ryan, attacked the government's hypocritical position in an angry letter to *The Australian*: 'The image of Australian democracy and political freedom that we are so assiduously trying to implant in Asian minds becomes a little distorted when students here are subjected to this kind of clumsy and impertinent supervision'.[38] Not surprisingly, the students refused to comment further when questioned by a *Daily News* journalist.[39] Toha later withdrew from an unrelated public debate on Australia's economic aid program to underdeveloped countries. When the rights and responsibilities of Colombo Plan students were raised in parliament, the government refused to yield.[40] The experience of Australia's liberal democracy remained strictly conditional and did not extend to the right to publicly criticise the government.

Criticism of Australian policy, especially by Asians, invariably drew a nationalist and racist ire, often from those at the forefront of Australia's relations with Asia. Indeed, some of the more conservative and reactionary views came from articulate and experienced diplomats. Roden Cutler VC, war hero and Australia's High Commissioner in Colombo, reacted defensively to a local newspaper article critical of Australian immigration law. In a brusque memo to Canberra, he said that Asians saw Australia as a Garden of Eden where jobs were plentiful and well paid:

> It has not occurred to those who declaim against the Australian immigration policy that they are in effect asking for a share in the fruits of labours of the Australian people from the pioneers until the present time, without the Asians being prepared to contribute the same qualities as the pioneers, namely initiative, hard work and perseverance against difficulties. These qualities, if they existed amongst the Asians who desired to migrate to Australia, could be used to sound advantage in the countries of Asia.[41]

It is important to remember that Cutler's views, and their many variations, were commonplace — those who believed in racial equality and cultural pluralism were still in the minority. But these conceptions of racial inferiority, which rejected the possibility of Asians ever having the necessary moral and physiological rectitude to share Australia's bounty, were already being quietly undermined.

For their part, Asian commentators did not always rally behind their students. Endorsing the government's policy, the editor of the Singapore daily *Straits Times* wrote that Malaysian students 'grumble too much and too publicly' and that disputes should be settled in a 'quiet and friendly manner'. As guests, the article went on, there are 'rules of propriety which they must learn to observe. To criticise the host country harshly and publicly offends against the very first of these rules'.[42] Nor was it in the interests of Asian governments to recommend obstreperous students to represent their countries. Recipient nations enforced their own regulations regarding the conduct of Colombo Plan scholars. For example, in June 1953, after two Ceylonese students made disparaging remarks about Australia, the Ceylon Government sent warnings to each of their Colombo Plan scholars that they would be immediately recalled or fined if they defaulted under the conditions on which they had been sent abroad.[43]

In response, Asian students discovered more constructive and unrestricted avenues for expression. From the 1950s on, newsletters and journals dedicated to Australian and Asian affairs sprang up on campuses across the country, and many overseas scholars contributed to established university newspapers. These journals combined articles from prominent journalists, academics, diplomats, as well as Asian and Australian students. Free from the editorial distortions of the major daily newspapers, Asian students wrote considered and critical pieces about Australia and their own countries. They commonly used pseudonyms, especially if their material was too politically charged for the ever-watchful DEA. The founding editors of such journals aimed to deepen the nascent interest in Asia they sensed among their fellow students. One such journal was the attractively produced *Asiana: Asian–Australian forum*, sponsored by the Asian Students' Council of NSW and the National Union of Australian University Students. Rumoured to be a potential rival to the external affairs brainchild, *Hemisphere*, *Asiana*'s mission was 'to make some contribution towards a deeper understanding between a relatively homogeneous "western" Australia and a kaleidoscopic rising Asia'. The time had come, wrote the journal's editor and former Colombo Plan student Mr Oedojo, 'to have a literary medium … to complement the oral interchange that has already become a daily occasion'. The editors of the short-lived journal *The Asian*, published by the University of Melbourne Asian Students' Federation, emphasised the importance of 'understanding and goodwill — goodwill which is spontaneous and real, and not necessarily on paper only'. The University of New England Overseas Students' Association periodical *Small World*, also guided by an idealistic and humanitarian ethos, aimed at bringing a degree of critical awareness to Australian understandings of Asia and the problems associated with cross-cultural education.[44] Most of these journals quietly disappeared after a few years. *Hemisphere* carried on — aided by a stable government subsidy — and became the pre-eminent forum for Australian–Asian writing.

There were always Colombo Plan students prepared to brave the public arena. Lee Yee Cheong, a Malaysian electrical engineering student at the University of Adelaide, thought that Australia had missed an opportunity to gain first-hand information on Asian affairs:

> *Asian students have found that the Australian's*
> *home is too much his castle. Although they have*
> *the opportunity of meeting many Australians*
> *through being invited to picnics, garden parties and*
> *other social functions ... very few Australians*
> *have seen fit, after an hour or so of handshaking*
> *and small talk, to invite the students home and*
> *develop more personal and deeper friendships.*

Some might have seen his letter as simply a comment
on Australian insularity, but others might have interpreted
it as a deft metaphorical jibe at immigration policy. Taking
the less controversial interpretation, the editor of the
Adelaide Advertiser responded somewhat cryptically. He
agreed with Cheong's sentiments and put it down to
'mainly shyness and thoughtlessness' on the part of
Australians. It was more common to see Asian students
socialising together, he suggested, because they 'naturally
find more in common with each other; there is something
missing somewhere. It is nothing to worry about, but it
deserves some thought'.[45]

Asian students politicised the image of Australia that
government officials hoped to project, both domestically
and internationally. For example, in 1957 the government
of Ceylon marked the sixth anniversary of the Colombo
Plan with an international exhibition. Promoted as an
opportunity for all donor nations to demonstrate the nature
of their regional aid projects and to present an informative
display about their own domestic economic development
programs, the Australian Cabinet appointed an inter-
departmental committee to consider possible ramifications.
With respect to the display on Papua New Guinea, the
Department of Territories thought it 'preferable only to
refer to white people' lest it 'create confusion in the minds

of the audience, particularly as photos would be shown ...
of Asian students taking part in various activities on the
mainland'. In a similar vein, the designers felt that
references to Aborigines should be avoided. They felt that
audiences might raise awkward questions, such as, 'if there
are dark-skinned people in Australia why are Asian people
excluded?' Any 'long explanations' of Australian history
were likely to raise more questions than they could answer.
Officials also feared that any mention of dependent people
under Australian trusteeship would give the impression that
colonial exploitation underpinned Australian prosperity.
Furthermore, the stark contrast in development between
the mainland and Papua New Guinea might lead to a
potentially embarrassing offer of aid from India or Japan![46]
Clearly unsettled by the prospect of international attention,
the exhibition forced government officials to recast their
representations of Australian life. The avoidance strategy
the DEA chose to adopt and the conscious presentation
of white Australia marked the realisation that the presence
of Asian students, and the attention that generated, had
drawn Australia into a much murkier and problematic
arena.

The draconian nature of Australia's immigration
restrictions meant that Asians expected a chilly reception.
As Walter Crocker explained to Casey in one of his fulsome
despatches, students had such low expectations that 'they
have been surprised and gratified by the friendly reception
... Their gratification is the greater because they go half
expecting to encounter something in the form of a colour
bar'.[47] Foreign students almost certainly encountered
discrimination and intolerance on a personal and institutional
level during their time in Australia. Yet they were also
significant witnesses to Australian tolerance and
adaptability. Student associations, church groups, and the

official Colombo Plan Liaison Office organised picnics, dinners and formal evenings as a means of facilitating social interaction with Australians. Significantly, overseas student groups themselves, such as the Colombo Plan Fellows Association of Sydney, established in June 1953, staged parties, cultural evenings, film nights, and excursions for Australian and overseas students. Newspapers acknowledged the difficulties faced by visiting students and appreciated the gradual nature of the changing attitudes: 'Obviously it isn't easy for Asians to settle into life here', confessed one writer in the *Adelaide News* in 1957, 'but it is probably easier than it was, say, six years ago', with instances of 'abysmal ignorance and intolerance [having] grown less'.[48] Cases of extreme alienation and personal hardship brought to the DEA's attention also declined, in large part because of the work of community support networks. The DEA rightly interpreted the rising level of academic success among the students as evidence of their ability to overcome intellectual and social obstacles present in Australia. A more worrying trend for the government was that the Colombo Plan might become a victim of its own success. For now, the DEA feared 'the reluctance of students who have become over-identified with the Australian way of life to return to their home countries'. The corollary, according to the DEA, was the possibility that by allowing Asians to linger too long in Australia they would develop unrealistic expectations for their own country and resent Australia for its prosperity.[49]

It was inevitable that many Australian students would begin romantic relationships with Asians they met on campus and elsewhere. Mariam Manaf, a distinguished scholar from Malaysia, won a Colombo Plan award to study medicine at the newly-founded Monash University in 1963. There she met fellow medical student Tim Hegarty.

The couple began courting in the mid-1960s and married before final year exams in 1969. Obliged to return home on finishing her degree, Manaf began her compulsory residency at General Hospital, Kuala Lumpur. Hegarty, who began his residency at Queen Victoria Hospital in Melbourne, convinced his employer to allow him to join his wife and complete his 'housemanship' in Malaysia. Although formally required to remain in Malaysia for five years, Manaf, like other Colombo Plan students, opted to repay part of her award in order to leave the country early. In 1971, having both completed their internships, they returned to Australia — and stayed.[50] In similar fashion, University of Western Australia student David Rome followed his girlfriend Daraka ('Dara') Vajarapan when she returned to Thailand after a year-long stay in Australia. An architecture graduate from Chulalongkorn University in Bangkok, she was awarded a Colombo Plan scholarship to study English at Perth Technical College in the late 1960s. Rome first saw Vajarapan when she appeared in the daily press with other Colombo Plan scholars shortly after their arrival in Perth. They met later through the Thai Students' Association. Obliged to return for a minimum of 12 months by the Thai government, Vajarapan worked as an architectural drafter with an American company based in Bangkok, before returning to Perth with Rome in 1970. They married shortly afterwards.[51] These encounters were not exactly what DEA officials had in mind when they warned of potential 'over-identification' with the Australian way of life.

The phenomenon of cross-cultural education sparked interest from social scientists, demographers, and psychologists. In 1969, Daphne Keats, from The Australian National University, conducted a follow-up study on Australian-trained Colombo Plan students. Among other things, she found that 83 per cent of the 503 respondents kept in regular contact with Australians.[52] Interestingly, the number of former students who maintained contact with formal graduate associations of ex-Australian students was much lower. This can be partly explained by the absence of such associations in some countries, but it might also suggest that personal relationships were a more enduring and meaningful basis for continued contact with Australia.

Another important dimension of the Colombo Plan and the cultural exchanges it fostered was the supply of technical expertise. Australian technical experts may have been lost among the growing contingent of international advisors, administrators, and technicians that descended on Asia in the 1950s, but they played a conspicuous role in the delivery of Colombo Plan projects and were therefore at the forefront of cultural interaction between Asians and Australians. By the mid-1960s, over 500 Australian experts had completed around 650 assignments in Colombo Plan countries. Over 40 per cent of Australian personnel contracted under the auspices of the program went to Malaysia. Singapore and Thailand received 116 and 105 experts respectively. Smaller numbers travelled to Indonesia (64), India (37), Ceylon (65), Pakistan (58), and Cambodia (33).[53] The DEA paid experts a basic living allowance for the duration of their assignments, and they typically continued to receive their normal wages and conditions. But they volunteered for these physically and emotionally demanding assignments, some going on for years, not for financial gain, but because they genuinely believed they were fulfilling part of Australia's obligations to its regional neighbours.

For many, it would be their first trip outside Australia to a region they knew little about. Norman Stringer, agricultural adviser with the South Australian Department of Agriculture, travelled to the Mianwali district of Pakistan in March 1954. Commissioned to monitor the Thal irrigation project, costing nearly £A1 million, Stringer approached his task with enthusiasm, diligence, and fortitude. He wrote to his boss in Adelaide:

> the place was in a terrible mess both from an administrative and cropping or agricultural aspect. My first job was to rectify the errors that the Australian had made before me and to try and retrieve the good name for Australia ... bringing sand dune country into an irrigable state and crop sufficient area to feed 400 head of milking buffalos [sic] and Dhni cattle, 1,000 head of sheep and produce sufficient grain for 1,000 head of poultry ... Being a foreigner not speaking the language all this has been no easy task particularly during the summer months with the shade temp. for several months over 120 degrees mark and at times getting up to 128 degrees in the shade.[54]

At the request of the Pakistan government, the DEA extended Stringer's assignment for 12 months. While it was inconvenient for Stringer's department to be without him for another year, his director felt it 'was one way in which the state can make some contribution to under-developed regions'.[55] In his final appraisal of Stringer's work, Eric Harrison, from the DEA, told South Australian Premier Thomas Playford that Stringer had 'established excellent relations with Pakistanis of all grades and this contributed greatly to his achieving the maximum success possible in the circumstances in improving farming'.[56]

The government also actively encouraged high-profile Australians to show off their technical prowess under the Colombo Plan mantle. In 1954, Casey approached prominent plastic surgeon Benjamin Rank about the prospect of travelling to Asia to do a 'series of ... operations on local people whose faces had gone wrong in one way or another'.[57] Rank, who famously performed reconstructive surgery on John Gorton during the Second World War, undertook a three-month tour of Singapore, where he completed over 80 operations and lectured on his surgical techniques. According to Casey, Malcolm MacDonald and Gerald Templer from the UK High Commission were 'falling over each other with enthusiasm'.[58] Even Walter Crocker, who was usually hostile to this style of Colombo Plan venture, saw the potential for a similar visit to India and asked the well-connected Casey if he might persuade Rank or other notables. The following year Rank completed an assignment in India, as did the acclaimed virologist and bacteriologist Macfarlane Burnet. The surgeon Sir Edward ('Weary') Dunlop and the physician Clive Fitts were among other prominent Australians to complete assignments under the Colombo Plan.[59]

Distinguished visitors such as Rank became conduits for the government's heavy-handed message about Australian values and the significance of Australian–Asian relations under the Colombo Plan. Leaving nothing to chance, the DEA gave Rank a ready-made speech, intended to help him answer any curly questions about the aid program or immigration laws. The speech emphasised the 'good neighbourly feeling' demonstrated by Australian aid, the presence of Indian students, and shared environmental problems, notably that large tracts of Australia remained 'incapable of supporting life and cultivation'. At its most sanctimonious, Rank's mock-speech explained that while Indian men had long been accustomed to avoiding 'manual work', through the scholarship program 'many Indian students in Australia have learned from us the dignity of labour'.[60]

Just as the presence of international students challenged racial stereotypes, so the expert program changed Australian perceptions of Asian people and work practices. In 1954, S.W. Dunkerley, a refrigeration expert from Melbourne, undertook an assignment to advise the Pakistan government on the creation of a cold storage industry and to determine what technical equipment Australia might supply. Accompanied by his wife, who proved 'an effective brace' to Dunkerley's morale, he travelled to Karachi, Hyderabad, Lahore, and other provincial cities. Much to his surprise, Dunkerley met intelligent, courteous, English-speaking Pakistanis, and 'big-hearted and big-thinking' Pakistani scientists, all of whom afforded him a warm welcome. He commented in his report to the DEA: 'Like many Australians, I knew little of what goes on inside the Eastern countries which are our neighbours'. While Dunkerley worked, his wife spent her time visiting places of interest and shopping in the bazaars, but 'never at any time did she experience fear or apprehension'. With his perceptions of Asia substantially de-mystified, Dunkerley returned to Australia with the 'conviction that the people of Pakistan are worthy of all the help that can be given them. Our Colombo Plan aid should be extended to the utmost, and Australians should see to it that it is so extended'. Maybe this would 'force the man in the street out of his sense of glorious isolation'.[61] Casey could scarcely have written a better promotional article for the plan himself. Yet neither Casey, nor anyone at the DEA, tampered with Dunkerley's impressions. Following a now well-established pattern in Casey's approach to the Colombo Plan, he welcomed Dunkerley's 'frank enthusiasm' and then saw to it that copies were sent to major Australian newspapers![62]

Australian officials searched for a politically and culturally appropriate way of working with Asians. The DEA was particularly aware of the potentially damaging nature of the technical appraisals provided to recipient governments. Overly emphatic reports and 'undiplomatic language' had caused offence to Asian officials in a number of cases, so in 1956 the DEA instructed technicians to first send their 'tactful reports' to Australian diplomatic representatives in their respective countries. The intention, Arnott explained to Australia's diplomatic posts across Asia, was not to stifle criticism, but to 'ensure that they did not contain offensive remarks' or promise further assistance that Australia might not be willing to give.[63] The DEA also watched for signs that its experts were losing their cool in often testing working environments — such as the technician sent home for taking on the role of colonial overlord and attempting to 'discipline local labour with his foot'.[64]

While technical aid and the scholarship program were valuable precursors to deeper professional and political links, the use of Colombo Plan experts as cultural ambassadors was as much an attempt to reduce latent anxiety over whether Asians would accept Australians as it was an attempt to promote Australian generosity. Professional exchanges (through the expert program), and the personal relations that contact inevitably fostered, became an important measure of the effectiveness of Colombo Plan aid and a litmus test of Australian character. In 1959, H.W. Moegerlein, an engineer with Commonwealth Railways, surveyed the use of Australian railcars and rolling stock in Singapore, Malaya (Malaya incorporated with Singapore, Sarawak and Sabah into Malaysia in September 1963), Thailand, Vietnam, and the Philippines. The practical problems he encountered proved manageable, and local authorities made good use of

Australian equipment. However, the highlight of his trip came when he met eight Thai engineers who had studied in Australia. 'As important as the service they render to their country is the goodwill they are spreading', he wrote. Moegerlein's pride was palpable: 'anyone who had doubts about the success of the Colombo Plan training scheme ... should have seen the expression on their faces when they were talking about Australia'.[65] An equally relieved — although slightly more muted — response came from the Prime Minister when in 1955 he told Thomas Playford that 'independent Australian observers [Colombo Plan experts] are now returning with reports that Asians are realizing that the Australian people are friendly and sympathetic to their aims and aspirations'.[66] The anxious search for approval spilled over into the wider community and was most evident in respect to the student program. 'Do they like us?' asked a headline in Perth's *Daily News*. Reassuringly, they did. But the sting for Perth readers was that while the students liked 'us and our way of life', they found the city 'dull and unsophisticated'.[67]

Rather than averting scrutiny, Asian students, the expert program, and the ubiquitous propaganda campaign that accompanied them actually exposed Australia to international censure. Few could ignore the invective coming from respected Asian media. The *Times of Indonesia*, for example, attacked the Colombo Plan as empty tokenism: 'the Australians cannot do enough to show how much Australians like Asians in absentia. The Colombo Plan and other such schemes are a kind of blood-money paid by the Australian to silence his guilty conscience towards Asians and Africans'.[68] At the same time, however, diplomats such as Tom Critchley, Australian High Commissioner in Malaya, could suggest that Colombo Plan students were Australia's 'most signal contribution to

Australian–Malayan amity'. And Peter Heydon, High Commissioner in New Delhi, could tell Canberra about a team of Indian editors who toured Australia and on their return to India wrote enthusiastically about the student scheme, 'the hard-working character of Australians generally and our egalitarianism'.[69]

The incongruous and contradictory relationship between immigration restrictions and the personal interactions between Anglo–Australians and Asians grew into the decade. By the mid- to late-1950s, diplomatic correspondence, student writings, and media coverage drew a distinction between the welcoming and positive reception Asian students received while studying in Australia and the harsh rigidity of the immigration restrictions themselves. Asian writers struggled to come to terms with the possibility that although protected by racially-based immigration laws, Australians themselves were not necessarily hostile or overtly racist. In 1955, after spending three years in Australia, writer Tennyson Rodrigo returned to Ceylon and reported that Asian students and educated Australians were convinced that a colour bar did not exist. The white Australia policy, he wrote, 'is purely a government policy and it does not point to the attitude of Australian society towards Asians', and the awkwardness that characterised encounters between non-Europeans and Australians was due to anxiety, unfamiliarity, and ignorance — not race. In a similar vein, the Indian daily paper *Hindu* explained quizzically, 'many forward Asian students find no difficulty in getting Australian girl partners to dance with them and a small number of Australian girls have married Asian husbands. The term colour bar is positively misleading when applied to Australia'. Asian diplomats in Australia, while ever critical, also appreciated the subtlety of social change. In 1960, the Indian High Commission in Canberra reported that despite continued intransigence over immigration, Australia's 'impregnable insularity' was beginning to subside and 'the Asian facet of the Australian personality has been taking clearer shape'.[70]

Increasing professional and commercial contact with Asia, the influx of students, and a growing regional awareness, deepened the cultural tissue of Australian society. The immediate and tangible contact facilitated by Asian students built momentum for a campaign to dismantle the white Australia policy. The *Ceylon Daily News*, for example, reported the radical views of the Anglican Archbishop of Brisbane, Reginald Halse, who supported the recognition of communist China, welcomed Colombo Plan students, and wanted to admit a quota of Asians 'who would add something to our way of living'.[71] The Reverend Thomas Rees-Thomas of the Brisbane City Congregational Church denied that a quota system would reduce living standards. According to a report in the Brisbane *Courier-Mail*, the Christian church believed that throughout 'universities and colleges … there were thousands of educated and cultured Asians who could not only live up to Australian standards, but could elevate them'.[72] The basic sentiment expressed by Halse and Rees-Thomas took a more politicised form when the influential Immigration Reform Group (IRG) used the Colombo Plan to expose the dangers of maintaining a policy offensive to Asian nations. The group, citing the cases of prominent Asian leaders educated in British institutions, asked rhetorically, 'could they have felt the same if the atmosphere of freedom and racial equality which they experienced in Britain had been tainted by an immigration policy that seemed to them a denial of the fundamental equality of mankind?' The IRG deliberately refrained from condemning the Colombo Plan as a total failure. Working from an assimilationist perspective, they proposed that Asian students had demonstrated their capacity for ready absorption into Australian society. Indeed, this integration would be enhanced if they could remain permanently: 'Australia cannot become "home" in their minds … Knowing that their stay here must be temporary, they have little encouragement to develop a sense of affinity with or affection towards this country'.[73]

Popular attitudes towards Asian immigration only began to soften from the mid-1950s. In 1943, 51 per cent of respondents to a Gallup Poll fell into the 'Keep Out' category. In 1954 it was 61 per cent. The number of respondents in this category fell steadily throughout the decade and stood at 33 per cent in 1960. After increasing to 39 per cent in 1961, it fell sharply to 16 per cent in 1965.[74] The pattern described here mirrored a gradual reduction in the number of respondents who believed that overall migration numbers were too high. That shift over a decade was a fundamental change in both national attitude and people's perception of what their nation should be. The government followed by making minor changes to Australia's immigration regulations, notably the scrapping of the infamous dictation test in 1958 in favour of a simpler entry system.

By the late 1950s, with the white Australia policy under regular attack, Asian students and the Colombo Plan played a crucial role in facilitating the turnaround in the government's immigration policy. In 1958, Harold Holt, Minister for Labour and National Service (he was Minister for Immigration between 1949 and 1956), dodged the accusation of racism by suggesting that the Australian people 'had no better ambassadors' of their tolerance and friendliness 'than those Asian students who come here to be trained'. Exclusion, he said, merely acknowledged 'the difficulties of assimilation for those with different racial and traditional backgrounds and customs'.[75] But with the idea that non-Europeans were unable to assimilate so visibly discredited, by 1966 Holt, now Prime Minister, emphasised, in an unabashed *volte-face*, the cultural affinity between Asia and Australia as a major reason to abandon the white Australia policy. As he explained in parliament:

> *Australia's increasing involvement in Asian developments, the rapid growth of our trade with Asian countries, our participation on a larger scale in an increasing number of aid projects in the area, the considerable number of Asian students — now well over 12,000 — receiving education in Australia, the expansion of our military effort, the scale of diplomatic contact, and the growth of tourism to and from the countries of Asia, combine to make such a review desirable in our eyes.*[76]

Although the 1966 reforms did not see the end of the white Australia policy, they signalled its imminent departure. The changing nature of Australia's interaction with Asian people during the 1950s and 1960s is succinctly encapsulated in one of Casey's diary entries. The day after a difficult meeting in October 1953 with members of the Ceylon Cabinet, Casey wrote:

> *Some things a good many people in Australia should learn about Asians*
> *— not to patronise them*
> *— not to believe we're superior to them*
> *— not to misinterpret their good manners*
> *— not to underrate their ability*[77]

By the end of the 1960s, Australia had indeed taken note of Casey's patrician reprimand. The nation's cautious embrace of Asia — both officially and in the wider community — was sufficient to allow the liberalisation of immigration law without significant political or social disruption.

———

Through the Colombo Plan education program and the broader integration of Asian scholars, the Menzies Government unwittingly unleashed a quietly subversive force upon the Australian community; a force made more powerful by its non-confrontational and temporary nature. Socio-cultural engagement between Asians students and Australians helped to change imperial accounts of Asian dependence and passivity into more complex and intimate appreciations. It also dented Australian dreams of racial superiority and regional dominance. The assimilationist credo that underpinned the embrace of the Colombo Plan and private scholars allowed Australia time to adjust, understand, and accept radical social and cultural changes associated with immigration. Interaction between Australian technical experts and Asians was an important factor in facilitating a change in outlook among the Australian people, and broke the myth — at least for middle-class Australians — that Asians were anathema to the 'Australian way of life'. Even Menzies, who had largely ignored Asia throughout his career, remarked in his memoirs that the 'daily association of Australians with students and scholars from Asian countries has greatly widened the experience and understanding of our own people'.[78]

With few exceptions, the experience of Asian students in Australia proved illuminating and beneficial, for student and host alike. Official reluctance to look beyond the narrow frame of foreign policy and cold war politics stood in stark contrast to the willingness of the Australian community to accept and engage with Asian students. Students may well have become 'valuable testimony' to Australian tolerance, but instead of generating sympathy for immigration policy, it intensified domestic and international criticism. But while international condemnation of racial discrimination was instrumental in encouraging the attitudinal changes that swept the country, international pressure alone would not have led the government to dismantle the white Australia policy. The ideals of equality, tolerance, and understanding were rendered less abstract by Colombo Plan students and the thousands of private scholars who spent time in Australia. The number of Asian scholars may appear small, but they marked a watershed in Australia's cultural development and their appearance on university campuses and in private homes across the country provided a sustained challenge to Australian insularity.

Footnotes

1   'Crossing the barriers: part 1, traces of dreamtime', Social history feature, ABC, Radio Australia, 1993

2   Commonwealth Bureau of Census and Statistics, *Census of the Commonwealth of Australia*, 30 June 1954, vol. 8, pp. 22–23 & 30 June 1961, vol. 8, p. 27; 'Review of Australian external aid: assessment of Colombo Plan training, Doc. AR/51', 16 December 1964, A1838, 2020/1/24/23, NAA

3   Memo, J.K. Waller, Assistant Secretary, to Casey, 2 May 1957, 1838, 2020/1/2 part 1, NAA

4   Memo, J.K. Waller, Assistant Secretary, to Casey, 2 May 1957

5   W. Crocker, 'Notes on Colombo Plan aid in India', 25 April 1953, A12099, C15, NAA

6   'General review of the Technical Co-operation Scheme', 1953, DO35/5768, PRO

7   'Review of Australian external aid: assessment of Colombo Plan training, Doc. AR/51', 16 December 1964, A1838, 2020/1/24/23, NAA; See also Letter, Casey to Fadden, 23 May 1957, 1838, 2020/1/2 part 1, NAA; Australian News and Information Bureau, *Australia in facts and figures*, various issues, 1950–70

8   Australian News and Information Bureau, *Australia in facts and figures*, various issues 1950–70; Memo, Dexter to Kevin, 20 September 1955, A1838, 563/6

part 1, NAA; 'Correspondence scholarships: new scheme under Colombo Plan: press release no. 33', 26 April 1955, A1838, 3004/11 part 3, NAA. Figures from Commonwealth Office of Education, 'Annual Report', *Parliamentary papers – general*, vol. 2, 1962–63, pp. 1068, 1086

9   Letter, Tange to Martin, 8 January 1962, A1838, 2008/6/1/2, NAA

10 Memo, Economic and Technical Assistance Branch to Shaw, 6 October 1955, A1838, 2048/2 part 7, NAA

11 'Statement by Department of External Affairs to the Committee on the Future of Tertiary Education in Australia', 8 January 1962, A1838, 2008/6/1/2, NAA

12 Letter, Langley to Menzies, A463, 1957/1046, NAA

13 Letter, Casey to Menzies, 19 July 1951, A10299, A18, NAA

14 *Sun* (Sydney), 6 November 1953

15 M. Loane, *Archbishop Mowll: the biography of Howard West Kilvinton Mowll*, London, Hodder and Stoughton, 1960, pp. 228–29.

16 *CPD (HoR)*, vol. 4, 17 August 1954, p. 315; Note, Arnott to Casey, 13 September 1951, A10299, A18, NAA; Editorial, *Daily Mirror*, 21 August 1953; *Sydney Morning Herald*, 12 May 1955

17 Report, 'Malayan Students' Association of Victoria', undated (*circa* 1956), A1838, 2008/1/3 part 1, NAA

18 *Sun* (Sydney), 20 December 1955

19 *Malay Mail*, 22 June 1956

20 Letter, Bland to Tange, 12 September 1957, A1838, 2008/1/1 part 2, NAA

21 'Progress of Colombo Plan students at Australian universities, 1956', A1838, 2020/1/11, NAA; 'Review of Australian external aid: assessment of Colombo Plan training, Doc. AR/51', 16 December 1964, A1838, 2020/1/24/23, NAA. Figures for 1959 can be found in 'Report of the Australian Universities Commission on Australian Universities, 1958–1963', A1203, 379/16/AUS, NAA

22 'Progress of Colombo Plan students at Australian universities, 1956'; E.F. Palmer, 'Report on Colombo Plan mining trainees — physics section', 7 June 1956, Correspondence 12/14255.2, SRNSW; C. Harrison, 'Burmese mining students – general comments', Correspondence 12/14255.2, SRNSW

23 Letter, Shaw to Casey, 6 February 1956, A1838, 2008/3/4 part 4, NAA

24 Editorial, *Daily Mirror*, 21 August 1953

25 Letter, K.P. Byrne to J. Weeden, 12 January 1955, K1217, 41/11/2, NAA; Memo, Dexter to Tange, 'Colombo Plan wives and trainees', 1 April 1957, A11604, 704/1 part 1, NAA

26 Memo, Dexter to Hay, 11 September 1957, A1838, 2008/1/1 part 2, NAA

27 Bevan Rutt to DEA, 18 May 1961, A1838, 2045/1/10 part 1, NAA

28 F.T. Borland, 'Circular letter — to all people offering accommodation to Adelaide University students', undated (*circa* 1960), A1838, 2045/1/10 part 1, NAA

29 C. Sanders, 'Asian scholars in Australia', K1217, 41/11/2, NAA: Western Australia

30 Memo, Worth to Casey, 6 July 1953, A10299, A18, NAA

31 *Age* (Melbourne), 29 May 1954

32 *Age* (Melbourne), 1 June 1954

33 Gwenda Tavan, '"Good neighbours": community, organisations, migrant assimilation and Australian society and culture, 1950–1961', *Australian Historical Studies*, vol. 28, no. 109, October 1997, pp. 77–89; '"Meet Your Neighbour" campaign: Mr Casey's support', press release 41, 26 April 1953, A1838, 3004/11 part 1, NAA

34 *My life in Australia*, Australian News and Information Bureau, 1956, in 'Publicity for the Colombo Plan', FO 953/1638, PRO

35 V. Sumathipala, W. Perera & D. Kodagoda, *We look at Australia*, Sydney, Australian News and Information Bureau, 1956

36 *Hemisphere*, March 1959, p. 29

37 *Daily News* (Perth), 9 August 1965

38 *Australian*, 14 September 1965

39 Daily News, 16 September 1965

40 D.O. Hay to Casey, 'Colombo Plan: expression of political views by students', 21 September 1965, A1838, 2045/9 part 2, NAA; *CPD (HoR)*, 16 September 1965, vol. 47, p. 1039

41 Memo, A.R. Cutler to Tange, 7 July 1954, A1838, 160/10/8, NAA

42 *Straits Times* (Singapore), 20 August 1965

43 'Ceylon newsletter', 6 June 1953, A1838, 160/11/1/1 part 2, AA

44 *Asiana*, vol. 1, no. 2, 1957, pp. 5–6; *The Asian*, June 1955; *Small World*, vol. 1, no. 7, 1966, p. 3

45 *Adelaide Advertiser*, 13 & 14 April 1961

46 Cabinet submission no. 270, 'Colombo Plan exhibition', 11 February 1955, A4940, C1208, NAA; B. Bray, 'Colombo Plan exhibition discussions', 27 April 1956, Department of Territories, A452, 57/1846, NAA; J. Plimsoll to Casey, 'Colombo Plan exhibition, 1957: inclusion of Australian dependent territories', 2 May 1956, A1838, 3004/11 part 4, NAA

47 Note quoting Crocker's despatch, Casey to Shaw, 29 December 1954, A10299, C15, NAA

48 *Adelaide News*, 1 July 1957

49 'Review of Australian external aid: assessment of Colombo Plan training, Doc. AR/51', 16 December 1964, A1838, 2020/1/24/23, NAA

50 Mariam & Tim Hegarty, pers. comm., 20 June 2003

51 Dara & David Rome, pers. comm., 2 July 2003

52 D.M. Keats, *Back in Asia: a follow-up study of Australian-trained Asian students*, Canberra, Australian National University, 1969, pp. 93, 98, 163

53 Australian Bureau of Census and Statistics, *Australia in facts and figures*, various issues 1950–66; Council for Technical Cooperation in South and South East Asia, *The Colombo Plan Technical Cooperation Scheme: report for 1953–1954*, London, 1953, pp. 21–28

54 Letter, Norman Stringer to A.R. Callaghan, Director of Agriculture, South Australia, no date, *circa* 1954, GRG 24/6 194/54, State Records, South Australia, (SRSA)

55 Letter, A.R. Callaghan to Minister for Agriculture, 6 January 1955, GRG 24/6 194/54, SRSA

56 Letter, E.J. Harrison, DEA to Thomas Playford, 15 February 1956, GRG 24/6 194/54, SRSA
57 Casey diaries, 8 June 1954, vol. 16, box 27, MS6150, NLA
58 Casey diaries, 27 September 1954, vol. 17, box 28, MS6150, NLA
59 Despatch, Heydon to Casey, 5 April 1956, A4231, 1956/New Delhi, NAA; Casey diaries, 22 December 1954, vol. 17, box 28, MS6150, NLA
60 Memo, Shaw to Arnott, 'Mr Rank's visit to India', 24 December 1954, A1838, 555/6/4 part 3, NAA
61 S.W. Dunkerley, 'Pakistan and the Colombo Plan: Australian expert's impressions', no date, circa 1954/55, A1838, 555/6/4 part 3, NAA
62 Letter, J.D. Keating, DEA, to H.A.M. Campbell, Editor, *The Age*, 15 February 1955, A1838, 555/6/4 part 3, NAA
63 Memo, L.J. Arnott to various posts, 22 March 1956, A4529, 65/1/4/1952/55, NAA
64 'Australian external aid: report to the Minister for External Affairs by the inter-departmental committee to review Australian external aid, 25 March 1965, A4311, 147/1, NAA
65 H.W. Moegerlein, 'Detailed report of work in Thailand' & 'Detailed report of work in Malaya', B300, 9268 part 3, NAA: South Australia (SA)
66 Letter, Menzies to Playford, 6 May 1955, GRG 24/6 194/54, SRSA
67 *Daily News* (Perth), 6 June 1959
68 Editorial, *Times of Indonesia*, 23 January 1958
69 P.J. Boyce, 'Twenty-one years of Australian diplomacy in Malaya', *Journal of South–East Asian History*, vol. 4, September 1963, p. 104; Memo, 'Visit to Australia by Indian editors', 18 June 1957, A1838, 3004/11/33 part 2, NAA
70 *Hindu* (Madras), 22 August 1960. See also, G.W. Jones & M. Jones, 'Australia's immigration policy: some Malaysian attitudes', *Australian Outlook*, vol. 19, December 1965, pp. 272–85; T. Rodrigo, 'Asian students in Australia experience no colour bar', *Ceylon Daily News*, 7 February 1955; F.R. Naragana, First Secretary, 'Monthly political report for November 1960: Australia', Ministry of External Affairs, 6(83) R&I Section/60, National Archives of India, New Delhi
71 *Ceylon Daily News*, 9 September 1954
72 *Courier-Mail* (Brisbane), 23 June 1954
73 Immigration Reform Group, *Immigration: control or colour bar? The background to 'White Australia' and a proposal for change*, Melbourne, Melbourne University Press, 1962, pp. 96–97
74 Figures from, J. Mackie, 'The politics of Asian immigration' in J.E. Coughlan and D.J. McNamara, Asians in *Australia: patterns of migration and settlement*, Melbourne, Macmillan Education Australia, 1997, p. 17
75 Sun News-Pictorial (Melbourne), 26 May 1958
76 CPD (HoR), 8 March 1966, vol. 50, p. 34
77 T.B. Millar (ed.), *Australian foreign minister: the diaries of R.G. Casey 1951–1960*, London, Collins, 1972, p. 121
78 R.G. Menzies, *The measure of the years*, London, Cassell, 1970, p. 48

7. A TOOTHPICK TO PROP UP A SWAYING SKYSCRAPER

The immediate and unexpected success of the student program in Australia threatened to overshadow the Colombo Plan's primary objective: the reduction of poverty in Asia. Simmering beneath the government's carefully manufactured publicity were deep-seated problems with aid management, the use of Australian projects, and the complexities of international trade. By the mid-1950s, much of the early optimism for the Colombo Plan — arising partly from the sheer novelty and boldness of the program — had faded, and a more searching and penetrating body of opinion began to emerge. The renowned journalist and interpreter of Asia, Peter Russo, accused aid donors of acting like witch-doctors who saw little in Asia that could not be 'cured with brass knuckles or a brew of politically flavoured handouts'. The Colombo Plan and other aid programs, he said, amounted to 'a toothpick to prop up a swaying skyscraper', incapable either of making a constructive impression on Asian economic development or of forestalling political turbulence.[1] The Royal Institute of International Affairs in London offered the judicious assessment that although the Colombo Plan represented the most effective means of conducting an 'onslaught on extreme poverty', its progress had been difficult and slow.[2] Chief among those qualified to judge Australia's aid program was the journalist Osmar White. At the conclusion of his six-month tour of the region, White offered his own assessment of the Colombo Plan aid program. His report, breathtaking in its scope and audacity, was a damning indictment of the international aid arena and, in particular, Australian practice. Corruption, wastage, gross mismanagement and ineptitude were recurring themes in White's appraisal of the much-vaunted Colombo Plan. The situation was at its most dispiriting in India (one of the largest recipients of Australian assistance in the 1950s), where aid was 'engulfed by the Greater Indian need — without leaving any measurable impression'. White told a foreign affairs committee that the task ahead was simply immense, 'as far as India is concerned, nothing foreigners can do will really affect the situation much at all. The problem is far too big. The most we in Australia can contribute is a mere drop in the ocean'.[3]

Inexperience and the lack of a systematic approach to international aid delivery fostered a cavalier attitude towards Australian aid to Asia in general, and the capital aid program in particular. From the outset, government officials seemed distinctly uninterested in what happened to goods once they left Australia and were reluctant to criticise publicly the uses to which Australian gifts were put. In keeping with the Colombo Plan's bilateral spirit, Australia resisted attempts to implement a systematic or centralised system of monitoring the technical aid program, and maintained that such evaluations were 'something which individual Governments should do to satisfy themselves'.[4] Delegates to the annual Consultative Committee meetings offered cautious — and always diplomatic — appraisals of Colombo Plan projects in their respective countries. Donors and recipients alike rarely used this forum to discuss the gritty realities of aid delivery and national development.

Assessment of the Colombo Plan within official circles was sporadic and inconsistent. An undue emphasis on extreme cases of abject failure or glowing success tended to obscure any underlying pattern in the efficacy of Australian assistance. Eager to avoid the charge of attaching political conditions on the use of aid, Casey ignored early cases of misuse and mismanagement. Anticipating the waste of aid or the unlikelihood of aid halting the growth of political extremism, Casey became fond of publicly quoting the generous pronouncements made by Asian politicians, and he always alluded to the non-material benefits of the program. 'The significance of such friendly assistance far transcends its material value', Casey told the parliament, recalling the words of India's finance minister, Chintaman Deshmukh.[5] Even the sober-minded academic commentators Gordon Greenwood and Norman Harper were caught up in the excitement, when they wrote about the 'meeting of East and West in fraternal association' and Australia's 'increasing maturity'. But few could deny that the impact of Australian foreign assistance and the complexities associated with building Asia's economic potential had yet to be evaluated.[6]

Aid contributions were often not coordinated with pre-established development plans because of limited official regulation or monitoring. This was so despite official decrees to the effect that support for the Colombo Plan was 'predicated on the belief that assistance should be within the context of well conceived development plans'.[7] Early projects, in particular, suffered from a combination of inadequate supervision, poor coordination, hasty execution, and 'unbusinesslike' procedures. For example, in 1952 the Pakistan government reported a 'most embarrassing situation', after a shipment of water pumps provided by Australia had been found to be completely unsuitable for the job at hand and discarded. With Australia eager to give and Pakistan eager to receive, neither country sent representatives to closely investigate the requirements of the project. A similar case occurred when Australia supplied 200 tractors for the Punjab Canal Links Project. After they arrived, officials discovered that much heavier vehicles were required to undertake land reclamation work. Compounding the error, Australia had supplied two technicians to train local staff how to operate and maintain the tractors, but the Pakistan government sent no personnel for training. The Australian experts left without conducting a single class. For Australia's part, Pakistani officials bemoaned the fact that Colombo Plan aid was not a simple supplement to their resources because they were often restricted to receiving 'Australian commodities, material, equipment and facilities' for a given project.[8] Goods and equipment manufactured in Australia consisted of around 65 per cent of the capital aid program to 1965. This procedure of 'tying' aid to the resources of the donor country was a common practice, intended to support local industrial capacity and agricultural production. Thus, high-wage nations, such as Australia, forced recipient nations to purchase expensive supplies and equipment that they might have been able to purchase more cheaply elsewhere.[9] Crocker, for one, felt helpless.

The practice hampered Australian short-term publicity objectives as much as it hindered effective economic development: 'what little it has accomplished has cost about three times what it would have in the free market. The same truth applies to American Aid and to the Technical Assistance of the UN'.[10]

Asian governments did not shirk responsibility for their role in project failure. Contrary to the tenor of many expert reports and Osmar White's pronouncements, the Pakistan government possessed a complex understanding of the aid-giving environment and the limitations of its own bureaucracy and work culture. The Pakistan Ministry for Economic Affairs (PMEA) took a savage view of its project directors:

> *most do not appreciate their responsibilities or fail to live up to them. Sometimes, they act like 'white collar' desk workers, signing papers and issuing orders rather than field operators, having direct and daily contact with the job. In certain cases, they showed deplorable ignorance of the details of their projects, particularly the list and specifications of equipment ordered.*

The Ministry also resolved to curb the growing tendency to request foreign expertise on the slightest pretext and to discourage the attitude that the employment of a foreign expert would magically solve difficult problems. This 'creates a sense of undue dependence and discourages Pakistani technicians', the report warned.[11]

Although the Department of External Affairs (DEA) rarely knew how much aid they had to spend on the Colombo Plan until Casey secured Cabinet approval, Pakistani officials criticised Australia for not disclosing how much aid would be available each year. Instead, the DEA preferred to see what projects the Pakistanis laid before them, and then to take its pick. When Australia did volunteer particular material and expertise, the preference for discrete and often isolated aid projects, while minimising the risk of a large-scale failure, had significant ramifications for Pakistan's national development program. As the PMEA contended in a major report:

> in the case of Australian aid, most of the projects taken up were not approved projects nor were their details drawn up in advance. The range of availabilities in Australia was limited. In the anxiety to use the aid offered, projects were sponsored to suit the equipment available: in other words, the aid led to the project rather than the project leading to the aid.[12]

Australia's narrow industrial export base, and the desire to reduce the export of goods with a high US dollar value, also restricted what Australia could provide, namely heavy capital equipment needed for complex projects such as power generation, mills, factories, and port facilities.

Domestic budgetary problems in recipient countries also hampered the effective use of equipment. In Indonesia, for example, the 100 diesel buses so conspicuously supplied to the Djakarta public transport authority soon required running repairs and modification for local conditions. Unable to afford the expensive parts — the result of an unfavourable exchange rate — the authority kept two Australian experts on site, and they had no option but to cannibalise 80 buses to keep 20 on the road.[13] But the news was not all bad. A cement pipe plant for the Karachi water supply project, for example, proved to be a more successful venture because, as the PMEA stated, a 'real need existed' and project managers implemented appropriate planning mechanisms.[14] Similarly, the Kangaroo Tractor Station in Anduradhapura, Ceylon, while not without its problems, appeared to run smoothly. The station served as a repair and maintenance depot for agricultural equipment hired to local farmers. On inspection in 1960, Murray Bourchier from the High Commission reported that the Australian tractors were well-serviced, in reasonable mechanical condition, and 'presented a very smart appearance'.[15] Other successful ventures included the supply of over £A5 million in railway cars to India and Pakistan, £A1 million in broadcasting equipment for All India Radio, and an extensive feeder road construction project in Thailand.

As with most aid projects, quiet success could be disappointingly anonymous, but failure could be very public. An Australian official reported that two earthmoving vehicles provided for refugee resettlement in Vietnam did not reach their intended communities because they were too heavy for local bridges, but also 'because no Vietnamese really knew how to operate' them. Public scrutiny was unavoidable because the large, yellow tractors stood conspicuously idle between the airport and Saigon. The Saigon Public Works department did, however, eventually use the tractors to extend the runway. If the provision of assistance proved difficult in Vietnam, it was nothing short of a disaster in Laos. An assessment of Australian technical equipment by R. Soudre was enough to test the fortitude of the staunchest advocates of the Colombo Plan. Of three excavation machines sent to the public works authority, one was irreparable after being started when the shipping bolts were still in place, another rested on the bottom of the Mekong River after a transport accident on the way from Bangkok, while the third was in poor condition because of poor handling and lack of maintenance. Of the seven bulldozers provided by

Australia, just two were in working order (and being operated by the Americans), and spare parts for 14 diesel rollers had been destroyed in a fire at Nong-Kai. Soudre's litany continued. No one knew whether three rock-crushing plants shipped to the area were in operation, or even where the equipment had been sent! A DEA representative from Saigon accompanied Soudre on a field trip and confirmed most of his observations. Together they also discovered structural equipment provided by Australia for a sawmill lying unprotected and weathered in the Saigon goods yards. The final insult to these conscientious public servants was the assault on their olfactory systems, with the equipment now serving the locals as a public lavatory. Soudre was angry at the misuse of Australian aid and said that equipment should 'never be sent to Laos without being accompanied by Australian engineers; nor should it be provided unless for use on specific and detailed projects'. He delivered his parting shot squarely at local people. The Australian government was unlikely ever to attract people to work in the region, he said, 'due to the appalling living conditions in Laos and the obstructiveness of Laotian officials'. DEA staff chided Soudre as being 'not the most tactful of people'. Nevertheless, his observations were disconcerting, not just because of his indictment of the Laotian authorities, but because he bluntly confirmed the worst fears of those administering the Colombo Plan.[16]

Australia's reluctance to engage in long-term, expensive infrastructure ventures stemmed partly from the obvious wastage, as well as from an inability to gain public recognition. D.O. Muller undertook an assignment to Pakistan in 1961 and reported on a deep level of distrust between himself and the local officials who attempted to 'suppress all the undesirable features' of the inspection sites. More importantly, Muller found no obvious recognition that the aid came from Australia; rather it was 'generally accepted that the scheme was conceived by the United Nations Food and Agriculture Organization'. He concluded that by the time the Tubewells irrigation program solved the problem of salinity in the Punjab, Australia's 'gift of 2 million worth of equipment ... will have been completely forgotten'. By the 1960s, with Casey now retired, diplomats reasserted their interest in funding sustainable and visible infrastructure development. The urbane and respected high commissioner in India, James Plimsoll, reported that 'what we need badly in India is some rather large project, in a place which is easily accessible and likely to be seen by a large number of Indians; which is almost completely financed by Australia'. He proposed the construction of a phytotron, a greenhouse with precise environmental controls used to study plant physiology and biochemistry. Simply giving aid to villages was wasteful, he said:

> *Some Australians come here, and many Americans in the Peace Corps, to work in villages. The young men themselves benefit from the experience and come back to Australia (or the US) the better for it. But the gain is often to them rather than to the Indians they have been working with. As a general proposition, it is not a choice between Australia assisting in villages, or in more sophisticated ways. It is often a choice of the latter or nothing.*[17]

The DEA's early fear of a 'trail of well-written' but 'useless reports' from its technical experts was being realised. In November 1956, the DEA requested that Australian diplomatic posts throughout the Colombo Plan region prepare a general assessment of the expert program, based on questionnaires completed by the technicians themselves. The results showed that while most achieved their basic objectives, they were hampered by ill-defined project proposals, worked in 'lower powered' positions than they anticipated, and had generally expected a higher degree of cooperation from local authorities than they found. Asians, some suggested, considered Western technicians a luxury: '"frills" from … the Colombo Plan cornucopia', as the Australian High Commission in Singapore put it.[18] Notably absent from the official report on the value of expert assistance was any mention of oversights by Australian officials and administrators. An independent survey conducted by Australian National University researcher Alan Boxer, however, found the DEA wanting. Boxer's report revealed that the most persistent problem associated with the provision of technical expertise was the lack of feedback and consultation initiated by the DEA. Experts identified themselves closely with the projects they undertook and the countries in which they worked. 'They had a lot to say about what they had done and how things could be better organised in the future', wrote Boxer, but had difficulty finding aid officials who were willing to listen. But such concerns had quietly disappeared from the department's list of priorities. Of course, the successful completion of their assignments was important, but the role of the expert as cultural emissary now overshadowed all other concerns. Once again, independent and governmental observers alike considered cultural interchange adequate compensation for expensive and economically dubious assignments: the value of the expert scheme, declared Boxer, 'greatly exceeds the actual money outlay incurred'.[19] The prestige associated with the Colombo Plan scholarship scheme, which always preceded the technicians, may also have been some compensation. Often local authorities enthusiastically received the Australians on assignment and politely waited for an appropriate period of time before asking them if they could organise further training places in Australia.

Casey's enthusiasm for the Colombo Plan blinded him to its faults. Yet observers, such as White, and senior diplomats also alleged that Australian officials concealed unpalatable aspects of the aid program from him. John Quinn, head of South and South–East Asia Branch, and Walter Crocker, suggested that ambitious officers would 'fawn on the Minister's foibles' and take advantage of what had become Casey's obsession.[20] Four years later, while on his investigatory tour, White reported that significant quarters of the public service had glossed over the failure of certain projects and generally neglected to 'inform Casey on what's been going on'. For his part, Casey preferred Asian authorities to manage their own aid allocations, thus avoiding potentially uncomfortable or destructive cultural and social misunderstandings. This official indifference to aid management and the reluctance to tread on Asian sensitivities helped perpetuate the ineffective management of Australian aid. White put it forcefully: Australia had been timorous and 'profitlessly diffident in failing to make it clear that reasonable utilization is a reasonable price to ask for continued aid-giving'.[21]

With limited resources at their disposal, Australian diplomatic staff were daunted by the magnitude of the developmental work facing many Asian countries. The growing administrative demands generated by Colombo Plan projects exacerbated official indifference towards what experts had to say and over the effectiveness of aid. In Indonesia, for example, senior diplomats were regularly spending the majority of their time on Colombo Plan matters. Casey concluded on his 1955 tour of the region that aid management was 'absorbing a good deal too much time'.[22] Rarely receiving explicit advice from Casey or the DEA in Canberra, this pattern of administration continued into the decade. According to Francis Stuart, Casey simply expected that he would 'get on with the job' with existing staffing levels.[23] According to Crocker, the spiralling burden had 'nothing less than a disastrous affect on the department'. Administration of aid came to be considered an incidental, additional chore to the routine duties of diplomatic posts, often relegated to inexperienced junior officers, untrained in the assessment of technical matters.[24] As the novelty receded and the continuing management responsibilities mounted, Arthur Tange saw his department becoming overloaded with the unwieldy task of administering an ever-expanding program of foreign aid. In the mid-1950s he decided that another department might better handle the growing responsibilities associated with the Colombo Plan. In fact, he hoped to retain policy control and, as he put it, simply 'off-load the administration'.[25] He found no takers. Australia's aid program stumbled on under the control of the DEA until 1974, when the Whitlam Labor Government created the Australian Development Assistance Agency, which brought together the various functions performed by different departments since a bilateral aid program (to Papua New Guinea) had begun in 1946. Renamed in 1976, and again in 1987, the agency finally settled on the title of Australian Agency for International Development (AusAID) in 1995.

Goodwill

Australian policy-makers placed considerable stock in the Colombo Plan's ability to generate benefits incommensurate with the limited funds channelled through the program. Personal rapport between officials and the somewhat amorphous concept of international 'goodwill' became an important measure by which the success of the Colombo

Plan could be judged; indeed, it was sometimes the only one. Assessment was also important to allay the concerns of those who thought that the Colombo Plan did not bring sufficient benefits to justify the costs. The constant repetition of the word 'goodwill' in departmental correspondence and public speeches throughout the 1950s and 1960s helped to establish its legitimacy as part of the international affairs lexicon. Such imprecise and flexible benefits also helped the boosters assuage those who decried the Colombo Plan as a wasted exercise.

Goodwill was often synonymous with the personal interactions facilitated by the Colombo Plan, and observers other than politicians also argued that even if aid did not raise living standards 'when related to the individual', it had 'been an instrument of mutual understanding *at the personal level*'.[26] To a great extent, this was the only meaningful way Australia could interpret the usefulness of foreign aid, especially considering the problems associated with large-scale project management and the piecemeal nature of the program itself. Former diplomat and senior DEA official Malcolm Booker suggested from retirement that despite the meagre and 'misdirected' nature of Western assistance, personal interaction succeeded in 'winning the trust and goodwill of the people' of Asia.[27] Australian politicians used the outwardly magnanimous Colombo Plan as a diplomatic tool to build a reserve of goodwill. 'Goodwill', said Menzies in 1955, was central to the Australia's 'good neighbour policy' toward Asia. Australia had made 'substantial contributions to the store of capital and other goods and of goodwill in several Asian countries'. Specifically, he contended that:

> *personal contacts between Asian students and the Australian people in Australia and between Australian experts and the countries they have visited, and the physical symbols of goodwill to be found in Colombo Plan programs, have all helped*

> to make our attitude and the integrity of our
> motives better understood and reciprocated in
> Asia.[28]

The impression left by Menzies here is that the
'stores' of goodwill being built through Australian
generosity were as tangible and quantifiable as the tractors,
rolling stock, wheat and flour donated via the aid program.
From the very beginning of the Colombo Plan, however, it
was always easy to claim widespread understanding and
acceptance of Australia's good intentions; it was much
harder to measure it. Nowhere was this more apparent than
with the student program.

The DEA's failure to instigate a methodical
evaluation procedure resulted from the lack of resources,
the difficulty in locating ex-students, and cultural barriers.
Often assessment was simply beyond the embassy's capacity
and its knowledge of the country. To gauge the real value of
their benefit to the national economy, said J.M. McMillan
from the Djakarta embassy, 'would require a far more
thorough knowledge of the apparatus of government in
this country than can readily be obtained by foreign
representatives'. The suggestion that returnees be
approached directly was also problematic. 'Indonesians tend
to be evasive', McMillan generalised, 'particularly in view
of their fear of losing face and of their desire always to
appear more important than they are'. Canberra insisted
that the post must offer some indication of the effectiveness
of the scheme. Going beyond the call of duty, the third
secretary resorted to staging informal social gatherings of
returned students at his home in order to circumvent these
cultural constrictions. Diplomatic staff in Ceylon were also
forced to 'tread warily when seeking information from
Government Departments' about the destinations of

returning Colombo Plan scholars. Once again, informal evaluations revealed a series of minor problems that marred the effectiveness of the program. Lack of planning and poor administration sometimes saw former students employed in work unconnected with their training. Some students regarded their Colombo Plan qualifications merely as something to mark them out for early promotion. The High Commission also heard reports of cliques forming of ex–Colombo Plan students (according to the country they studied in) and 'for these cliques to be jealous or critical of one another'. On another occasion, two Ceylonese nationals who interviewed Colombo Plan students in Australia, told the commission about the dissatisfaction felt by students who had experienced a 'better life materially in Australia'. They claimed that these students 'did not relish the thought of returning to Ceylon' for the five years required of them by the Ceylon government and 'thought of establishing themselves in the UK or Canada if Australia would not have them'.[29] To a greater or lesser extent, Australian diplomatic posts throughout Asia expressed these concerns about the viability of the student program.

Wastage and the potential for abuse by ambitious, middle-class Asians offended some commentators. The middle-class leanings of most Colombo Plan students prompted journalist Peter Coleman to describe the scheme as a 'racket for yes-men only'. Coleman suggested that the scheme shift its focus to provide poorer Asians with Leaving Certificates. This, he believed, would encourage economic development and discourage 'careerist' scholars. Chiming in, John Quinlem suggested that money would be better spent by establishing centres for technical education in Asia, and reserving scholarships to Australia for talented Asian post-graduates. Not only would this be more efficient for building the necessary skills among Asians, but it would also address the wastage which occurred because of the language and cultural difficulties experienced by many undergraduate scholarship holders. Raffles Professor of History at the University of Singapore Ken Tregonning flayed the Colombo Plan for giving Asians an 'irrelevant' education 'opposed to conditions in their own environment'. His rather thin body of evidence came from personal experience. Suffering from a painful earache, Tregonning got no relief from his Australian-trained Chinese doctor. Only a locally-trained physician recognised his ailment as a tropical ear infection. 'I could not help wishing the first doctor knew more about the diseases of his country', Tregonning wrote. The point that training needed to be better tailored to local conditions may have been valid. But as Asia's appetite for Colombo Plan stipends, other international scholarships, and overseas tertiary experience in general grew apace, he seemed wide of the mark when he suggested that 'in many cases' outside education led to 'estrangement, even possibly an emasculation, of those involved'. And his fanciful suggestion that 'deculturised' Asians returned home from Australia unable to communicate in their native language was based on a deeper fear about the corruptive impact of Western values.[30] Nevertheless, Australia continued to resist the establishment of education centres in Asia, preferring to educate Asians in Australia. Cultural exchange and the search for the elusive store of 'international goodwill', even at the cost of achieving developmental objectives in Asia, remained an overwhelming government priority.

The DEA was generally less perturbed by the precise destinations of Colombo Plan graduates. Robert Birch in Rangoon reported that although Australia had lost contact with most of the returning scholars, some trainees went on to provide valuable links to the Burmese government service. The embassy in Djakarta posed questions about an Indonesian Colombo Plan student, Mr Saud, who studied commerce and price control, then returned to Indonesia, and within a short time became head of the Criminal Division of the Djakarta Police. Did he gain valuable public administration experience while in Australia, the DEA wondered? Did he just get enough kudos to obtain a promotion? Did it matter? Indirectly addressing these very issues, Asian student Chai Hon-Chan acted as an unwitting propagandist when he took issue with the likes of Quinlem and Coleman. Encapsulating the government's prevailing concerns, he wrote that Coleman's argument was moot because Asia's emerging middle classes were precisely the social group that needed to experience Australia's liberal democracy if progressive development was to be encouraged in the region. Officials and policy-makers alike accepted some waste and mismanagement because they were convinced that 'the growing cadre of people associated directly or indirectly with the training aspect of the Colombo Plan' was a boon for Australia and stood in stark contrast to the capital aid program. Copying the American practice, the DEA proposed to present Colombo Plan certificates at Australian diplomatic posts throughout Asia. This presentation, they believed, would help establish personal contact between the Australian representatives and returned students and help to ensure Australian involvement in solving any problems they might encounter when 'adapting their Australian experience to local conditions', such as the provision of equipment or further technical assistance.[31]

A conference of government agencies involved in the training of Colombo Plan students that met in Canberra in 1960 was one indication of increased effort to evaluate the impact of educational assistance. Although delegates complained about getting inadequate information on trainees, they acknowledged that Asian governments, motivated by the rising demand for the highly prized scholarships, were beginning to institute rigorous selection processes and methods of evaluation. By the mid-1960s, the DEA, in conjunction with the Bureau of Census and Statistics, set about developing a more sophisticated means of surveying ex–Colombo Plan scholars.[32]

Australians expected to be applauded as good and generous neighbours. But the response of Asian authorities to the Colombo Plan was equivocal, ranging from appreciation through to indifference and even hostility. Asians, while happy to receive aid, did not wish to appear as lesser or subservient people in need of advice, charity, and surplus goods. Nor did they accept passively the role of grateful and pliable recipient. Many Australians working in Asia were genuinely surprised and hurt by such ambivalence, and, in turn, responded defensively. Osmar White reported the Indian attitude to aid as being 'ungracious and at times obliquely contemptuous'.[33] For others, the ingratitude and righteousness displayed towards donor nations seemed to grow as they became accustomed to receiving aid. As Crocker committed to his diary: 'another thing to strike one is the widespread feeling amongst Indonesians, as amongst so many Asian people, that the better-off-world and especially the West, owes it to them to give aid a'la [sic] Colombo Plan'.[34] Australian experts on assignment in Asia may well have reported on a changing attitude towards Australians, but that did not necessarily extend to a sense of appreciation for aid. With surprising regularity, those working in the region suggested that very few Asians were aware of Australia's aid contributions and only an educated minority thought more positively about Australia. Once again, it was only former students and those who worked alongside Australian technicians who displayed any gratitude towards donor countries.[35]

The goodwill that Australia did generate often had more to do with timing than the particular effectiveness of aid projects. Osmar White noted that in Pakistan even though much of Australia's aid contribution was inadequate and mismanaged, it was supplied on a consistent basis at a time when the Western world regarded the nation with suspicion. Like Indonesia's admission to the Colombo Plan, the 'spectacularly well-timed' gift of aid to Pakistan allowed Australia to gain 'room for manoeuvre and fields of contact with Pakistani opinion beyond the normal diplomatic field'.[36] But using aid to bolster diplomatic relations was fraught with problems. As White explained to the DEA in July 1959: 'Goodwill built up in this way is a fragile thing. It can be destroyed by one ill-timed political speech. That is the tragedy of it'.[37] Of course, the government already knew this well, but they received an explicit reminder the following year. In May 1960, the Indian newspaper the *Hindu* attacked Menzies's failure to speak out when South African police opened fire on black demonstrators at Sharpeville, killing 67. The paper claimed that by describing it as simply a domestic and 'internal affair', he destroyed 'at one blow much of the work of Mr. Casey in creating a friendly image of Australia'.[38]

Western allies could be just as fickle towards Australia's aid efforts as Asian leaders. In the field, US aid managers were cooler in their attitude towards Australia's use of the Colombo Plan. According to DEA reports, Australia's aversion to submerging her smaller contributions within larger American projects was 'unsympathetically received in some instances', as was the tendency to avoid difficult projects in favour of 'politically rewarding' ones.[39] But in diplomatic circles, American representatives in

Canberra were forced to concede that the Colombo Plan still had the 'highest reputation of any of the international aid programs and has been fully successful in establishing a framework for Australian assistance'. And, regardless of the effectiveness of individual aid projects, the Colombo Plan reduced Australia's sense of dislocation from Asian affairs. It facilitated access to all levels of government and enabled Australian diplomats to get to know a wider range of people than they might have in its absence. The DEA, quite rightly, reasoned that the Colombo Plan had 'much to do with the opening of doors and the readiness of ministers and officials in most countries of Asia to give Australian representations a sympathetic hearing'.[40]

Yet Australian leaders could forget the Colombo Plan as easily as they could invoke it. Bipartisan support (and the concomitant lack of public debate) and competition from Soviet aid programs took attention from Western aid, and prompted former Secretary of the DEA, and now Commissioner in South–East Asia, Alan Watt, to tell Casey that 'some of the novelty of the Plan has worn off and the impact of the Plan upon Asian consciousness has lost some of its freshness'.[41] Menzies' major statement on international affairs, made to his own party in 1957, ignored the Colombo Plan entirely.[42] Even Casey, the plan's champion, grew less interested: his diaries hardly mentioned it by the end of his time as minister. It was the same outside Australia. The institutional success and public cohesiveness of the Consultative Committee did not make exciting copy, especially as Asian governments came to expect and rely on regular aid payments. 'The Colombo Plan has lost its initial novelty. It has become an accepted fact, and a successful institution in the community of nations', said Ceylon's finance minister, M.D.H.

Jayewardane, during his opening address at the 1955 Consultative Committee meeting.[43]

Despite the Colombo Plan's fading lustre, the annual meeting of the Colombo Plan Consultative Committee prevailed as the diplomatic high point of the aid-giving calendar — an event that promised opportunities for Western donors to test, and perhaps draw on, their stocks of international goodwill. Social events, excursions, and informal meetings accompanied the formal business of the week-long conferences. Although the rigours of the heavy social agenda tested Casey's stamina, he revelled in the power and influence at his command. Seasoned diplomat that he was, Casey worked the floor and took the opportunity to drop hints about the forms of assistance that Australia could supply. For example, during the Ottawa meeting he mentioned informally the availability of Australian-built light trucks and tractors to the Burmese delegation: 'their eyes opened wide' at the remark, he recorded.[44] The pressure brought to bear on Asian recipients during these meetings was always subtle. When donor governments did exert pressure and make suggestions, this occurred in the congenial atmosphere of a dinner party or over cocktails. Indeed, often the recipients of aid had the upper hand, able to canvass a range of glad-handing representatives, who were in turn eager to appear generous and obliging.[45] Nevertheless, the increasing importance of informal discussion, and the corresponding decrease in the significance of official business, was institutionalised, albeit casually. During the Melbourne meeting of the Consultative Committee in 1962, the chairman apologised for pushing delegates to conclude their business quickly, but said that the formal business was less significant than the informal discussions after the close of proceedings. They agreed.[46]

Quiet diplomacy

Australia's Colombo Plan aid may have been sporadic, limited, and loaded with political and cultural preconceptions, but it was rarely capricious. The DEA did not suspend aid in retaliation if a country took a stance at odds with Australian foreign policy. They also avoided accusations of providing assistance on a political basis alone because even though political relations with Indonesia deteriorated over the West New Guinea dispute, there was no corresponding reduction in assistance. Certainly, some officials and politicians would have preferred to use foreign aid as a direct political lever. The conciliatory and incremental nature of Australian diplomacy, which played an important role in securing Indonesian participation in the Colombo Plan, was lost on some members of the Australian parliament, who demanded explicit political concessions in return for aid. Henry 'Jo' Gullett, son of the late Sir Henry Gullett, saw Indonesia's involvement with Australia as an opportunity to bully Indonesian elites over West New Guinea:

> I trust that the Australian Government, though under the Colombo Plan it is giving aid to Indonesia, among other Asian countries, will speak firmly and bluntly to the Indonesians. I have never believed that one buys popularity in this world ... Australia should tell Indonesia bluntly that if it wants assistance from us, we should like it to adopt a more reasonable attitude towards West New Guinea.[47]

Extreme and out-of-touch as Gullett was, he represented the imperial apologists who lurked ever more furtively in Australia's halls of power. But the example highlights an important evolution in the history of Australia's diplomatic service. The gulf between those who recognised that Australia's engagement with Asia required a more mindful approach and those who maintained a paternalistic and imperial view of regional affairs continued to grow. Decision-making power, however, rested with those who insisted that the political usefulness of the Colombo Plan arose from the spirit of bipartisan cooperation it had come to represent. The Assistant Secretary of the DEA, Keith Waller, rejected suggestions from his staff to direct Colombo Plan aid to Australia's SEATO partners and cut assistance to neutral governments. The Colombo Plan 'flourished because political issues have been kept at bay', he told Casey. 'No country has ever had to vote in a minority in Colombo Plan councils because all decisions are taken unanimously and harmoniously. It would destroy the fabric of the Plan to give political considerations undue weight'. Of course, this did not mean that the Colombo Plan was about to shed its strategic and political essence. Aid to India, Ceylon, and Pakistan slowly tapered off towards the end of the 1950s and flowed in the palatable form of scholarships and technical equipment to South–East Asia, notably Malaya, Indonesia, and later Vietnam; regions 'where we have an obvious political target', explained Waller.[48] That shift to the 'near north' also reflected a growing consciousness among Australians of the relative importance of the immediate region over the old ties of Empire and Commonwealth.

The immediate region to the north was of particular significance. With a communist nation potentially sharing a land-border with Australian territory, Australian relations with Indonesia had greater repercussions for Australia's security than any other country in the region. They would continue to do so for many decades. John Kevin, Australia's Minister and Charge d'Affaires in Djakarta, told Casey in 1953, 'both as near neighbour and for reasons of self-interest', Indonesia was a nation Australia could ill afford to ignore.[49] As an aid-giver, Australia had established a greater rapport with Asian leaders and officials, but the goodwill created by the Colombo Plan was not always enough to offset the negative consequences of other aspects of Australian foreign policy. For example, Australia's refusal to support Indonesian claims to West New Guinea, according to White, 'obliterated memory of Australian support for Indonesian claims to independence … and had certainly overshadowed any warmth that might in other circumstances had been derived from appreciation of attempts at economic, technical and educational assistance'.[50] Australian self-delusion over this issue featured in a political report written by Samar Sen, the Indian High Commissioner in Canberra in 1959. Among a myriad of topics, he suggested that the Australian government had not realised that Colombo Plan aid could not repair the 'ill-will and suspicion caused by its attitude over West Irian'.[51]

By the mid-1950s, Australian predictions of Indonesian militancy were being realised. Indonesia lobbied the UN General Assembly to force The Netherlands to enter negotiations over the West New Guinea issue; and in 1955 the Bandung conference of Afro–Asian nations — that quintessential expression of Asian nationalism — rallied behind Indonesia. Rising nationalist sentiment, combined with Sukarno's increasingly restive and unpredictable behaviour, prompted Australian officials to think carefully about the consequences of a breakdown in diplomatic relations. With Australia still unlikely to change its position on the issue, the DEA looked to the Colombo Plan to maintain stable relations. In November 1957, former Ambassador in Bangkok, David Hay, wrote a draft memo to Casey:

*The Colombo Plan is perhaps our best way of
keeping open the door to Indonesia ... There is
little doubt that our Colombo Plan activities
constitute a very positive aspect of our foreign
policy and that good relations have been cemented
with responsible people in Indonesia by means of
our training programmes, supply of useful
equipment and willingness to undertake such
integrated projects as the printing school and the
central Sumatran medical school. Should there be
any termination or suspension of our aid it would
be extremely difficult to ever recapture the present
atmosphere of our unique partnership under the
Colombo Plan.*[52]

Kevin had also told Casey that providing
scholarships to Indonesia continued to be the 'best
propaganda' on offer because opportunities to study in
Australia were 'greatly appreciated ... much sought after
and [receive] wide publicity'. The decision to maintain
Colombo Plan aid to Indonesia, Casey explained to James
Plimsoll, Assistant Secretary of the DEA, represented a
'mild piece of generosity' that would pay off in the long
run.[53] At this time, however, he was not to know how
quickly things would deteriorate. One week later,
Indonesia's Foreign Minister since 1957, Dr. Achmed
Subandrio, made the ominous announcement that
Indonesia would no longer seek redress through the
General Assembly, but would pursue 'action outside the
United Nations'. In December 1957, the Indonesian army
took control of Dutch businesses, banned Dutch
publications, revoked the landing rights of the Dutch
airline KLM, and took steps to repatriate Dutch citizens.
The Dutch responded by calling for a mass exodus and

more than 40,000 Dutch citizens left Indonesia in a matter of weeks. Throughout this chaotic time Australia's Colombo Plan aid program continued relatively smoothly. Projects continued to be developed, technical experts travelled and worked throughout the archipelago, and students continued to study in Australia. In fact, in 1957 almost 500 Indonesians were attending Australian educational institutions, or had completed their studies and returned home – the highest of any Colombo Plan nation supported by Australia. By 1970, that total approached 1,500.[54]

Australia also maintained Colombo Plan assistance when Indonesia aggressively resisted the formation of the Malaysian federation in September 1963, and President Sukarno's policy of 'confrontation' saw Australian troops fighting in Borneo in an undeclared war against Indonesia. In January 1965, in the face of pressure from the opposition and the press, Cabinet elected to restrict the negotiation of new Colombo Plan projects, but to maintain existing projects operating in Indonesia and the flow of scholarship holders. Cabinet determined that the 'abrupt discontinuance' of Colombo Plan aid risked 'adverse repercussions without yielding any balancing advantage to Australia'.[55] Menzies defended the decision by saying that he strove to 'preserve our contact with Indonesia in such directions as are open to us in the hope that this may produce opportunities to work towards peace and stability in the area'.[56] Here was the Colombo Plan clearly fulfilling an important purpose in maintaining visible, positive, and non-political contact in the face of hostilities that, at the time, had the potential to escalate into a much wider conflict with Indonesia. The government rescinded its restriction on the negotiation of new Colombo Plan aid projects as soon as the prospect of a resolution appeared likely.[57] Using the Colombo Plan to chart a quiet but persistent path through seemingly intractable regional disputes had become an important feature of Australian diplomacy.

A difficult business

However, the Colombo Plan's usefulness as a diplomatic tool and facilitator of cross-cultural relations stood in marked contrast to its ability to generate economic growth. Piecemeal as it was and wedded to political and strategic incentives, Australian Colombo Plan aid was spread so thinly across a wide range of countries that it had little measurable impact on capital formation. Indeed, the billions of dollars supplied by Colombo Plan donors did little to alter the trajectory of South and South–East Asia's economic evolution. But in the mid-1960s, the shadow cast by Rostow's theorem was long. Although the language employed by planners and economists became increasingly sophisticated, the message was the same. 'No country can arrive at the "take-off" point purely through foreign aid', the DEA advised in 1964 during the first major review of Australia's aid program: 'domestic effort is vital to any economic development program'.[58] The role of trade was more pronounced than ever before, but responsibility for economic performance rested squarely with Asian authorities themselves. And, by regularly claiming that the Colombo Plan would make people richer in the future, donor nations could at least distract attention from the fact that the recipients were poorer at present. Asians were always encouraged to keep looking towards the future.

Donor nations paid cursory attention to the complex interplay between trade, aid, and economic development. This annoyed Asia's more truculent leaders, who were only too willing to point out the flaws and contradictions inherent in the giving of foreign aid. 'Make no mistake', President Sukarno blustered at a state banquet for Colombo Plan delegates in Jogjakarta in 1959, 'the greatest evils and dangers facing humanity are the perverted products of a technical civilization centering in the West'. Of course, he welcomed aid but confessed, with heavy irony, to being 'very puzzled when a market manipulation of prices destroys in one day all the aid and assistance received in one year'.[59] Shattering the collegial and cordial atmosphere, most delegations found his bellicosity in 'extremely bad taste and inappropriate to the traditional harmonious spirit' of Colombo Plan meetings. Nevertheless, Sukarno had a point. In the short term, the Korean War boom pushed up commodity prices for many Asian countries (and Australia) and increased their foreign exchange earnings. In turn, this allowed them to spend more of their own finance on development projects. But from the end of 1951, as export prices fell, developing countries lost as much through the deterioration in their terms of trade as they received in aid. Sukarno's provocative speech reminded Colombo Plan donors that recipients of aid were alive to the impact world markets and trade barriers had on their economic progress and were unwilling to fall into the role of grateful and supine recipients. However, according to the US delegation, Sukarno's speech was 'rebutted without creating sharp dissension'. That congeniality prevailed was, according to the Americans, a 'remarkable tribute' to the atmosphere of the Colombo Plan. However, it was equally a 'tribute' to the reluctance of delegates to confront the complex relationship between aid and trade that might otherwise have been expected to accompany such an outburst. But then the Consultative Committee never was a forum for discussing the gritty and often depressing realities of development aid.[60]

Australia, like other nations with primary industries to protect, found itself in the contradictory position of offering aid on one hand — presumably to help Asian nations expand their export potential — and invoking trade barriers to deny competitive access to the Australian markets on the other. Australian policy-makers found themselves in a double bind. By resisting pressure to give unrequited tariff concessions, they increased the obligation to give more aid. Alternatively, giving trade concessions might reduce pressure to give aid. The decision to bolster the Colombo Plan and multilateral aid agencies instead of negotiating trade concessions emerged as the path of least resistance. Helping Asia with aid spread the burden and did not single out the local manufacturers likely to be adversely effected by freer trading arrangements. Of course, Australian manufacturers were keen to exploit the increased exposure made possible by Colombo Plan gifts, yet they were ambivalent — and often hostile — to the prospect of tariff reduction and increased competition from Asian imports. The trade concessions, which might have made a far greater economic impact than aid, threatened national economic interests. While gaining access to Asian markets was a relatively minor factor in the genesis of the Colombo Plan, policy-makers envisaged that the promotion of Australian technology, expertise, training facilities, and commercial produce would generate substantial commercial business.[61] In fact, only very occasionally did the exposure of Australian equipment under the Colombo Plan generate commercial interest. Of course, some grew frustrated at the tantalising but unrealised potential. In 1955, Alexander Downer (Snr) asked Phillip McBride, Acting Minister for External Affairs, whether Australia could supply a shipment of dried fruit to Colombo Plan countries, thus exploiting a 'hitherto undeveloped market' and stimulating a struggling local industry. McBride was circumspect, explaining that it was usual for Australia to respond only to explicit requests for goods and equipment. The government had received no request for dried fruit.[62] But it was not policy or a fine sense of morality that distanced the Colombo Plan from the pursuit of new export markets. Indeed, the DEA reassured conscientious officials who expressed concern about taking advantage of their Colombo Plan connections to foster additional commercial sales that such transactions were 'within normal business methods'.[63]

In some cases, winning a contract to provide goods under the Colombo Plan boosted a company's production levels and saved them the expense and responsibility of shipping. However, many Australian manufacturers with 'comfortable and sheltered' domestic markets had little incentive to give priority to filling Colombo Plan orders, especially when they had little prospect of further sales. In addition, the ubiquity of US aid (usually tied to the purchase of American goods) also affected the chances of Australian manufacturers gaining their share of the market.[64] The typically caustic Tange wrote that in addition to the 'faltering, uncertain, tardy and relatively inefficient Australian manufacturing industry', the inability to break the 'franchise arrangements where South East Asia belongs to the American parent company' meant that Australia did 'not seem to have very much ice upon which to skate'.[65] In the 1950s around 10 per cent of Australian exports went to South and East Asia, mostly in the form of foodstuffs, only marginally higher than it had been in the 1930s, and slightly lower than in the 1910s. By the early 1970s this figure had risen to 15 per cent, largely on the back of limited tariff concessions granted by Australia in the mid-1960s and not from any cumulative impact of Colombo Plan aid. With the exception of Japan, trade between Australia and Asia struggled to expand because of low commodity prices, political instability, concurrent population growth, debt repayments, and the crushing weight of tariff barriers. The small market for Australian foodstuffs and the growing relationship with Japan created a basis for future trade and regional economic integration. But, in general, in the poorest nations of Asia there was simply no appreciable increase in purchasing power to sustain fresh imports.

Perhaps because of Australia's negligible trade ties with the region, the Department of Trade and Industry exerted a powerful influence over the aid review committee. While defence and political considerations were important, its officials wanted aid to be given in a form that contributed 'most towards Australia's trade policies and through them towards Australia's economic objectives'. The national mantra of sustainable growth and full employment meant that Australia had to look towards Asia for fresh export markets. 'If Australia is to obtain her share of the markets in the Less Developed Countries, particularly in South East Asia, aid must become recognised as a technique of export expansion', the departmental report stated.[66] The Department of Trade's interest in commercial benefits and the Department of Treasury's continuing reluctance to embrace the program soon brought them into conflict with the DEA.

While no one could accuse Tange of being an uncritical supporter of the Colombo Plan, to some extent he took over Casey's battle with those who sought to hobble the already tightly-funded program. In the midst of the review, he declared to his senior officers that the preoccupation with fostering trade advantages, the persistent 'gamesmanship' from the Treasury department, and general 'inadequacy' of the Colombo Plan added 'up to a rather negative commercial interest in our external aid' policy. Tange disagreed with the passive and ambiguous nature of the Colombo Plan. Australia's aid program, he reasoned, should be determined by the specific needs of particular Asian economies and 'specific Australian policy objectives', and not 'flow from some general preconceived idea as what level and kind of aid ... we ought to give the outside world'.[67] Even those outside the inner sanctum of inter-departmental policy-making could see the bureaucratic strictures at play. Heinz Arndt, one of Australia's leading economists, wrote that the 'trickle' of aid to Indonesia was 'pushed along by a handful of Australian officials in the face of heart-breaking frustrations arising from conditions in both countries'. Australia's aid program, he continued, suffered from inadequate administrative support and relentless pressure from a Department of Trade 'interested only in export promotion and the pulls from a Treasury jealous of the taxpayers' money and sceptical about the value of foreign aid'.[68] No doubt Tange would have appreciated Arndt's analysis.

By insisting that the chance of trade promotion 'should not be allowed to divert [Australia] from the basic aims of our aid policy', Tange did manage to temper the Trade Department's forceful presence. But it was not his intention to emphasise the humanitarian dimensions of the Colombo Plan. Rather he sought to embed hard-headed political and strategic imperatives within the broader thrust of Australian aid policy — of which humanitarian concern was only one facet. After 15 years, the essence of that policy remained largely unchanged. The inter-departmental committee concluded that Australian assistance was intended to help develop the nations in areas of political and strategic importance to Australia, lessen the attractions of communism, stimulate additional markets for Australian goods, and foster circumstances to dispose of surplus commodities. Importantly, the committee believed that the Colombo Plan continued to demonstrate to the United States that Australia was prepared to assist the Western effort to resist regional aggression and subversion, reinforce the collegial spirit inherent in Colombo Plan dealings, and give substance to the 'Commonwealth concept'.[69] Cabinet approved the review's broad direction. However, it scotched recommendations to restrict involvement with the soon-to-be-opened Asian Development Bank, an institution the DEA considered of 'doubtful utility'.[70] Japan and the United States strongly supported this UN-managed organisation, which provided loans and technical assistance and brought together 30 regional governments and 14 nations from Europe and North America. Fearing regional ostracism, Australia soon fell into line.

The DEA had learnt valuable lessons from 15 years of giving aid. Drawing on this experience, the review spelt out the attributes essential to the successful and efficient completion of an aid project. This basic framework, while elementary stuff for aid managers today, was not obvious to a department with such limited experience in supplying overseas aid. Where aid was accompanied by training and carefully targeted to 'break a bottleneck in the local economy', it was more likely to meet its objectives. Projects without diplomatic support, local involvement, and continuing financial backing would inevitably falter, languish, or fail altogether. The absence of a forward-planning provision in the annual budget restricted the ability of developing nations to predict the amount of funds likely to come from Australia and so allow them to initiate large-scale projects. The restriction on supplying equipment when the imported content exceeded 33 per cent or if the US dollar content exceeded 10 per cent meant that very few manufactured goods could be donated. Australia could not contribute to the hydro-electricity schemes in India because the generators were not made in Australia. Significantly, the DEA realised 'the same limitation applies to most "prestige" projects or industrial ventures'. The restriction also stopped Australia undertaking many 'complete projects' if there was an item of equipment required from overseas. For example, Australian aid workers could not complete the construction of a school in Khulna, Pakistan, because some steel rods were only available outside Australia. The DEA's review also acknowledged that the failure to provide flexible loans or credits, which allowed recipients to buy in the cheapest markets, meant that the department was unable to initiate major projects and 'very few worthwhile development projects cost less than £1 million'. Not only did this hamper attempts to promote the importation of Australian goods, it denied Australia the opportunity to create 'interest and capital repayment obligations [which] could act as a stimulus to ensure the optimum economic use of the resources provided'.[71] In other words, by encouraging poor countries to repay loans, Australian authorities could argue that they were building economic incentives into the aid projects themselves. These incentives would then ensure that the projects worked efficiently and generated income. Yet the economic situation in developing Asia was not this simple. The Consultative Committee reported in its final communiqué in 1966 that already a 'substantial proportion of the assistance obtained by developing countries is being repaid in the form of interest and installment payments on debts contracted earlier'. By the 1970s, many developing countries were trapped in a vicious cycle of producing cash crops to satisfy loan requirements that restricted their capacity to sustain their own development programs. In turn, this process kept industrial powers supplied with cheap primary commodities. Political economists labelled the intractable problem 'dependency theory'.[72]

By the mid-1960s, Australia spent a greater portion of national income on aid than at any time in its history, supporting a growing array of multilateral aid agencies in addition to a further £A1 million a year for the Colombo Plan. Australians, too, had grown accustomed to giving aid to the region. Opinion polls reflected this attitude, with the proportion of respondents supporting the provision of humanitarian and educational assistance hovering between 50 and 60 per cent throughout the decade. More significantly, the proportion of those who thought the government should reduce or cease giving aid altogether fell from 40 to 24 per cent. The student program was by far the most popular feature of Australian aid. In 1960, around 90 per cent of respondents were aware of the program, and 80 per cent were in favour of it. Seventy per cent thought that Australia should extend the invitation to African students.[73] Support for expanding government assistance also came from unlikely quarters, such as the Victorian Country Party, which passed a resolution in support of giving one per cent of national income as foreign aid. The government now sought to appease those among them who sought to open the national coffers, in contrast to the succession of foreign ministers who had spent years haggling and cajoling their uninterested colleagues. In 1967, Holt pacified Country Party whip Winton Turnbull by telling him that Australia already supplied 0.65 per cent of national income as foreign aid, second only to France and Belgium. It made more sense, he wrote, to examine what was being done with Australian money rather than simply spending more.[74]

The proliferation of non-government aid agencies also reflected community interest in assisting the developing world. In 1965, non-government aid organisations in Australia formed the Australian Council for Overseas Aid (ACFOA). The ACFOA functioned as an interface between the government, the UN, and a growing number of community and religious groups that had organised voluntary aid programs since the Second World War. Among its members were Apex, Lions Clubs, the YMCA, the YWCA, the Australian–Asian Association of Victoria, the Australian Council of Churches, the Australian Council of Aid to Refugees, the Australian Red Cross Society, Community Aid Abroad, the Society for Relief in India and South–East Asia, and the Freedom from Hunger Campaign. Non-government organisations conspicuously picked up the humanitarian shortfall of the government's aid policy, and by the 1980s the ACFOA's original membership of around 20 groups had tripled.

In the early 1960s, a group of Melbourne academics, including the economists Anthony Clunies-Ross and Richard I. Downing, formed a lobby group advocating the spending of one per cent of national income on foreign aid. Taking an idea already espoused by Community Aid Abroad, the 'One per cent' group employed a more detailed, and, it might be said, more coherent application of the government's own argument for assisting the region. Although driven by a strong humanitarian impulse, they stressed the political, strategic, and economic benefits likely to come from economic expansion in Asia. 'Imagine the changes that would come about if the major low income areas of the world attain appreciably better living standards by 1980', the writers enthused. 'The people of these areas will be more numerous, and will consume more per head of industrial materials … [and] much of the extra food and agrarian raw materials they consume will have to come from imports'. And they also knew that in order to embrace this new age of economic expansion Australians would have to relinquish their fears of Asian population growth and start to see 'our neighbours as real people rather than as vast (and necessarily predatory) hordes'. However, it was over trade policy that Clunies-Ross and his co-authors departed from government policy. The 'cautious liberalization' of the tariff and import restrictions they recommended, structures which had hitherto hindered Asia's industrial growth, were still decades away.[75] Government leaders pushed the idea that Australia herself was a 'developing' country and refused to offer loans as part of aid because of her own large-scale borrowing from overseas: an idea that academic economists such as Heinz Arndt dismissed publicly as 'sheer humbug'. Yet, the powerful sentiment struck a deep cord with how Australians perceived their own role as developers of a vast, underpopulated land, and it was successful in restraining the Colombo Plan and other aid initiatives. John McEwen made Australia's special status official at the United Nations Conference on Trade and Development meeting in 1964, when he lobbied for Australia (and other net importers of capital) to be excluded from a resolution asking wealthy nations to offer one per cent of their national income as foreign aid.[76]

For Australia, the failure to imagine Asia as anything other than a homogenous collection of buffer states obscured the specific economic and cultural factors that determined the effectiveness of each aid project. Although a believer in the Colombo Plan, Osmar White was among those who challenged the prevailing faith in the ability of aid projects to fit seamlessly into existing development programs and benignly launch Asia's economic growth. The DEA 'failed to understand that effective aid-giving poses a different set of problems in every country', he told his boss at the Melbourne *Herald*. The 'Paks, Indians, Nepalese, Burmans and the rest have different temperaments, skills, prejudices and reactions. Except in the broadest sense you can't have a Colombo Plan policy; you've got to have 17 separate policies guided by a unifying set of principles'. In parliament, some members were beginning to sense that issues of regional development were becoming more complex and the policy options less assured. As one member said in September 1959: 'Take a country like Malaya ... It is an under-developed and under-populated country. But it is a wealthy country. It produces rubber and tin ... I think we use this term far too broadly when we say that there are starving millions in the near north'. At the very least, public debate exhibited a more inquiring approach to Asian–Australian affairs and marked a departure from the formulaic conventions that had shaped earlier Australian perceptions of the region.[77]

How did Australia's aid program respond to these subtle cultural and attitudinal shifts? Behind the DEA's application of the universal logic of 'take-off' theory, there appeared to be an emerging appreciation of the complexity of giving aid to an economically, politically, and culturally diffuse region. Improving the effectiveness of aid delivery required more than improving accounting, auditing, and the supervision of public expenditure, the review said. Policy-makers also needed to consider the 'susceptibilities of sovereign states and the complex psychological reactions that former colonial non-European peoples have towards richer Western nations'.[78] Significant as this change was, it is important to remember that the DEA couched these sensitivities less in terms of meaningfully addressing developmental issues and more in terms of easing the passage of Australian economic and foreign policy objectives. The government based its expanded aid commitments of the mid- to late-1960s on the assumption that communist China (and north Vietnam) would maintain expansionist pressure against the 18 non-communist countries in the region. In the face of overwhelming problems associated with development assistance, the DEA in general, and aid policy-makers in particular, retreated behind the glib maxim that had governed aid-giving over the last 15 years: the idea that, given time, development and peaceful prosperity would take care of themselves. The primary objective of international assistance revolved around generating economic and political dividends for the donor government. The major goals for Australia remained the cultivation of political contacts, minimising the impact on Australia's balance of payments, and maximising the 'opportunity to introduce Australian goods to new markets'.[79] So too, when Australia's diplomatic representatives met in 1964 to discuss aid policy administration, they agreed that increased pressure to contribute to multilateral agencies, such as the Asian Development Bank, would reduce bilateral spending. The Colombo Plan's annual meeting, they said, risked losing its 'pride of place amongst regional economic meetings'.[80] And with it, they might have added, Australia's conspicuous reputation as an aid-giving regional power.

Australia's attempts to generate political influence through aid worked against a growing raft of difficult international issues likely to alienate Asian leaders. The major issues included support for US defence policy, support for Dutch control of West New Guinea, endorsement of British action at Suez, maintenance of a protective tariff system, and the failure to condemn the South African government's apartheid policy. But while the 1965 review warned against over-estimating the extent to which

Australian policy had been accepted, it also reiterated the view that aid could 'demonstrate our good intentions' and alleviate the handicaps imposed by what had become the pillars of Australian foreign policy.[81] The government's predominately realist approach to international affairs continued to be girded by an optimistic faith in the Colombo Plan's ability to convince the world of Australia's probity.

Since 1950 Australia policymakers subordinated the selection, monitoring, and evaluation of foreign aid to a narrower quest for political and strategic advantage and regional status. The tendency to spread aid projects thinly over a wide array of small-scale undertakings was based on a preference for maximum exposure over substance. In turn, this reduced the impact of Colombo Plan projects in Asia, both in terms of their capacity to foster economic change and, ironically, in terms of their ability to generate positive publicity for Australia. The inexperience and indifference displayed by diplomats and high-level policy-makers, combined with widespread waste and mismanagement of Colombo Plan resources, also severely limited the potential of the program to effect economic growth in the region's poorest countries.[82] For the most part, Casey and the DEA worked in full knowledge of these limitations. Experts, independent observers, and academics suggested ways to release the Colombo Plan from the constraints through which it operated, but the government's unwillingness to divorce aid from foreign policy entrenched an inflexible and doctrinaire approach. In thinking about the Colombo Plan's capacity to initiate substantive economic change in Asia, we might take a broad interpretation of what irrigation expert D. Muller said when he returned after completing his assignment: 'we in Australia' have developed a distinct capacity to 'mislead ourselves'.[83]

Footnotes

1   *Argus*, 8 March 1955

2   A.L. Minkes, *The Colombo Plan: an economic survey*, London, Royal Institute of International Affairs, 1954, p. 9

3   'Foreign Affairs Committee: notes on discussion with Mr. Osmar White', 2 July 1959, Osmar White Papers (OWP); O. White, 'Colombo Plan Survey for Australian Press, December 3 to June 1, 1958/59: summary of conclusions on which further newspaper articles and background memoranda to editors will be based', OWP; Cable, White to Casey, 28 February 1959, OWP

4   'Consultative Committee meeting 1957: evaluation of technical assistance provided under the Colombo Plan', A1838, 2020/1/11, NAA

5   *CPD (HoR)*, vol. 217, 4 June 1952, p. 1371

6   G. Greenwood & N. Harper, eds., *Australia in world affairs, 1950–1955*, Melbourne, F.W. Cheshire, 1957, pp. 90–91, 147

7   A. Basch, 'The Colombo Plan: a case of regional economic cooperation', *International Organization*, vol. 9, no. 1, February 1955, p.12; Consultative Committee, *The Colombo Plan: the second annual report of the Consultative Committee on Economic Development in South and South East Asia, New Delhi, October 1953*, London, HMSO, 1953, p. 87

8   Government of Pakistan, *Foreign Aid Review Committee*, Ministry of Economic Affairs, Karachi, July 1957, A1838, 2020/1/11, NAA

9   'Australian external aid: report to the Minister for External Affairs by the Inter-departmental Committee to Review Australian External Aid, 25 March 1965, A4311, 147/1, NAA

10 Crocker diaries, 17 October 1955, roll 2: G20735, NLA

11 Government of Pakistan, *Foreign Aid Review Committee*

12 Government of Pakistan, *Foreign Aid Review Committee*; D.C. Corbett, *Australian aid in South and South–East Asia*, Canberra, Australian Institute of International Affairs, 1965, p. 26

13 'Foreign Affairs Committee: notes on discussion with Mr. Osmar White', 2 July 1959, OWP

15 M.G.M. Bourchier to DEA, 28 October 1960, A1838, 2020/1/11, NAA

16 'Colombo Plan: use of heavy equipment in Viet Nam', Dexter to Casey, 20 October 1957, A1838, 2020/1/11, NAA; 'Record of interview with Mr R.E.A. Soudre: Australian equipment in South Viet Nam, Laos and Cambodia', 17 April 1957, A1838, 2020/1/11, NAA

17 Memo, Muller, 'Colombo Plan – Punjab Tubewells project', 24 January 1961, A1838, 2020/1/11, NAA; J. Plimsoll to DEA, 8 December 1964, A1838, 2020/1/24/1, NAA

18 C. Gamba, 'Some thoughts on Australian–Asian understanding', *Australian Quarterly*, vol. 30, September 1958, p. 29; D.O. Hay to Casey, 'Colombo Plan – assessment of the value of experts', 21 February 1958, A10302, 1958/170, NAA

19 A.H. Boxer, *Experts in Asia: an inquiry into Australian technical assistance*, Canberra, Australian National University Press, 1969, pp. 5–11

20 Crocker diaries, 17 & 29 October 1955, roll 2: G20735, NLA; Cable, White to Edwards, 30 March 1959, OWP; C. Burns, 'The Colombo Plan', *The Year Book of World Affairs*, vol. 14, 1960, p. 199

21 White, 'Colombo Plan survey for Australian press', OWP

22 Casey diaries, 15 October 1955, vol. 19, box 28, MS 6150, NLA

23 F. Stuart, interview with author, 5 April 2001, Canberra

24 Sir W. Crocker, interview with author, 28 August 2001, Adelaide. See also Crocker diaries, 21 July 1957, roll 3: G20736, NLA; Crocker diaries, 6 May 1955, roll 2: G20735, NLA; Crocker diaries, 20 May 1958, roll 3: G20736, NLA

25 A. Tange, *Monologue: recording of a personal narrative made in February and August 1989 intended as a supplement to the 1989 interview with J.D.B. Miller*, TRC 2447, Oral History Collection, NLA

26 C. Gamba, 'Some thoughts on Australian–Asian understanding'

27 M. Booker, *The last domino: aspects of Australia's foreign relations*, Sydney, Collins, 1976, pp. 110–11

28 *CPD(HoR)*, vol. 6, 20 April 1955, pp. 44, 49–50

29 Memo, J.M. McMillan, Djakarta to DEA, 1 February 1957, A11604, 706/1, NAA

30 *Observer* (Sydney), 2 May 1959, vol. 2, no. 9, pp. 264–65; *Bulletin*, 4 February 1967

31 Memo, R.P. Throssell to various, 14 August 1967, A1838, 2008/10/8 part 3, NAA

32 Memo, R.N. Birch to DEA, 23 September 1959, B142, SC1958/31, NAA:VIC; Memo, J.M. McMillan, Djakarta to DEA, 1 February 1957, A11604, 706/1, NAA; *Observer*, 4 October 1958, pp. 518–19; *Observer* (Sydney), 1 November 1958; 'Consultative Committee meeting 1957: evaluation of technical assistance provided under the Colombo Plan', A1838, 2020/1/11, NAA; 'Minutes of the Colombo Plan conference of training institutions, Canberra, 31 September 1960', A1422, 14/20/2, NAA; see file: A1838, 2008/9 part 3, NAA

33 Cable, White to Casey, 28 February 1959, OWP

34 Crocker diaries, 23 December 1956, roll 3: G20736, NLA

35 T.B. Paltridge, 'Report on some aspects of Colombo Plan aid in Ceylon', 23 October 1957, A1838, 160/10/2/4, NAA

36 'Foreign Affairs Committee: notes on discussion with Mr. Osmar White', 2 July 1959, OWP

37 O. White, 'Colombo Plan survey for Australian press', OWP; 'Foreign Affairs Committee: notes on discussion with Mr. Osmar White', 2 July 1959, OWP; D. Copland, *Australia and the changing world in Asia: eighth Roy Milne Memorial Lecture, Hobart*, Melbourne, The Australian Institute of International Affairs, 1957, pp. 14–15

38 *Hindu*, 25 May 1960
39 Cable, American Embassy, Canberra to Department of State, Washington, 'Australian views on future of Colombo Plan', 7 August 1959, RG59 890.00/8-759, USNA
40 'Review of Australian external aid: general evaluation of Australian aid – relations with recipients, major allies and multilateral institutions', 15 December 1964, A1838, 2020/1/24/23, NAA
41 Despatch, Watt to Casey, March 1956, A1838, 2020/1/7 part 1, NAA
42 *Current Notes on International Affairs*, vol. 28, no. 10, October 1957, p. 822
43 *Morning Times of Ceylon*, 18 October 1959
44 R.G. Casey diaries, 6 October 1954, MS 6150, vol. 17 Box 28, NLA
45 C. Burns also makes this suggestion in 'The Colombo Plan', *The Year Book of World Affairs*, vol. 14, 1960, pp. 186–87
46 L.P. Singh, *The politics of economic cooperation in Asia: a study of Asian international organizations*, Columbia, University of Missouri Press, 1966, p. 200
47 *CPD (HoR)*, vol. 4, 17 August 1954, p. 319
48 Memo, J.K. Waller to Casey, 'The Colombo Plan', 2 May 1957, A1838, 2020/1/2 part 1, NAA; Waller to Casey, 2 May 1957, A1838, 2020/1/24 part 4, NAA
49 Despatch, J.C.G. Kevin to Casey, 30 May 1953, A4231, 1953/Djakarta, NAA
50 O. White, 'Colombo Plan survey for Australian press', OWP
51 S. Sen, 'Annual political report for 1959: Australia', 11 November 1960, Ministry for External Affairs, 3 (31) R&I Section/60, National Archives of India, New Delhi
52 Memo, D.O. Hay to Casey, Djakarta, 'Relations with Indonesia: Colombo Plan aspects', 21 November 1957, A1838, TS2020/2/4, NAA
53 Casey diaries, 6 March 1955, vol. 18, box 28, MS 6150, NLA; Note, Casey to Plimsoll, 20 November 1957, A1838, TS2020/2/4, NAA
54 Indonesian Department of Foreign Affairs, *The question of West Irian in the United Nations, 1954–1957*, Jakarta, Ministry of Foreign Affairs, 1958, p. 480; *Australia in facts and figures*, various issues, 1956–71
55 'Cabinet Decision 695', 26 January 1965, A4940, C4095, NAA
56 *CPD (HoR)*, vol. 45, 23 March 1965, p. 236
57 Letter, Menzies to Drury, 10 March 1965, A1209, 65/6228, NAA; Cabinet minute: Decision 290, 'Economic assistance to Indonesia', 1 June 1966, A4940, C4095, NAA
58 'Review of Australian external aid: economic significance of Australian bilateral aid to Asian countries', 29 December 1965, A1838, 2020/1/24/23, NAA
59 A. Sukarno, *Speech by H.E. President Sukarno at state banquet for Colombo Plan delegates at Gedung Negara Jogjakarta, 10 November 1959*; R.V. Wolpert, 'The Colombo Plan under review', *Eastern World*, vol. 7, October 1953, p. 37

60 'Classified report of the United States delegation to the eleventh meeting of the Consultative Committee of the Colombo Plan on Economic Development in South and South–East Asia, Jogjakarta, Indonesia, 26 October – 14 November, 1959', RG 59, 890.00/12-2259, USNA

61 Cable, McEwan to Casey, 7 October 1955, A1838, 156/5, NAA. See also Casey diaries, 10 March 1954, vol. 16, box 27, MS6150, NLA

62 CPD (HoR), vol. 8, 4 October 1955, pp. 1168–69

63 Cable, B.C. Hill, Saigon to DEA, 12 February 1963, B300, 9268/2 part 3, NAA: SA

64 'Australian external aid: report to the Minister for External Affairs by the Inter-departmental Committee to Review Australian External Aid', 25 March 1965, A4311, 147/1, NAA

65 A. Tange, 'Australia's external aid policy', 22 December 1964, A1838, 2020/1/24 part 2, NAA

66 'Review of Australian external aid: aid and its relationship to trade policy objectives', 23 February 1965, A1838, 2020/1/24/23, NAA

67 A. Tange, 'Australia's external aid policy', 22 December 1964, A1838, 2020/1/24 part 2, NAA

68 H.W. Arndt, 'Australian economic aid to Indonesia', Australian Outlook, vol. 24, no. 2, August 1970, p. 124; F. Stuart, interview with author, 5 April 2001, Canberra

69 'Australian external aid: report to the Minister for External Affairs by the Inter-departmental Committee to Review Australian External Aid', 25 March 1965, A4311, 147/1, NAA

70 'Australian external aid: report to the Minister for External Affairs by the Inter-departmental Committee to Review Australian External Aid', 25 March 1965. Cabinet minute, 'Decision 1002', 9 June 1965, A1838, 2020/1/24 part 3, NAA

71 'Review of Australian external aid', 21 December 1964, A1838, 2020/1/24/23, NAA

72 'Communiqué: seventeenth meeting of the Consultative Committee, 1966', M. Haas, ed., Basic documents of Asian regional organizations, New York, Oceana Publications, 1974, p. 204

73 Australian Gallup Polls, Melbourne, Roy Morgan Research Centre, 1950–67

74 Letter, H. Holt to W.G. Turnbull, 20 July 1967, A1838, 2020/1/24 part 4, NAA

75 A. Clunies-Ross with R.I. Downing et al., One per cent: the case for greater Australian foreign aid, Melbourne, Melbourne University Press, 1963, p. 27–28

76 Arndt, Australian foreign aid policy, p. 12

77 Cable, White to Edwards, 30 March 1959, OWP; CPD (HoR), vol. 24, 2 September 1959, p. 833; P. Torney-Parlicki, Somewhere in Asia: war, journalism and Australia's neighbours 1941–1975, Sydney, University of New South Wales Press, 2000

78 'Review of Australian external aid: types of aid given and its effectiveness or ineffectiveness, duplication or overlapping', 6 January 1965, A1838, 2020/1/24/23, NAA

79 'Review of Australian external aid', 21 December 1964, A1838, 2020/1/24/23, NAA

80 'Head of mission meeting: discussion of aid policy and administration, 10 December 1964', A1838, 2020/1/24 part 4, NAA

81 'Review of Australian external aid: general evaluation of Australian aid', 15 December 1964, A1838, 2020/1/24/23, NAA

82 Sir W. Crocker, interview with author, 28 August 2001, Adelaide; A.H. Borthwick, interview with author, 21 May 2001, Canberra

83 Memo, Muller, 'Colombo Plan – Punjab Tubewells project', 24 January 1961, A1838, 2020/1/11, NAA

8. CROSSING THE FRONTIER

Since the Second World War a pervasive uncertainty about Australia's regional presence has spread across the political landscape. True, that anxiety had been there since settlement, but the experience of war and its aftermath intensified national ambivalence towards the region. A monolithic 'Asia' emerged as Australia's northern frontier, a place whence future enemies might come, but a place most knew needed to be more deeply understood. Paul Carter, in his history of Australian settlement, *The road to Botany Bay*, argued that the notion of the frontier as a barrier, a 'one-sided, unified line of defence or attack', was of limited value in explaining the settlers' relationships to each other, the land and the indigenous people. It was better, he argued, to look at the frontier not as a barrier, but as a place of communication and exchange: 'It enables the settler to establish who and where he is. This is my clearing, that beyond is not'. We can understand the settler's presence, not in exclusive opposition to those around him, but only in relation to his surrounding. 'The settler himself takes advantage of his distinction to make his own position clear. The boundary is not a barrier to communication. Quite the opposite: it gives the settler something to talk about'.[1]

Carter's interpretation is particularly useful for understanding the nature of Australia's relationship to Asia since the end of the Second World War. In 1950, when Spender told parliament of the immutable limitations and responsibilities of Australia's geography, it was as much an admission of territorial and cultural vulnerability, as it was a call to recast the outmoded concept of the frontier which had retarded Australia's engagement with the region. The fluidity of political and social change in the region, the uncertainty of decolonisation and the mounting tension of the Cold War moved Australia to question where the boundary with Asia lay. The frontier could not be a 'unified line of defence' — the nature of communism (as defined by Percy Spender and others) would not allow it. Australia's conception of — and approach to — the Cold War meant that two frontiers were in operation. One, a tangible strategically defined boundary measured by borders and armed encounters, and the other, an indeterminate and vague mental frontier requiring a sustained propaganda battle. The frontier had become amorphous and Australia's security and prosperity would not come from isolation, but only through helping others to develop and resist. The cornerstone of this policy, Spender declared, was engagement via a 'sustained and determined effort in every field of human activity, including the political, economic and spiritual fields'.[2]

If the intangible nature of ideological conflict helped bring the Colombo Plan into existence, the outbreak of war in Vietnam cast the merits of the aid program into much sharper — and starker — relief. On 13 August 1964, the first full debate on the regional and global implications of conflict in Vietnam took place in the House of Representatives. Although the debate was ostensibly over the merits of the Menzies Government's decision to issue a statement wholeheartedly supporting the US decision to increase its involvement in Vietnam in the wake of the Gulf of Tonkin incident,[3] it was quickly transformed into a much wider debate about the use of foreign aid versus military might in the struggle against communism. The faithful continued to use foreign aid to attack the government's claim that there was 'no current alternative' to military intervention. Labor leader Arthur Calwell spoke of the need for an 'expanded programme of economic and social aid' which would help to 'ensure that the inevitable economic and social revolution in South East Asia is not a Communist revolution'. To back his claim, he stated that the Labor Party pledged one per cent of national income for overseas aid, roughly twice the Menzies Government's allocation. Another member, drawing inspiration from Colombo Plan initiatives and the personal contacts they fostered, protested vainly: 'We must convince both the South and North Vietnamese that we have a better way of life than the Communists have. That is the only answer. We must live amongst them, talk to them and work with them as the Communists are doing'.[4]

Yet fifteen years of giving aid to the Asian region had failed to 'draw the teeth of Communist imperialism' and remove popular sympathy for revolution.[5] In the mid-1960s, on the crest of Asia's most bitter and divisive conflict, rarely had the commitment to Asian economic development seemed so marginal to Australia's approach to containing the spread of communist ideology. Evatt's idealistic vision of first securing 'freedom from want' and thus removing the systemic basis of instability had been turned on its head.[6] The Minister for the Navy, Fred Chaney (Snr), unwittingly reversed Evatt's rhetorical hook when he said that 'people should first be given freedom from attack and freedom from the fear of attack' before experts could offer advice on health and social welfare. More colourfully, Henry Turner, Member for Bradfield (NSW), asked: 'How can the man who fears, when he leaves his village, that, while he is away his child may be kidnapped, his wife may be murdered, or his village burnt down, give attention to instruction from an agricultural expert on how to tend his rice paddy?'[7] Opposition protests were in vain and with the outbreak of war, it became clear to all that the plan to create a model Western-style democracy, and thus forestall regional disquiet, was little more than a fantasy of the post-war imagination. The technical and financial aid Australia gave to political trouble spots in Asia did little to allay feelings of insecurity and the need for a military alliance. Armed resistance was part of Australia's strategy to check the advance of communism, Paul Hasluck told Parliament: 'behind the shelter provided by regional security arrangements the countries of South and South–East Asia wish to pursue their objectives of social and economic progress. To help them to do that is the purpose of the Colombo Plan'.[8] In the official rhetoric, the success of the Colombo Plan now depended on the military intervention it was nominally supposed to have precluded.

The apparent failure of aid to prevent conflict, however, did not stop Hasluck from generating greater interest in the Colombo Plan, in large measure because of his strong Cabinet performance. Between 1964 and 1967, Hasluck increased the bilateral aid budget (excluding Papua New Guinea) from $14.1 million to over $34 million.[9] Indeed, from retirement, Hasluck wrote that the expansion of Australia's aid program gave him the greatest sense of achievement while foreign minister.[10] He also took an interest in the administration and organisation of aid programs, and he confronted the tendency to tie bilateral assistance to Australian produce and the crippling effect this had on the real value of foreign assistance.

Most welcomed the Colombo Plan as a valuable contribution to regional relations, but open, generous, and responsive engagement with Asia did not always command broad endorsement. Although giving aid to Asia became a consistent and important facet of Australian foreign policy, it was not central to the government's political agenda and was often overlooked when more important and immediate issues were raised. To suggest that Australian policy-makers worked towards a clear set of policy objectives for the Colombo Plan would be to attribute, somewhat artificially, a coherence and direction to Australia's foreign aid policy that did not exist. The imprecise and largely unquantifiable nature of many of the Colombo Plan's objectives frustrated those eager for a more concrete basis on which to base their aid policies. The administration of aid projects involved many bureaucrats and diplomats in detailed and difficult work, associated them with corruption and failure, and strained the resources of their posts. Many were dismayed and angry at the lack of gratitude displayed by Asian leaders, and preferred to get on with tasks which they saw as central to diplomacy. Casey's obsession with publicity and propaganda was as much an attempt to overcome bureaucratic resistance and enlist the support of those who were otherwise indifferent, as it was to burnish Australia's national image in the fight for the hearts and minds of Asia. A successful public relations campaign offered an alternative way to assess the Colombo Plan other than by using quantitative economic measures.

The equivocal attitude of Australian diplomats toward the Colombo Plan stemmed as much from inexperience and uncertainty about Australia's relationship with Asia as it did from a diminished faith in foreign aid to secure Australian interests. The ambivalent attitude of Australian officials towards the broader impact of the aid scheme is one measure of the anxiety the program caused, rather than allayed. Throughout the 1950s, Australian officials greeted the Colombo Plan with a range of emotions, from cautious approval to outright hostility. Sometimes, they held both views simultaneously. No one had more experience with the high-level administration and policy direction of the Colombo Plan than Arthur Tange, Secretary of the DEA from 1954 to 1965. 'We count too much on the Colombo Plan', he told Casey, the program's patron saint, in 1955:

> Australia's contributions can be of no major
> significance in the eyes of the political leaders of
> India, Burma, Indonesia or Thailand … It has no
> effect upon their assessment of where Australia
> stands in international political issues because it is
> a thing apart, except in so far as it demonstrates a
> willingness to offer a small amount of friendly help
> … I also fear that, by overemphasis in our
> publicity, we may arouse a counter reaction, not
> always indulgent, against patronage and what may
> be regarded as an effort to compensate for lack
> of Australian support on more fundamental

questions such as 'American intervention' or 'colonialism'.

Yet he claimed with equal conviction that Australia's 'standing is certainly better than if we contributed nothing. We pick up the goodwill disseminated by students, and technical ministries with whom we co-operate. We take the edge off our immigration policy ... It is a most valuable arm in our foreign policy'.[11]

Politicians and policy-makers felt that after fighting in two world wars Australia had earned a right to act in concert with the great powers. Liberal parliamentarian Kent Hughes captured this sentiment candidly in 1954, when he remarked that Australia deserved to have its 'voice heard in the councils of the world' but 'must avoid the two extremes of making too much noise and of sitting silent on the sidelines'.[12] As Australia juggled its commitment to alliance politics and regional engagement, the Colombo Plan offered a gentle means of building rapport with Asia. Even a cursory survey of inward correspondence from Asian posts shows how frequently the Colombo Plan formed the basis of diplomatic contact, being often used as an icebreaker before broaching weightier issues. Neighbourly goodwill, although built on shaky foundations, still had the capacity to determine the mood of the next diplomatic meeting, the next regional conference, or, at worst, the next confrontation. It was crucial to building relations, especially where previous dealings had been limited or even hostile. The establishing of closer economic relations with Japan and the maintenance of diplomatic contact during Indonesia's policy of 'confrontation' form but two examples.

While the Colombo Plan was a step towards engagement and mutual understanding, it did little to challenge the geo-political precepts that shaped the official imagination. The basic premise from which Australian policy-makers approached the region in the decades after the end of the Second World War (namely, that South and South–East Asia were keystones in Soviet and Chinese plans to dominate Asia) remained largely unchanged. Asia, as it existed in the shadow of the Cold War, was both threatened and threatening. The looming threat of communist expansionism and Australia's proximity to a people they perceived as desperately poor, weak, and vulnerable struck at the centre of Western ideas about progress and stability and formed a powerfully unsettling image. The military and strategic objectives — and their associated cultural and economic objectives — that drew Australian policy-makers into Asia defined and limited the terms on which Asia was represented and understood. Trapped by the seemingly inescapable polarities of the Cold War, this reductive view gave the Colombo Plan much of its momentum. Of course, the simplistic and fearful interpretation militated against the recognition and acceptance of differences between Asian countries and their peoples. In time this would change, but it would take a bitter, divisive, and ultimately futile war to convince them that Asia was more than a collection of politically malleable and culturally homogenous buffer states.

And yet, on university campuses and in homes and hostels across the country, interactions between Australians and Asian students enriched and challenged Australia's knowledge of the region. Partly because these exchanges brought about by the scheme precluded overt control, they were able to circumvent the distortions imposed by the Cold War agenda. The government had no way of predicting how Australians would respond to Asian students, or how students would interpret and tell of their experiences once they returned home. For many Australians, the exposure to

Asia that the Colombo Plan facilitated came in a remarkably contradictory form. The devious and ruthless communist insurgents penetrating vulnerable minds throughout Asia and beyond, as described in parliament, the popular press, and official appraisals, must have seemed a world apart from the urbane, middle-class Asians seen in ever increasing numbers in Australian universities. The experience for the thousands of experts sent to Asia on their first assignments was similarly challenging.

Cultural exchange proved to be the most enduring aspect of the program. In Australia, some welcomed the exchange, others were apprehensive, but few could deny the growing awareness of Asia taking place in Australian society. Under the Colombo Plan those Asians perceived as poor, numerous, diseased, different, and threatening stayed at home, and those who were young, clean, English-speaking, and not seen as competitors for Australian jobs journeyed to Australia — and they came temporarily. Generally, they were welcomed. They were Australia's guests and Australians thought themselves good and generous neighbours by having them. Suspicion of inferiority, racial pollution, political disruption, and moral contamination — long associated with Asian people — began to fade. Instead, the presence of Asian students stimulated a desire for genuine social pluralism and a distaste for the hollow trappings of government and media propaganda. One student, writing in the University of Sydney newspaper *Honi Soit*, asked earnestly, 'How long will it be before they notice that each time they are invited to a social function they meet the same small group of people — those thoughtful few to whom "international friendship" is something more than a phrase occasionally heard in overseas news items, something in fact personal and relevant to our own daily lives'.[13] The acceptance of

Colombo Plan scholars and the arrival of more students, who were seen in a similar light, resulted in a significant weakening of the basic arguments that bolstered the white Australia policy. People who were manifestly different were not necessarily a threat. Colombo Plan scholars did not provoke racist incidents or endanger social and economic stability, and they paved the way for the acceptance of thousands of private Asian students, who have become an important element of today's tertiary education system.

The Colombo Plan also exposed the ambiguities of Australian loyalty to Britain and America. In June 1961, the heads of Australia's diplomatic posts across Asia met in Bangkok. They agreed that while the flow of Colombo Plan students afforded Australia a distinctive regional presence, they wanted an identity that would help them avoid the undercurrent of 'envious resentment' directed against the United States and the automatic assumption that Australia was the same as Britain. The process could be accelerated if they could 'discard some of the constitutional forms and terminology which to unsophisticated minds suggest dependence on the UK'. For a start, they wondered whether 'the Queen might be described more often simply as the Queen of Australia and that Australian representatives might perhaps be "Her Australian Majesty's Representatives" rather than "Her Majesty's Australian Representatives"'. While not the cry of a rabid republican, such gentle resistance to the trappings of empire signalled that those representing the country to the outside world thought Australian interests would be better served by an 'independent country with its own identity'.[14] And foreign aid had proved a valuable and relatively inexpensive tool for the assertion of that distinctiveness.

This argument is not a case of 'leaching the "empire" out of Menzies', to borrow Greg Pemberton's colourful phrase. Nor is it to imply that political leaders always exuded strongly nationalist sentiments, as opposed to imperialist inclinations. Instead, the point is to suggest that the Colombo Plan was part of a realisation that Australia would have to establish intimate bilateral relations with Asia on a myriad of economic, political, and defence issues, irrespective of its military connections to the United States. Again, this is not to argue that Australia did not agree with and support the approach of Western powers. Rather, that loyalty did not denote servility or pliable dependence. In relation to the Colombo Plan, Pemberton's argument that 'Menzies and his close associates admitted to themselves that their policies meant the denial of national sovereignty in foreign policy' is clearly overstated.[15] Australia capitalised on the inflexibility or absence of US aid as a means of creating a distinctively Australian connection with Asia. Australia took a leading role in actively drawing as many non-Commonwealth Asian nations as possible into the Colombo Plan, partially as a means of enhancing the Australian flavour the scheme came to possess. Indeed, the independent nature of the approach irritated officials in Washington and London. Australian diplomats and policy-makers alike quickly seized upon the unprecedented and unexpected success of the student program as an ideal way of projecting Australian values into the region and conferring a uniquely Australian influence upon Asian scholars. The aid program also helped to create a dialogue between Asians and Australians, on an official and personal level, that had hitherto scarcely existed. Through the Colombo Plan, Australia came to see the virtue, if not the necessity, of sustaining an identity that was at arm's length from the United States and outside the old bonds of empire.

The Colombo Plan's bilateral aid structure gave the program its particular salience in the fractious regional climate and allowed donor nations to secure their own foreign policy objectives. For Australia, this feature was particularly useful in order to build a regional identity via its aid contributions. These congenial and non-coercive administrative arrangements, and the Consultative Committee's lack of decision-making power, rendered the Colombo Plan something of an international curio. According to an appraisal from the UK Foreign Office, the plan resembled 'a building which, though constructed in defiance of the rules of architecture, gives admirable service only as long as no one attempts major changes liable to overload the structure and bring about its collapse'.[16] Indeed, the shallow inclusiveness of the Colombo Plan continued to be one of its defining characteristics. Four 'fringe members' joined the program in the early 1960s: Korea and Bhutan (1962), and Afghanistan and the Maldive Islands (1963). Australia lobbied vigorously for each inclusion, with the aid relationship 'our only real point of contact with these states, in none of which does Australia have resident representation'. First Assistant Secretary Ralph Harry told Tange that tiny states such as Bhutan, wedged between India, China, and Tibet, needed 'some added Western stiffening', but he also admitted that Australia's aid to these new members was 'purely of a token character'.[17] The tradition of providing small amounts of assistance to an increasing number of geographically and politically diffuse nations continued into the 1970s, with the membership of Iran (1966), Singapore (1966), Fiji (1972), Bangladesh (1972), and Papua New Guinea (1973) bringing the total number of member nations to 27.

Despite the limitations of the Colombo Plan and the pre-eminence of geo-strategic considerations, Australia's relations with Asia had become increasingly complex since 1945. In spite of the hope of the principal designers and advocates of the Colombo Plan, Spender and Casey, the aid program had not rendered the complexities of Asia less threatening and more comprehensible. Although conceived at a time of great uncertainty, the plan embodied the optimistic view that, with but slight encouragement, progressive, liberal development had the capacity to solve a panoply of international issues. Commonwealth policy-makers genuinely believed that the plan would go some way to building a cooperative, anti-communist regional association under the protective wing of the United States. Yet if Australian policy-makers hoped that the Colombo Plan would make their lives easier, they must have been sorely disappointed. Rather than stimulate an Asian economic recovery, the Colombo Plan drew greater attention to the massive task of building economic and social infrastructure and exposed a haphazard and piecemeal handling of complex development projects. Australian policy-makers also found it far more difficult to cozen Asian societies into Western modernity than they expected. Rather than foster a grateful and supine body of Asian political elites, the process of giving aid exposed Australia to Asian nationalism and the practical difficulties of building positive rapport with independent nations.

Given that the Colombo Plan development program, as it functioned in Asia, appeared to be riddled with inefficiency and inconsistency, why, then, did it survive to become an entrenched feature of the regional aid-giving environment? A number of interrelated factors sustained the Colombo Plan: the relatively low burden on Australian taxpayers, the limited official analysis undertaken by the Consultative Committee, and, irrespective of its practical limitations as a development scheme, the fact that it functioned symbolically as a bridge between disparate and divergent political and economic systems, thus becoming a unifying force in the fractious climate of the Cold War. It comforted Australian politicians and diplomats who could point to the plan as concrete evidence of Australia's regional awareness and generosity. Any success associated with the Colombo Plan was Australia's success because Australians could claim that they were responsible for the plan's conception and implementation. Failures could be blamed on inefficiencies in the recipient countries and on the vicissitudes of international markets. The critical and moderate opinions offered by the likes of Macmahon Ball threatened to undermine the popular rationale for Australia's aid program. Although some in the DEA would have had sympathy with Macmahon Ball's analysis, diplomatic staff and senior policy officials were already overworked and nervous about attaching too many strings to foreign aid. The imposition of further conditions would have been next to impossible. For their part, the Labor Party began to target the government's preoccupation with strategic objectives at the expense of humanitarian aid. Delegates to Labor's 1961 national conference specifically advocated a 'widening of the Colombo Plan to assist Asian nations on a basis of common need and mutual co-operation and not in the narrow limits of so-called "enlightened self-interest"'.[18] Most importantly, the program yielded other benefits and objectives, not necessarily present or obvious at its creation. The conspicuous benefits generated by the student program were incommensurate with the relatively small outlay of government funds, which the international affairs commentator Douglas Wilkie claimed as one of the 'cheapest strokes of foreign policy in all history'.[19]

In the volatile and uncertain aftermath of the Second World War, Australia searched for an active remedy for the dangers inherent in decolonisation and the beginning of the Cold War. Australians did not seek to become part of Asia; rather, they gradually came to see Australia's future as inexorably linked with the 'near north'. Since then Australia has sought to maintain strategic interests, express neighbourly goodwill, fulfil humanitarian obligations, and establish a cultural, diplomatic, and economic dialogue with the region — all without appearing to violate Asian sovereignty. Historian Manning Clark observed that during the 1950s Australia faced Asia with twin offerings: with one hand, she offered 'welfare, and with the other, a sword'.[20] As Australia faced Asia in 1964, on the verge of its longest and most divisive military commitment, his observation seemed apt. But what this book has shown is that, through the genesis of the Colombo Plan in the late-1940s and its implementation in the 1950s, attitudes and understandings of Australia's place and security in the Asian region expanded to incorporate a more organic and flexible appreciation of economic, social, and cultural engagement. Australian geo-strategic, economic, and cultural security was — and is — intertwined with the management of its relations with Asia. The decision to create the Colombo Plan and maintain it for so long signalled Australia's official admission that engagement with Asia simply had to occur and that Australia should be among those taking the initiative. Although the financial commitment was small, the Colombo Plan had considerable cultural and political significance. It brought together those who wanted Australia to be a humane and generous neighbour, those who thought modern, liberal values could be transplanted easily into Asia, and those hard-nosed realists who hoped for little more than a slim strategic advantage in the Cold War struggle. The Colombo Plan captured this amorphous and changing approach to regional engagement — one that spanned a remarkable diversity of governmental considerations of a strategic, cultural and economic nature.

Full of quasi-imperial intent, the Colombo Plan was a defensive response to a particular construction of Asia and the anxieties, threats and promises that lay within that region. Yet its creation represented a shift away from the often insular concerns of the Menzies Government and actively — if with considerable ambivalence and trepidation — breached the barriers, both geographic and mental, of Australia's northern frontier. This cautious and conditional opening embodied a much broader tension of post-war Australian life: the preservation of Australia's political, economic, and military sovereignty meant engaging with the region and reconceptualising its regional identity outside the boundaries of a defensive and insular nationalism. That tension is with us still.

Footnotes

1 P. Carter, *The road to Botany Bay: an exploration of landscape and history*, Chicago, University of Chicago Press, 1989, pp. 158–59

2 P. Spender, *Politics and a man*, Sydney, Collins, 1972, p. 328

3 The Gulf of Tonkin resolution was passed with overwhelming support by the US Congress on 5 August 1964, in response to two allegedly unprovoked attacks by North Vietnamese patrol boats. Its stated purpose was to approve and support President Lyndon Johnson's determination to take all necessary measures to repel any armed attack against the forces of the United States and to prevent further aggression.

4 *CPD (HoR)*, vol. 43, 11 August 1964, p. 21; *CPD (HoR)*, vol. 43, 13 August 1964, pp. 180–81, 257

5 *CPD (HoR)*, vol. 206, 9 March 1950, p. 632

7 *CPD (HoR)*, vol. 43, 13 August 1964, pp. 247, 260

8 *CPD (HoR)*, vol. 45, 23 March 1965, p. 235

9 R. Porter, *Paul Hasluck: a political biography*, Perth, University of Western Australia Press, 1993, p. 270

10 P. Hasluck, 'Foreign affairs', vol. 2, p. 14, box 37, Hasluck papers, MS 5274, NLA

11 Memo, Tange to Casey, 'Policy critique', 22 June 1955, Tange papers, Department of Foreign Affairs and Trade

12 *CPD (HoR)*, vol. 4, 10 August 1954, pp. 132–33

13 *Honi Soit*, 8 May 1956

14 'Heads of mission conference — Bangkok', 19–22 June 1962, A1838, 3004/11 part 7, NAA

15 G. Pemberton, 'An imperial imagination: explaining the post-1945 foreign policy of Robert Gordon Menzies', F. Cain, ed., *Menzies in peace and war*, Sydney, Allen & Unwin, 1997, p. 156–59

16 Joint memorandum by South–East Asia and Economic Relations Department, Foreign Office, 'The future development of the Colombo Plan', 28 August 1961, FO 371/160010, PRO, UK

17 Note, Harry for Tange, 26 February 1965, A1838, 2020/1/24 part 3, NAA

18 Quoted in, A.A. Calwell, *Labor's role in modern society*, Melbourne, Lansdowne Press, 1963, p. 181

19 *Sun News-Pictorial* (Melbourne), 6 November 1953

20 M. Clark, *A short history of Australia*, New York, New American history, p. 257.

EPILOGUE

The Colombo Plan still operates and is one of the longest running aid programs in the world. Yet awareness of the Plan has diminished, largely because its main functions have slowly been eclipsed by the multitude of cooperative forums that have emerged since the Second World War. The United Nations Development Program (UNDP), the Economic Commission for Asia and the Pacific (ECAP), the Asian Development Bank (ADB), and regional groupings such as the Association of Southeast Asian Nations (ASEAN) and the South Asian Association for Regional Cooperation (SAARC) have all diverted attention, and finance, from the Colombo Plan. Greater prosperity in some Asian countries has also reduced the need for external technical assistance. In the 1980s, donor nations even contemplated the end of the historic scheme when Britain and Canada dropped out. But salvation came from Japan, a country that had once struggled to gain acceptance into the Colombo Plan fraternity. In fact,

Japan has been the largest donor nation since 1977, and in 1989 gave more than twice the amount provided by the United States.

The Colombo Plan survived the Cold War and the anti-communist objective foisted upon it by Western donors to become a broader, more permanent international organisation. Today, it still manages to retain a nominally non-political agenda. Membership of the Consultative Committee still includes nations that are geographically diverse and politically divergent. Indeed, having begun with seven founding Commonwealth nations, the Colombo Plan now includes 25 countries stretching from Iran in the west to the Fiji Islands in the east. By 1980, membership included almost every Southeast Asian nation and the Colombo Plan was extended indefinitely. The admission of the Socialist Republic of Vietnam in November 2001 left Brunei as the only outstanding regional country. Mongolia attends as a provisional member.

Throughout all these changes in membership, the basic philosophy of the Colombo Plan has remained essentially unchanged. The Consultative Committee serves as a non-coercive discussion forum and member nations negotiate bilateral cooperative programs. More recently, Colombo Plan activities have emphasised human resource management, intra-regional trade, public administration, and private sector development. The drug advisory program, initiated in 1972, continues to work with international bodies and non-government organisations to control the availability of drugs and provide assistance to addicts. Technical training is still supported through the Colombo Plan Staff College for Technical Education, established in 1973 to train management and specialist personnel.

Australia retains its Colombo Plan membership by bearing some of the administration costs of the bureau in

Sri Lanka. But since the mid-1970s, when the Whitlam Government oversaw a major restructure of the aid bureaucracy, Australian aid has been channeled through a wider variety of multilateral and bilateral programs. Since that time, the number of Colombo Plan scholarships has fallen steadily from a peak of over 3,000 per year as alternative means of sponsoring students have become available and, more significantly, demand from Asians prepared to pay for education in Australia has risen markedly.

Yet the legacy of the Colombo Plan is more directly evident in the scope and structure of Australia's current overseas aid program and the language used to promote it. On the 50th anniversary of the Colombo Plan in 2001 the Malaysian–Australian Alumni Council, with support from the Australian government and other organisations, launched the Malaysia–Australia Colombo Plan Commemoration (MACC) scholarship program. Intended to encourage the two-way exchange of students between Australia and Malaya, the inaugural program offered 56 scholarships for undergraduate and postgraduate study. Of the 62 places offered in 2004, 46 were offered to Australian applicants to study at 12 Malaysian institutions. The MACC initiative hopes to build on the sentiment and aspirations of the Colombo Plan by strengthening the educational and cultural links between the two countries. In a similar vein, the Australian government and the World Bank launched the 'Virtual Colombo Plan' in August 2001. The program is intended to provide developing countries with distance education programs and access to Australian research via the Internet and extends as far as East Timor, China, Indonesia, Mongolia, Papua New Guinea, Samoa, the Philippines and some African countries. Here the talk of using information and communication technology to 'leap frog' ahead in the development process is reminiscent of the overly optimistic language that characterised the development models of the 1950s and 60s. Predictably, this revival of the 'Colombo Plan' as a byword for education and positive cross-cultural exchange ignores the scheme's complex history and the self-interested political and cultural motivations that underpinned the program.

Another contemporary incarnation of the Colombo Plan development scheme is the Australian Youth Ambassadors for Development Program (AYAD), launched in 1998 and organised by the Australian Agency for International Development (AusAID). Drawing inspiration from the Plan's technical expert program, skilled young Australians undertake short-term assignments of up to 12 months in developing countries, often in partnership with Australian companies, educational institutions, government agencies, non-government organisations and community groups. Like the expert program of the past, the youth ambassadors' role as cultural representatives is just as important as the contributions they make to specific development projects.

Certainly, Australian aid providers today place much greater emphasis on cultural sensitivity and tailoring development to the local and national needs of developing countries. But Australia's commitment to the provision of modern infrastructure, the promotion of sustainable development, and the emphasis on technical training, distance education and institutional strengthening, all have strong links to the Colombo Plan's basic vision of regional development. Indeed, the preference for economically tied infrastructure projects, such as the My Thuan bridge in Vietnam, which was built by Australian companies, confirms Minister for Foreign Affairs and Trade Alexander Downer's directive that Australia's 'aid program will remain identifiably Australian — it is a reflection of Australian values and is a projection of those values abroad'.[1] The anti-communist rhetoric that gave foreign assistance its momentum may have gone, but the nexus between international aid and national economic, social and cultural imperatives is as intricate as it was 50 years ago.

Footnotes

[1]   A. Downer, *Better aid for a better future: seventh annual report to Parliament on Australia's development cooperation program and the Government's response to the Committee of Review of Australia's Overseas Aid Program*, Canberra, Australian Agency for International Development, 1997

LIST OF
ABBREVIATIONS

ABC	Australian Broadcasting Commission
ACFOA	Australian Council of Overseas Aid
ACFU	Australian Commonwealth Film Unit
AIIB	Australian Institute of International Affairs
ANIB	Australian News and Information Bureau
ANU	Australian National University
ANZAM	Australia, New Zealand and Malaya
ANZUS	Australia, New Zealand and the United States
ASIO	Australian Security Intelligence Organisation
ASIS	Australian Security Intelligence Service
AusAID	Australian Agency for International Development
COE	Commonwealth Office of Education
CRO	Commonwealth Relations Office, United Kingdom
DEA	Department of External Affairs
DPR	Deparment of Postwar Reconstruction
ECAFE	Economic Commission for Asia and the Far East
GATT	General Agreement on Tariffs and Trade
IBRD	International Bank for Reconstruction and Development
IMF	International Monetary Fund
IRG	Immigration Reform Group
IRO	International Refugee Organisation
NATO	North Atlantic Treaty Organisation
NSW	New South Wales
OEEC	Organisation for European Economic Cooperation
OPC	Overseas Planning Committee
PNG	Papua New Guinea
SEATO	South–East Asian Treaty Organisation
SPC	South Pacific Commission

UK	United Kingdom
UN	United Nations
UNEPTA	United Nations Expanded Program for Technical Assistance
UNESCO	United Nations Educational, Scientific and Cultural Organisation
UNICEF	United Nations International Children's Emergency Fund
UNKRA	United Nations Korean Reconstruction Agency
UNP	United National Party
UNRRA	United Nations Relief and Rehabilitation Administration
UNRWAPR	United Nations Relief and Works Agency for Palestine Refugees
US/USA	United States of America
USSR	Union of Soviet Socialist Republics
WNG	West New Guinea

KEY FOR ENDNOTES

CPD (HoR)	*Commonwealth parliamentary debates, House of Representatives*
FO	Foreign Office
FRUS	*Foreign Relations of the United States*
HMSO	Her Majesty's Stationery Office
NAA	National Archives Australia
NLA	National Library Australia
OWP	Osmar White papers
PRO, UK	Public Records Office, United Kingdom
SRNSW	State Records, New South Wales
SRSA	State Records, South Australia
USNA	United States National Archive

BIBLIOGRAPHY

ARCHIVAL SOURCES

Australia

National Archives of Australia — Canberra

A452	Correspondence files: Department of Territories, Central Office
A462	Prime Minister's Department
A463	Correspondence files: Department of Prime Minister
A621	Department of Commerce and Agriculture
A816	Correspondence files: Defence Department, 1928–58
A1068	Department of External Affairs, Central Office
A1203	Department of Prime Minister, Central Office
A1209	Department of Prime Minister and Cabinet, Central Office
A1838	Correspondence files: Department of External Affairs, 1948–
A3320	Correspondence files, 1948–1963
A4231	Bound volumes of despatches from overseas posts, 1940–
A4311	Cumpston Collection of Department of External Affairs Records, 1901–1969
A4529	Correspondence files: Saigon, 1952–1957
A5462	Secret/Top Secret Correspondence files: Australian Embassy, Washington
A4638	Cabinet decisions, 1949–1951
A4639	Cabinet submissions, 1949–1951
A4905	Fifth Menzies ministry: cabinet submissions, 1951–1954
A4907	Cabinet minutes, 1951–1954
A4933	Fourth and fifth Menzies ministries: folders of Cabinet committee papers

A4940	Cabinet files: Menzies and Holt ministries, 1949–67
A4968	Correspondence files: Australian Commissioner for South–East Asia
A5827	Eighth Menzies ministry: Cabinet submissions and associated decisions
A5954	Sheddon Collection: Department of Defence, Central Administration
A6364	Inward cables
A6366	Outward cables
A6537	Department of External Affairs, South East Asia Top Secret
A6895	Correspondence files: Australian News and Information Bureau, Canberra
A7452	Correspondence Files, 1949 onwards
A7936	Correspondence files: Department of Defence, Strategic Policy and Planning Branch, Intelligence Policy Section
A9879	Papers relating to post war economic matters, particularly General Agreement on Tariffs and Trade
A10299	Ministerial correspondence files of R. G. Casey: alphabetical series
A10302	R. G. Casey: ministerial correspondence files, 1952–1960
A11604	Correspondence files: Djakarta/Jakarta
A10617	Colombo Plan: records of meetings of the Consultative Committee
CP529	General correspondence: trade information and trade relations
CP553	General correspondence: trade relations various countries

National Archives of Australia — Adelaide

| B300 | Correspondence files: Commonwealth Railways |

National Archives of Australia — Melbourne

| B142 | Correspondence files: Department of Labour and National Service, Central Secretariat |

MP275/5   General correspondence: Department of Labour
            and National Service, Central Secretariat
MP463   Correspondence and reports: Department of
            Labour and National Service, Industrial Training
            Division
M1145   Photographs: R.G. Casey

National Archives of Australia — Perth
K403   Correspondence file: Department of Immigration,
            Western Australia
K1217   Administration: Commonwealth Office of
            Education, Western Australia

State Records — New South Wales
12/14255.2 General correspondence

State Records — South Australia
GRG 24/6 194/54   General correspondence

United Kingdom
Public Records Office — London
CAB 129   Cabinet memoranda, 1945–69
DO 35   Dominions Office and Commonwealth Relations
            Office: original correspondence, 1915–71
FO 371   Political departments: general correspondence,
            1906–66

United States of America
National Archives of the United States — Washington DC
RG 59   State Department Central Decimal Series

India
National Archives of India — New Delhi
6(83) R&I Section/60   Ministry of External Affairs:
                         correspondence
3(31) R&I Section/60   Ministry of External Affairs:
                         correspondence

PRIVATE PAPERS

Richard G. Casey papers	MS 6150, NLA
Walter Crocker, diaries	MS Microfilm: G20734-20741, NLA
Paul Hasluck papers	MS 5274, NLA
Percy Spender papers	MS 4875, NLA
Osmar White papers	Held by Sally White, Melbourne

NEWSPAPERS AND PERIODICALS

Advertiser (Adelaide)
Age (Melbourne)
Argus (Melbourne)
Australian
Australian Outlook
Bulletin
Canberra Times
Ceylon Daily News (Colombo)
Ceylon Observer (Colombo)
Courier-Mail (Brisbane)
Daily Mirror (Sydney)
Daily Telegraph (Sydney)
Eastern World (London)
Globe (Toronto)
Herald (Melbourne)
Hemisphere
Hindu (Madras)
Hindustan Standard
Japan News
Morning Times of Ceylon
New Light of Burma
New York Times
Nippon Times (Tokyo)
Sun-News Pictorial (Melbourne)
Sun (Sydney)
Sydney Morning Herald
The Times (London)

Times of India (Bombay)
The Reporter (Burma)
The Truth (Sydney)
Times of Indonesia
West Australian

PUBLISHED GOVERNMENT SOURCES

Australia

Australian News and Information Bureau, *Australia in Facts and Figures*, 1950–1970

Commonwealth Bureau of Census and Statistics, *Official year book of the Commonwealth of Australia*, Canberra, 1950–1970

—— The Victorian yearbook, Melbourne, 1960–67

Commonwealth parliamentary debates, House of Representatives, 1949–1966

Commonwealth parliamentary debates, Senate, 1950–1966

Department of External Affairs. *Australia's international aid*, Canberra, Government Printing Service, 1969

—— *The Colombo Plan: report presented to the Australian parliament on 9th April, 1954*, Canberra, 1954

—— *Current Notes on International Affairs*, Australian Government Publishing Service, Canberra, 1950–1967

—— *Information handbook no.2: Australia's aid to developing countries*, Canberra, 1964

Downer A., *Better aid for a better future: seventh annual report to Parliament on Australia's development cooperation program and the Government's response to the Committee of Review of Australia's overseas aid program*, Canberra, Australian Agency for International Development, 1997

Ceylon/Sri Lanka

Arulpiragasam, A., *A short review of the Colombo Exhibition*, Colombo, Government Press, 1953

Ceylon House of Representatives debates (Hansard), 1950–1956

India

Indian Council of World Affairs, *Rural development schemes in India*, New Delhi, 1954

Indonesia

Indonesian Department of Foreign Affairs, *The question of West Irian in the United Nations, 1954–1957*, Jakarta, Ministry of Foreign Affairs, 1958

New Zealand

Department of External Affairs. *New Zealand and the Colombo Plan*, Wellington, 1962

New Zealand parliamentary debates, House of Representatives, 1950–1955

United Kingdom

Economic Information Unit, *New hope for Asia: The Colombo plan for co-operative economic development in South and South–East Asia*, Canberra, Commonwealth Office of Education for the Department of External Affairs, 1951

Treasury Department. *Aid to developing countries*, London, HMSO, 1963

United States of America

Department of State Bulletin, Office of Public Communication, Bureau of Public Affairs, Washington, DC

Foreign relations of the United States, United States Government Printing Office, Washington, DC

International Bank for Reconstruction and Development, *The economic development of Ceylon*, Baltimore, John Hopkins Press, 1952

United Nations Department of Economic Affairs, *Technical assistance for economic development available through the United Nations and the specialized agencies*, Lake Success, New York, Department of Economic Affairs, Division of Economic Stability and Development, 1948

United States-Vietnam relations, 1945–1967, US Government Printing Office, Washington, DC

Colombo Plan Publications

Chona, P. R., *The Colombo Plan, 1951–1976: vision into reality*, Colombo, Information Department, Colombo Plan Bureau, 1976

Commonwealth Consultative Committee, *The Colombo Plan for Co-operative Economic Development in South and South–East Asia, a report by the Commonwealth Consultative Committee*, London, HMSO, 1950

Colombo Plan Bureau, *The seventh year: progress of the Colombo Plan*, Colombo, Colombo Plan Bureau, 1959

——— *Youth on the Colombo Plan, a symposium of essays in the international contest*, Colombo, 1971

Colombo Plan Council, *Report for the Council for Technical Cooperation in South and South East Asia*, Colombo, Colombo Plan Bureau. Various issues, 1951–65

Consultative Committee, *First annual report of the Consultative Committee, Karachi, March 1952*, London, HMSO, 1952

——— *Second annual report of the Consultative Committee, New Delhi, October 1953*, London, HMSO, 1953

——— *Third annual report of the Consultative Committee, Ottawa, 1954*, Ottawa, Government Printer, 1954

——— *Fourth annual report of the Consultative Committee, Singapore, October 1955*, London, HMSO, 1955

——— *Fifth annual report of the Consultative Committee, Wellington, December 1956*, Wellington, Government Printer, 1957

——— *Sixth annual report of the Consultative Committee, Saigon, October 1957*, Saigon, 1957

——— *Seventh annual report of the Consultative Committee, Seattle, November 1958*, London, HMSO, 1958

——— *Eighth annual report of the Consultative Committee, Jogjakarta, November 1959*, Jogjakarta, 1959

——— *Ninth annual report of the Consultative Committee, Tokyo, November 1960*, Tokyo, 1960

——— *Tenth annual report of the Consultative Committee, Kuala Lumpur, October–November 1961*, London, HMSO, 1961

——— *Eleventh annual report of the Consultative Committee, Melbourne, November 1962*, London, HMSO, 1962

——— *Twelfth annual report of the Consultative Committee, Bangkok, November 1963*, London, HMSO, 1963

—————— *Thirteenth annual report of the Consultative Committee,
        London, November 1964*, London, HMSO, 1964
—————— *Fourteenth annual report of the Consultative Committee,
        Karachi, November 1966*, London, HMSO, 1966
Council for Technical Co-operation in South and South–East
        Asia, Information Unit, *The Colombo Plan: co-operative
        economic development in South and South–East Asia*,
        Colombo, Colombo Plan Bureau, 1954
Goonetilleke, L.P., *A compendium of some major Colombo Plan
        assisted projects in South & South–East Asia*, Colombo,
        Colombo Plan Bureau, 1972

ORAL SOURCES: INTERVIEWS

R. Bodinagoda, 8 September 1999, Colombo
Alex H. Borthwick, 21 May 2001, Canberra
Dr John Burton, 21 September 2000, Canberra
Sir Walter Crocker, 28 August 2001, Adelaide
Francis Stuart, 5 April 2001, Canberra

Other oral sources

P. Spender, *Conversation with Sir Percy Spender, Hazel de Berg
        collection*, 1968, TRC 354-355, Oral History Collection, NLA
A. Tange, *Monologue: recording of a personal narrative made in
        February and August 1989 intended as a supplement to the
        1989 interview with J.D.B. Miller*, TRC 2447, Oral History
        Collection, NLA
'Crossing the barriers: parts 1 to 6', social history feature, Radio
        Australia, 1993

FILMS

Screen Sound: National Film and Sound Archive — Canberra
Australian Commonwealth Film Unit, Canberra, *Our Neighbour
        Australia*, 1952
Australian News and Information Bureau, Canberra, *Australia for
        the Student*, 1957
Australian Commonwealth Film Unit, Canberra, *The Builders*, 1959

Cinemedia — Melbourne

Australian Commonwealth Film Unit, Canberra, *The Unlucky Country*, 1967

Halas and Batchelor Cartoon Film, United Kingdom, *The Colombo Plan*, 1961

Malayan Film Unit for the Office of the Commissioner-General for the United Kingdom in South–East Asia, *The Summer School in Singapore*, c.1960

National Media Production Center, Department of General Services, United States of America, *The Colombo Plan and You*, 1961

SECONDARY SOURCES

Anderson, B., *Imagined communities: reflections on the origin and spread of nationalism*, London, Verso, 1965

Arndt, H.W., *Australia and Asia: economic essays*, Canberra, Australian National University Press, 1972

—— 'Australian economic aid to Indonesia', *Australian Outlook*, vol. 24, no. 2, August 1970

—— *Australian foreign aid policy*, Adelaide, Griffin Press, 1964

—— *A small rich industrial country: studies in Australian development, aid and trade*, Melbourne, F. W. Cheshire Publishing, 1968

Arthur Lewis, W,. *The principles of economic planning*, London, Unwin University Books, 1970

Asher, R.E., 'Multilateral versus bilateral aid: an old controversy revisited', *International Organization*, vol. 16, no. 4, Autumn 1962

Asian Relations Conference, *Asian relations: being report of the proceedings and documentation of the first Asian Relations Conference, New Delhi, March–April 1947,* New Delhi, Asian Relations Organization, 1948

Ball, W. Macmahon, *Japan: enemy or ally?*, Melbourne, Cassell and Company, 1948

—— *Nationalism and communism in East Asia*, Melbourne, Melbourne University Press, 1952

Barwick, G. et al, *Living with Asia: a discussion on Australia's future*, Sydney, Australian Institute of International Affairs, 1963

Basch, A., 'The Colombo Plan: a case of regional economic
    cooperation', *International Organisation* vol. 9, no. 1, 1955,
    pp. 1–18
Benham, F., 'The Colombo Plan', *Economica* (London), May
    1954
—— *The Colombo Plan and other essays*, London, Royal
    Institute of International Affairs, 1956
—— ed., *Survey of international affairs 1954*, London, Oxford
    University Press, 1957
Blainey, G., *A centenary history of the University of Melbourne*,
    Melbourne, Melbourne University Press, 1957
Boehm, E.A,. *Twentieth century economic development in Australia*,
    Melbourne, Longman Cheshire, 1979
Bolton, G., *The Oxford history of Australia: the middle way, 1942-
    1988*, Melbourne, Oxford University Press, 1993
Booker, M., *The last domino: aspects of Australia's foreign policy*,
    Sydney, Collins, 1976
Borden, W.S., *The pacific alliance: United States foreign economic
    policy and Japanese trade recovery, 1947–1955*, Madison,
    University of Wisconsin Press, 1984
Boxer, A.H., *Experts in Asia: an inquiry into Australian technical
    assistance*, Canberra, Australian National University
    Press, 1969
Boyce, P.J., 'Twenty-one years of Australian diplomacy in
    Malaya', *Journal of South–East Asian History*, vol. 4,
    September 1963, pp. 91–135
Brawley, S., *The white peril: foreign relations and Asian immigration
    to Australasia and North America 1919–78*, Sydney,
    University of New South Wales Press, 1995
Bridge, C., ed., *Munich to Vietnam: Australia's relations with Britain
    and the United States since the 1930s*, Melbourne,
    Melbourne University Press, 1991
Brown, N., *Governing prosperity: social change and social analysis in
    Australia in the 1950s*, Melbourne, Cambridge University
    Press, 1995
Burke, A., *In fear of security: Australia's invasion anxiety*, Sydney,
    Pluto Press, 2001

Burns, C.L., 'The Colombo Plan', *The Year Book of World Affairs*, vol. 14, 1960, pp. 176–206

———— 'The Colombo Plan and Australian foreign policy', *Australian Outlook*, vol. 12, no. 1, 1958

———— 'Progress report on the Colombo Plan', *Australia's neighbours*, January 1954

Burton, J., *The alternative: a dynamic approach to our relations with Asia*, Sydney, Liberty Press, 1954

Butler, R. & Pelly, M.E., eds., *Documents on British policy overseas, Series 2: The London Conferences — Anglo–American Relations and Cold War strategy, January–June 1950, volume 2*, London, HMSO, 1987

Cairns, J., *Living with Asia*, Melbourne, Lansdowne Press, 1965

Calwell, A.A., *Be just and fear not*, Melbourne, Lloyd O'Neil, 1972

———— *Labor's role in modern society*, Melbourne, Lansdowne Press, 1963

Campbell, D., *Writing security: United States foreign policy and the politics of identity*, Minneapolis, University of Minnesota Press, 1992

Carr-Gregg, J.R.E., 'The Colombo Plan: a Commonwealth program for South–East Asia', *International Conciliation*, no. 467, 1951, pp. 16–21

Carter, P., *The road to Botany Bay: an exploration of landscape and history*, Chicago, University of Chicago Press, 1989

Casey, R.G., *The conduct of Australian foreign policy: third Roy Milne memorial lecture, Brisbane*, Melbourne, Australian Institute of International Affairs, 1952

———— *Friends and neighbours: Australia and the world*, Melbourne, Cheshire, 1954

———— *The future of the Commonwealth*, London, Fredrick Muller Limited, 1963

Clark, M., *A short history of Australia*, New York, New American Library, 1969

Clunies-Ross, I., *Prerequisites for the establishment of democratic institutions in South–East Asia, fifth Roy Milne memorial lecture, Adelaide, 15 October 1954*, Melbourne, Australian Institute of International Affairs, 1954

Clunies Ross, A., *One per cent: the case for greater Australian
        foreign aid*, Melbourne, Melbourne University Press, 1963
Coombs, H.C., *Trial balance*, Melbourne, Macmillian, 1981
Copland, D., *Australia and the changing world in Asia*, Melbourne,
        Australian Institute of International Affairs, 1957
Corbett, D.C., 'Immigration and foreign policy in Australia and
        Canada', *International Journal*, vol. 13, 1958, pp. 110–123
—————— *Australian aid in South and South–East Asia*, Canberra,
        Australian Institute of International Affairs, 1965
Crocker, W.R., *Australian Ambassador: international relations at
        first hand*, Melbourne, Melbourne University Press, 1971
—————— *Travelling back: the memoirs of Sir Walter Crocker*,
        Melbourne, Macmillan, 1981
Day, D., ed., *Brave new world: Dr H.V. Evatt and Australian
        foreign policy*, Brisbane, Queensland University Press, 1996
Deakin, A., *Federal story: the inner history of the federal cause
        1880–1900*, Melbourne, Melbourne University Press, 1963
DeSilva, K.M. & Wriggins, H., *J.R. Jayewardene of Sri Lanka:
        a political biography: volume one: 1906–1956*, London,
        Anthony Blond/Quartet, 1988
Edwards, P. with Pemberton, G., *Crises and commitments:
        the politics and diplomacy of Australia's involvement in
        South–East Asian conflicts 1948–1965*, Sydney, Allen &
        Unwin, 1992
Evatt, H.V., *Foreign policy of Australia — speeches*, Sydney, Angus
        and Robertson, 1945
—————— *Australia in world affairs*, Sydney, Angus and Robertson,
        1946
Fitzhardinge, L.F., *William Morris Hughes: a political biography*,
        vol. 2, Sydney, Angus and Robertson, 1979
Fry, G., 'Australia's regional security doctrine: old assumptions,
        new challenges', G. Fry, ed., *Australia's regional security*,
        Sydney, Allen & Unwin, 1991, pp. 1–11
—————— 'The South Pacific "experiment": reflections of the
        origins of regional identity', *Journal of Pacific History*,
        vol. 32, no. 2, 1997, pp. 180–202

Gaddis, J.L., *Strategies of containment: a critical appraisal of postwar American national security policy*, New York, Oxford University Press, 1982

———— 'The strategy of containment', T.H. Etzold & J.L. Gaddis, eds, *Containment: documents on American policy and strategy, 1945–1950*, New York, Columbia University Press, 1978, pp. 25–38

Gamba, C., 'Some thoughts on Australian–Asian understanding', *Australian Quarterly*, vol. 30, September 1958

Gibbons, I., ed., *Undiplomatic dialogue: letters between Carl Berendsen and Alister McIntosh, 1943–52*, Auckland, Auckland University Press in association with the Ministry of Foreign Affairs and Trade, 1993

Goldman, M.I., *Soviet foreign aid*, New York, Fredrick A. Praeger Publishers, 1967

Goldsworthy, D., ed., *Facing north: a century of Australian engagement with Asia, vol. 1: 1901 to the 1970s*, Melbourne, Melbourne University Press, 2001

Gordon, L,. 'Economic regionalism reconsidered', *World Politics*, vol. 13, no. 2, 1961, pp. 231–253

———— 'The Organisation for European Economic Cooperation', *International Cooperation*, vol. 10, no. 1, 1956, pp. 1–11

Grant, B., *The Australian dilemma: a new kind of Western society*, Sydney, MacDonald Futura, 1983

Greenwood, G. & Harper, N, eds., *Australia in world affairs, 1950–55*, Melbourne, F.W. Cheshire, 1956

———— eds., *Australia in world affairs, 1956–1960*, Melbourne, F.W. Cheshire, 1963

Gupta, S., *India and regional integration in Asia*, London, Asia Publishing House, 1964

Gurry, M., *India: Australia's neglected neighbour? 1947–1996*, Brisbane, Griffith University, Centre for the Study of Australia–Asia Relations, 1996

———— 'Neither threat nor promise: an Australian view of Australian–Indian relations since 1947', *South Asia*, vol. 13, no. 1, 1990, pp. 85–101

Haas, M., ed., *Basic documents of Asian regional organizations*, New
    York, Oceana Publications, 1974
Harper, N., 'Asian students and Asian studies in Australia',
    Pacific Affairs, vol. 31, no. 1, March 1958, pp. 154–64
——— 'Australia and South–East Asia', *Pacific Affairs*, vol. 28,
    no. 3, September 1955
Harrison, W.E.C., *Canada in world affairs, 1949–1950*, Toronto,
    Oxford University Press, 1957
Harry, R., *No man is a hero: pioneers of Australian diplomacy*,
    Sydney, Arts Management, 1997
——— *The diplomat who laughed*, Melbourne, Hutchinson, 1983
——— *The north was always near*, Brisbane, Centre for the Study
    of Australia–Asia Relations, Griffith University, 1994
Harrod, R., *Towards a dynamic economics*, London, Macmillan,
    1948
Hasluck, P., 'A policy for New Guinea', *South Pacific*, vol. 5, no. 1,
    1951, pp. 224–28
——— *Mucking about: an autobiography*, Melbourne, Melbourne
    University Press, 1977
——— *The chance of politics*, N. Hasluck, ed., Melbourne, Text
    Publishing, 1997
——— 'The economic development of Papua and New Guinea',
    Australian Outlook, April 1962, pp. 5–25
Hazlehurst, C., *Menzies observed*, Sydney, Allen & Unwin, 1979
Hodge, E., *Radio wars: truth, propaganda and the struggle for Radio
    Australia*, Melbourne, Cambridge University Press, 1995
Hoffman, S., 'The role of international organisation: limits and
    possibilities', *International Organisation*, vol. 10, no. 3, 1956
Hogan, M.J., *The Marshall Plan: America, Britain, and the
    reconstruction of Western Europe, 1947–1952*, Cambridge,
    Cambridge University Press, 1987
Holder, R.F., 'Australia's trade relations with the Far East', G.
    Greenwood, ed., *Australian policies toward Asia: Australian
    papers, Institute of Pacific Relations conference, 1954*,
    Melbourne, Australian Institute of International Affairs,
    1954
Hudson, W.J., *Casey*, Melbourne, Oxford University Press, 1986

Hughes, W.M., *The splendid adventure: a review of empire relations within and without the Commonwealth of Britannic nations*, London, Ernest Benn Limited, 1929

Hyam, R., ed., *British documents on the end of empire, vol. 2: The Labour Government and the end of empire 1945–1951, Part 2: Economics and international relations*, London, HMSO, 1992

Immigration Reform Group, *Immigration: control or colour bar?: the background to 'White Australia' and a proposal for change*, Melbourne, Melbourne University Press, 1962

Ingleson, J. & Walker, D., 'The impact of Asia', N. Meaney, ed., *Under new heavens: cultural transmission and the making of Australia*, Melbourne, Heinemann Education Australia, 1989, pp. 287–324

Inglis, K., *This is the ABC: the Australian Broadcasting Commission 1932–1983*, Melbourne, Melbourne University Press, 1983

Jain, R.K., *Soviet South Asian relations 1947–1978, vol. 2: Pakistan, Bangladesh, Nepal, Sri Lanka*, Oxford, Martin Robertson, 1979

James, C.W., 'The Colombo Plan passes halfway', *Australian Outlook*, vol. 9, no. 1, March 1955, pp. 29–42

Jarrett, F., *The evolution of Australia's aid program*, Canberra, Australian Development Studies Network, 1994

Jones, C., *Something in the air: a history of radio in Australia*, Kenthurst, Kangaroo Press, 1995

Jones, G.W. & Jones, M., 'Australia's immigration policy: some Malaysian attitudes', *Australian Outlook*, vol. 19, December 1965

Jupp, J., *Australian retrospectives: immigration*, Sydney, Sydney University Press, 1991

Kahin, G., *The Asian–African Conference, Bandung, Indonesia, April 1955*, Ithaca, Cornell University Press, 1956

Kaufman, B.I., *Trade and aid: Eisenhower's foreign economic policy, 1953–1961*, Baltimore, John Hopkins University Press, 1982

Keats, D.M., *Back in Asia: a follow-up study of Australian-trained Asian students*, Canberra, Australian National University, 1969

Kesavan, K.V,. *Japan's relations with South–East Asia, 1952–1960*, Bombay, Somaiya Publications, 1972

Kilby, P., ed., *Australia's aid program: mixed messages and conflicting agendas*, Melbourne, Monash Asia Institute and Community Aid Abroad, 1996

Kolko, G., *Confronting the third world: United States foreign policy 1945–1980*, New York, Pantheon Books, 1988

Lakshmana Rao, G., *Overseas students in Australia: some major findings from a nation-wide survey*, Canberra, Australian National University, 1976

Laugier, H., 'The first step in the international approach to the problems of underdeveloped areas', *The Milbank Memorial Fund Quarterly*, vol. 23, no. 3, 1948, pp. 256–59

Lee, D., 'Australia and the British Commonwealth, 1950–1953', *Journal of Imperial and Commonwealth History*, vol. 20, no. 3, 1992

—— *The search for security: the political economy of Australia's postwar foreign and defence policy*, Sydney, Allen & Unwin, 1995

Leong, C.C., 'An enduring allurement', S. Bochner & P. Wicks, eds., *Overseas students in Australia*, Sydney, New South Wales University Press, 1972

LePan, D.V., *Bright glass of memory: a set of four memoirs*, Toronto, McGraw-Hill Ryerson, 1979

Lewis, J.P., *Quiet crisis in India: economic development and American policy*, Washington, D.C., The Brookings Institute, 1962

Lewis, W., *The principles of economic planning* (1949), London, Unwin University Books, 1970

—— 'Industrialization of the British West Indies', *Caribbean Economic Review*, vol. 2, 1950, p. 36

Loane, M., *Archbishop Mowll: the biography of Howard West Kilvinton Mowll*, London, Hodder and Stoughton, 1960

Lowe, D., 'Percy Spender and the Colombo Plan 1950', *Australian Journal of Politics and History*, vol. 40, no. 2, 1994, pp. 162–76

—— 'The Colombo Plan', D. Lowe, ed., *Australia and the end of empires*, Geelong, Deakin University Press, 1996, pp. 105–18

—— *Menzies and the 'great world struggle': Australia's Cold War, 1948–1954*, Sydney, University of New South Wales Press, 1999

——— 'Mr Spender goes to Washington: an Ambassador's
    vision of Australian–American relations, 1951–58',
    Journal of Imperial and Commonwealth History, vol. 24, no. 2,
    May 1996, pp. 278–95
McCullough, D., *Truman*, New York, Simon and Schuster, 1992
Mackie, J.,'The politics of Asian immigration', J.E. Coughlan
    & D.J. McNamara, eds., *Asians in Australia: patterns of
    migration and settlement*, Melbourne, Macmillan Education
    Australia, 1997
Manne, R., *The Petrov affair: politics and espionage*, Sydney,
    Pergamon, 1987
Manning, R., 'Australian aid to developing countries', L.T. Evans
    & J.D.B. Miller, eds., *Policy and practice: essays in honour of
    Sir John Crawford*, Canberra, Australian National
    University Press, 1987
Marshall, H., *Ignorance to enlightenment: fifty years in Asia:
    Australians in Asia series, no. 18*, Brisbane, Griffith
    University, Centre for Australian–Asia Relations, 1997
Meaney, N., 'Australia and the world', N. Meaney, ed., *Under
    new heavens: cultural transmission and the making of
    Australia*, Melbourne, Heinemann Education Australia,
    1989, pp. 379–450
——— ed., *Australia and the world: a documentary history from the
    1870s to the 1970s*, Melbourne, Longman Cheshire, 1985
——— 'The end of 'White Australia' and Australia's changing
    perceptions of Asia, 1945–1990', *Australian Journal of
    International Affairs*, vol. 49, no. 2, 1995, pp 171–89
Menzies, R.G., *Afternoon light*, Melbourne, Cassell, 1967
——— *The measure of the years*, London, Cassell, 1970
Millar, T.B., *Australia's defence*, Melbourne, Melbourne
    University Press, 1965
——— *Foreign policy: some Australian reflections*, Melbourne,
    Georgian House, 1971
——— ed., *Australian foreign minister: the diaries of R.G. Casey,
    1951–60*, London, Collins, 1972
Minkes, A.L., *The Colombo Plan: an economic survey*, London,
    Royal Institute of International Affairs, 1954

Montgomery, J.D., *The politics of foreign aid: American experience in South–East Asia*, New York, Praeger, 1962

Murphy, J., *Harvest of fear: a history of Australia's Vietnam war*, Sydney, Allen & Unwin, 1993

Neale, R.G., 'Australian interests in and attitudes towards economic assistance to Asia', G. Greenwood, ed., *Australian policies toward Asia, Australian papers, Institute of Pacific Relations conference, 1954*, Melbourne, Australian Institute of International Affairs, 1954

Nester, W.R., *Power across the Pacific: a diplomatic history of American relations with Japan*, New York, New York University Press, 1996

Nurkse, R., *Problems of capital formation in underdeveloped countries*, Oxford, Basil Blackwell, 1953

O'Connell, D.P., 'Sedentary fisheries and the Australian continental shelf', *American Journal of International Law*, vol. 49, no. 2, 1955, pp. 185–209

Oakman, D., 'The seed of freedom: regional security and the Colombo Plan', *Australian Journal of Politics and History*, vol. 46, no. 1, 2000, pp. 67–85

———— 'The politics of foreign aid, counter-subversion and the Colombo Plan, 1950–1965', *Pacifica Review: Peace, Security and Global Change*, vol. 13, no. 3, 2001, pp. 255–72

———— '"Young Asians in our homes": Colombo Plan students and white Australia', *Journal of Australian Studies*, no. 72, 2002, pp. 89–98

Organisation for Economic Cooperation and Development, *Australia's international development assistance*, Paris, Organisation for Economic Cooperation and Development, 1969

Padelford, N.J., 'Regional Cooperation in the South Pacific, Twelve Years of the South Pacific Commission', *International Organization*, vol. 13, no. 3, 1959, pp. 380–93

Palfreeman, A.C., *The administration of the White Australia Policy*, Melbourne, Melbourne University Press, 1967

Panikkar, K.M., *In two Chinas: memoirs of a diplomat*, London, George Allen and Unwin, 1955

Pearson, L., 'The Colombo conference', *External Affairs of Canada*, vol. 2, no. 3, March 1950

Pemberton, G., 'An imperial imagination: explaining the post-1945 foreign policy of Robert Gordon Menzies', F. Cain, ed., *Menzies in peace and war*, Sydney, Allen & Unwin, 1997, pp. 154–75

Porter, D., *United States economic foreign aid: a case study of the United States Agency for International Development*, New York, Garland Publishing, 1990

Porter, R., *Paul Hasluck: a political biography*, Perth, University of Western Australia Press, 1993

Rajan, M.S., *India in world affairs, 1954–56*, New York, Asia Publishing House, 1964

Remme, T., *Britain and regional cooperation in South–East Asia, 1945–49*, London, Routledge, 1995

Reubens, E.P., 'Economic aid to Asia: progress report', *Far Eastern survey*, 1951, pp. 6–12

Rix, A., *The Australian–Japan political alignment: 1952 to the present*, London, Routledge, 1999

—— *Coming to terms: the politics of Australia's trade with Japan 1945–57*, Sydney, Allen & Unwin, 1986

Rosenstein-Rodan, P.N., 'International aid for underdeveloped countries', *Review of Economics and Statistics*, May 1961

—— 'Problems of industrialisation in Eastern and South–Eastern Europe', *Economic Journal*, vol. 52, pp. 202–11

Rostow, W.W., *The stages of economic growth: a non-communist manifesto*, Cambridge, Cambridge University Press, 1963

Rotter, A., *The path to Vietnam: origins of the American commitment to South–East Asia*, Ithaca, Cornell University Press, 1987

Rymalov, V.R., 'Soviet assistance to underdeveloped countries', *International Affairs (Moscow)*, September 1959, pp. 23–31

Said, E., *Orientalism*, London, Routledge, 1978

Singer, H.W., 'International aid for economic development: problems and tendencies', *International Development Review*, March 1964, pp. 16–21

Singh, L.P., *The Colombo Plan: some political aspects*, Canberra, Department of International Relations, Australian National University, 1963

—— The politics of economic cooperation in Asia: a study of
    Asian international organizations, Columbia, University of
    Missouri Press, 1966
Smith, J.B., Portrait of a cold warrior, New York, G.P. Putnam's
    Sons, 1976
Sukarno, A., Speech by H.E. President Sukarno at the state banquet
    for Colombo Plan delegates, Djakarta, Indonesian
    Department of Information, 1959
Sumathipala, V., Perera, W. & Kodagoda, D., We look at
    Australia, Sydney, Australian News and Information
    Bureau, 1956
Spender, J., Ambassador's wife, Sydney, Angus and Robertson,
    1968
Spender, P., Exercises in diplomacy: the ANZUS Treaty and the
    Colombo Plan, Sydney, Sydney University Press, 1969
—— 'Partnership with Asia', Current Notes on International
    Affairs, vol. 22, January 1951
—— Politics and a man, Sydney, Collins, 1972
Sudo, S., The Fukuda Doctrine and ASEAN: new dimensions in
    Japanese foreign policy, Singapore, Institute of South–East
    Asian Studies, 1992
Tarling, N., ed., The Cambridge history of South–East Asia, volume
    four: from World War Two to the present, Melbourne,
    Cambridge University Press, 1999
Tate, M., 'The Australasian Monroe Doctrine', Political Science
    Quarterly, vol. 76, no. 2, 1961, pp. 264–84
Tavan, G., '"Good neighbours": community, organisations,
    migrant assimilation and Australian society and culture,
    1950–1961', Australian Historical Studies, vol. 28, no. 109,
    October 1997, pp 77–89
Tennant, K., Evatt: politics and justice, Sydney, Angus and
    Robertson, 1970
Thompson, R.C., Australian imperialism in the Pacific: the
    expansionist era 1820–1920, Melbourne, Melbourne
    University Press, 1980
Toohey, B. & Pinwill, W., Oyster: the story of the Australian Secret
    Intelligence Service, Melbourne, William Heinemann
    Australia, 1989

Torney-Parlicki, P., *Somewhere in Asia: war, journalism, and Australia's neighbours 1941–75*, Sydney, University of New South Wales Press, 2000

Tweedie, S., *Trading partners: Australia and Asia 1790–1993*, Sydney, University of New South Wales Press, 1994

University of New South Wales, *Australia, a part of Asia?: Papers presented at the symposium held at the University of New South Wales on November 17th, 1968*, Sydney, University of New South Wales, 1968

Vandenbosh, M.B & Vandenbosh, A., *Australia faces South–East Asia: the emergence of a foreign policy*, Lexington, University of Kentucky Press, 1967

Varma, R., *Australia and South–East Asia: the crystallisation of a relationship*, New Delhi, Abhinav Publications, 1974

Vithal Babu, V., *Colombo Plan and India*, Dehli, Atma Ram & Sons, 1951

Walker, D., *Anxious nation: Australia and the rise of Asia 1850–1939*, Brisbane, University of Queensland Press, 1999

Warner, D. & Gilmore, R.J., eds., *Near north: Australia and a thousand million neighbours*, Sydney, Angus and Robertson, 1948

Warner, D., *Australia's northern neighbours*, London, Longmans, Green & Co., 1957

Waters, C., 'A failure of imagination: R.G. Casey and Australian plans for counter-subversion in Asia, 1954–1956', *Australian Journal of Politics and History*, vol. 45, no. 3, 1999, pp. 347–61

——— *The empire fractures: Anglo–Australian conflict in the 1940s*, Melbourne, Australian Scholarly Publishing, 1995

——— 'The Macmahon Ball mission to East Asia, 1948', *Australian Journal of Politics and History*, vol. 40, no. 3, 1994, pp. 351–63

Watt, A., *The evolution of Australian foreign policy, 1938–1965*, Cambridge, Cambridge University Press, 1968

——— *Australian diplomat: memoirs of Sir Alan Watt*, Sydney, Angus and Robertson, 1972

Webb, J.B., *Towards survival: A programme for Australia's overseas aid*, Melbourne, Community Aid Abroad, 1971

Weintraub, D., 'International approaches to economic development of undeveloped areas', *The Milbank Memorial Fund Quarterly*, vol. 26, no. 3, 1948, pp. 260–70

White, O., *The seed of freedom: Australia and the Colombo Plan*, Canberra, Department of External Affairs, Australian News and Information Bureau, 1961

Whitwell, G., 'Economic policy', S. Prasser, J.R. Nethercote & J. Warhurst, eds., *The Menzies era: a reappraisal of government, politics and policy*, Sydney, Hale & Iremonger, 1993

——— 'The social planning of the F & E economists', *Australian Economic History Review*, no. 26, 1985

Williams, P., ed., *The diary of Hugh Gaitskell, 1945–1956*, London, Cape, 1983

Wolf, C., *Foreign aid: theory and practice in Southern Asia*, Princeton, Princeton University Press, 1960

Wolfstone, D., 'The Colombo Plan after ten years', *Far Eastern Economic Review*, vol. 33, no. 5, 1961, p. 219

Wolpert, R.V., 'The Colombo Plan under review', *Eastern World*, vol. 7, October 1953, pp. 37–38

Wood, J., *History of international broadcasting*, London, Peter Peregrinus, 1992

Woodard, G., 'Ministers and mandarins: the relationship between Ministers and Secretaries of External Affairs 1935–1970', *Australian Journal of International Affairs*, vol. 54, no. 1, 2000, pp. 79–95

Zainu'ddin, A., *A short history of Indonesia*, Melbourne, Cassell, 1968

INDEX

www.ingramcontent.com/pod-product-compliance
Lightning Source LLC
Chambersburg PA
CBHW040141270326
41928CB00023B/3294